The Practical Office XP

Includes a multimedia Book-on-CD with the entire contents of the the printed book, interactive step-by-step animations, pop-up definitions, skills tests, and more!

June Jamrich Parsons

Dan Oja

THOMSON
COURSE TECHNOLOGY
™

25 Thomson Place, Boston, MA 02210

Australia • Canada • Mexico • Singapore • Spain • United Kingdom • United States

The Practical Office XP is published by Course Technology.

Developmental Editor	Catherine Perlich
Managing Editor	Rachel Crapser
Senior Editor	Donna Gridley
Senior Product Manager	Kathy Finnegan
Product Manager	Melissa Hathaway
Technology Product Manager	Amanda Young
Associate Product Manager	Brianna Germain
Media Specialist	Donna Schuch
Book-on-CD Development	MediaTechnics Corp.
Prepress Production	GEX Publishing Services
Text and Design Composition	MediaTechnics Corp.
Production Editor	Debbie Masi
Cover Art Designer	MaryAnn Southard

ISBN 0-619-10185-7

Printed in the United States of America

3 4 5 6 7 8 9 10 __ BM   06 05 04 03

Preface

About this book

The Practical Office XP provides a state-of-the-art introduction to Microsoft Office XP, written in an easy-to-read style. Every book includes an action-packed multimedia Book-on-CD. Each page of the Book-on-CD looks exactly like its corresponding page in the printed book and contains interactive elements such as pop-up definitions, interactive animations, and interactive end-of-chapter material. The Book-on-CD requires no installation, so it's easy to use at home, at school, or at work.

The Practical Office XP provides a focused introduction to the most important features of Microsoft Office XP. It is designed to teach you what you really need to know about Office XP in order to use it for practical tasks at school, at work, or at home.

The first page of each chapter introduces the chapter topic and lists the chapter contents. Each chapter includes:

■ **FAQs**, or "frequently asked questions," which explain and demonstrate how to use key features of Microsoft Office XP, and give specific tips for becoming a more proficient office user.

■ An **Assessment** page that contains self-test activities including two sets of QuickCheck questions and four interactive Skill Set tests. These assessment activities provide you with essential feedback that indicates how well you have mastered the material in the chapter. Data from the Skill Sets can be stored on a Tracking Disk. An instructor can consolidate data from all students, generating a variety of reports.

About the Book-on-CD

Every book includes the innovative Book-on-CD, which is loaded with the following features to enhance and reinforce learning:

 Play It! buttons provide animated screen tours that demonstrate how to accomplish various tasks.

 Do It! buttons launch interactive simulations that let you try your hand at the activities presented on that page.

 The Get It? section at the end of each chapter contains an auto-graded interactive review of skills.

QuickChecks   Interactive end-of-chapter QuickCheck questions provide instant feedback on the concepts that you've learned.

Pop-up Definitions & Glossary   Clickable boldface terms display pop-up definitions. A Glossary button provides easy access to all definitions from any page.

Projects   A set of projects located at the end of the book provides structured practice for the Office XP skills presented in each chapter.

Use this book because...

■ **You want to learn how to use Microsoft Office XP**. *The Practical Office XP* will help you learn how to use the essential features of Microsoft Word, Excel, Access, and PowerPoint in the most efficient possible manner. You won't find excess pages or coverage of features that you'll never need—instead you'll find a focused, efficient approach to learning how to use Office XP to complete real-world tasks.

■ **You want to learn Office XP, but don't have Office XP on your computer**. *The Practical Office XP* uses interactive simulations to show you how Office XP works. You don't need to have Office XP on your computer to use *The Practical Office XP* CD. You'll only need to use Office XP if you decide to complete the projects at the end of the book.

■ **You're looking for a product that teaches you how to use Microsoft Office XP, but that also serves as a handy reference**. *The Practical Office XP* is designed to work as both a learning environment and as a quick reference. We recommend using the CD to learn new features. After you've mastered Office XP, keep the printed book nearby as a quick reference.

■ **You've used word processing or spreadsheet software in the past, but haven't used the latest versions of the Microsoft Office XP applications**. *The Practical Office XP* makes it quick and easy to get up to speed on the latest versions of Microsoft Word, Excel, PowerPoint, and Access.

■ **You're a beginning or intermediate computer user**. *The Practical Office XP* is great for beginners, but it also serves as a useful quick reference or refresher for intermediate users. You can skim over the features that you already know and quickly learn how to use features that are new to you.

Teaching Tools

ExamView: Our Powerful Testing Software Package. With ExamView, instructors can generate printed tests, create LAN-based tests, or test over the Internet.

An **Instructor's Manual** outlines each chapter, offers valuable teaching tips, and offers solutions to the end-of-book projects.

WebTrack is an exciting new feature that provides automated delivery of tracking data from any student directly to the instructor with minimal setup or administrative overhead.

Check with your Course Technology sales representative or go to www.course.com to learn more about other valuable Teaching Tools.

Acknowledgments

The successful launch of this book was possible only because of our extraordinary "ground crews." We would like to extend our profound thanks:

To the students at Northern Michigan University, the University of the Virgin Islands, and countless other universities who have participated in classes and corresponded with us over the 25 (or so) years since we began teaching.

To our development team: Donna Schuch, Tensi Parsons, and Keefe Crowley for content and media development; to Kevin Lappi, Deanna Martinson, Karen Kangas, Sue Oja, and Jackie Kangas for testing; to Chris Robbert for narrations; and to Jill Batistick for her detailed copyedit.

To our team members' patient and supportive parents, spouses, and significant others.

To the New Perspectives team at Course Technology, who once again provided professional and enthusiastic support, guidance, and advice. Their insights and team spirit were invaluable.

To Rachel Crapser and Donna Gridley for their editorial support and to our Product Manager, Melissa Hathaway.

To Brianna Germain for her excellent work on the supplements, Brian Raffeto for managing the acceptance testing, and the Software Quality Assurance Team for their valuable QA test comments.

To Gary and the crew at GEX, Dean Fossella and Patty Stephan for their valuable input on the book design, and Debbie Masi for her careful and cheerful production proofing.

To the professors and reviewers who expressed their ideas and shared their teaching strategies with us for the Practical series: Dennis Anderson, St. Francis College; Mary Dobranski, College of Saint Mary; Mike Feiler, Merritt College; Shmuel Fink, Touro College; Dennette Foy, Edison Community College; Nancy LaChance, DeVry Institute of Technology; Janet Sheppard, Collin County Community College; Pauline Pike, Community College of Morris; Linda Reis, Garland County Community College; and Janet Sheppard, Collin County Community College.

Media Credits

All media elements for *The Practical Office XP* are copyrighted by MediaTechnics Corporation.

▪Brief Contents

Introduction
Preface iii
Before You Begin ix

PART A: Microsoft Windows
Chapter 1: Using Windows 2

PART B: Microsoft Word
Chapter 2: Creating a Document 16
Chapter 3: Formatting a Document 28
Chapter 4: Finalizing a Document 38

PART C: Microsoft Excel
Chapter 5: Creating a Worksheet 48
Chapter 6: Formatting a Worksheet 58
Chapter 7: Finalizing a Worksheet 68

PART D: Microsoft PowerPoint
Chapter 8: Creating a Presentation 80
Chapter 9: Finalizing a Presentation 90

PART E: Microsoft Access
Chapter 10: Creating a Database 102
Chapter 11: Finalizing a Database 114

PART F: Projects
Projects 124
Introduction to Projects 125
Projects for Windows 130
Projects for Word 134
Projects for Excel 146
Projects for PowerPoint 158
Projects for Access 166

Index 174

▪ ▪ ▪

▪Contents

PART A: Microsoft Windows

Chapter 1: Using Windows   **2**

How do I start my computer?   3

What's on the Windows desktop?   4

How do I start and stop an application program?   5

How do I change the size of a window?   6

How do I switch between programs?   7

How do menus work?   8

How do toolbars work?   9

How do Windows controls work?   10

How do I open a file?   12

How do I save files?   13

How do I turn off my computer?   14

Assessment   15

PART B: Microsoft Word

Chapter 2: Creating a Document   **16**

What's in the Word program window?   17

How do I create a document?   18

How do I select text for editing?   19

How do I move, copy, and delete text?   20

How can I undo a command?   21

How do I use a document template?   22

How do I save a document?   23

How do I use a document wizard?   24

How do I print a document?   26

Assessment   27

Chapter 3: Formatting a Document   **28**

How do I select different fonts, font sizes, and text colors?   29

How do I apply bold, italic, and underlining attributes?   30

How do I use the Font dialog box?   31

How do I center and align text?   32

How do I add numbering and bullets to a list?   33

How do I adjust the line spacing?   34

How do I use tabs?   35

How do I indent text?   36

Assessment   37

Chapter 4: Finalizing a Document   **38**

How do I check spelling and grammar?   39

How do I use the thesaurus?   40

How do I create headers and footers?   41

How do I set the margins?   42

How do I create a table?   43

How do I use the Print dialog box?   44

How do I use styles?   45

How do I save my document as a Web page?   46

Assessment   47

PART C: Microsoft Excel

Chapter 5: Creating a Worksheet   **48**

What's in the Excel window?   49

How do I enter labels?   50

How do I enter values?   51

How do I enter formulas?   52

How do I create complex formulas?   53

How do I use functions?   54

How do I use the AutoSum button?   56

Assessment   57

Chapter 6: Formatting a Worksheet   **58**

How do I add borders and background colors?   59

How do I format worksheet data?   60

How do I use the Format Cells dialog box?   61

How do I adjust the width of a column?   62

How do I center and align cell contents?   63

What happens when I copy and move cells?   64

How do I know when to use absolute references?   65

How do I delete and insert rows and columns?   66

Assessment   67

▪   ▪   ▪

Contents

Chapter 7: Finalizing a Worksheet   68

How do I check the spelling in a worksheet?   69

How do I sort data in a worksheet?   70

How do I test my worksheet?   71

How do I create a chart?   72

How do I use the print preview and page setup options?   74

How do I add headers and footers to a worksheet?   76

How do I use the Print dialog box?   77

How do I save a worksheet as a Web page?   78

Assessment   79

PART D: Microsoft PowerPoint

Chapter 8: Creating a Presentation   80

What's in the PowerPoint window?   81

How do I create a presentation?   82

How do I add a title slide?   83

How do I add a bulleted list?   84

How do I add a graphic?   85

How do I add a chart?   86

How do I add a table?   87

How do I view a slide show?   88

Assessment   89

Chapter 9: Finalizing a Presentation   90

How do I use the Normal View?   91

How do I use the Slide Sorter View?   92

How do I add transitions?   93

How do I format text on a slide?   94

How do I add animation effects to a bulleted list?   95

How do I check the spelling in a presentation?   96

How do I add and print speaker notes?   97

How do I print handouts?   98

How do I save a presentation as Web pages?   99

Can I show my presentation with an overhead projector?   100

Assessment   101

PART E: Microsoft Access

Chapter 10: Creating a Database   102

How is data organized in a database?   103

What's in the Access window?   104

How do I create a new database or open an existing database?   105

How do I create a table using a wizard?   106

How do I enter and edit data in a table?   109

How do I create a table in Design view?   110

How do I create a query using a wizard?   111

Assessment   113

Chapter 11: Finalizing a Database   114

How do I create a form using a wizard?   115

How do I create a report using a wizard?   118

How do I print a report?   121

How do I save a report as a Web page?   122

Assessment   123

PART F: Projects

Projects   124

Introduction to Projects   125

Projects for Windows   130

Projects for Word   134

Projects for Excel   146

Projects for PowerPoint   158

Projects for Access   166

Index   174

▪Before You Begin

You're going to enjoy using *The Practical Office XP* and the accompanying Book-on-CD. It's a snap to start the Book-on-CD and use it on your computer. So don't delay—get started right away! The answers to the FAQs (frequently asked questions) in this section will help you begin.

▪FAQ   Will the Book-on-CD work on my computer?

The easiest way to find out if the Book-on-CD works on your computer is to try it! Just follow the steps below to start the CD. If it works, you're all set. Otherwise, check with your local technical support person. If you are technically inclined, the system requirements are listed inside the front cover of this book.

▪FAQ   How do I start the Book-on-CD?

The Practical Office XP Book-on-CD is easy to use and requires no installation. Follow these simple steps to get started:

1. Make sure your computer is turned on.

2. Press the button on your computer's CD-ROM drive to open the drawer-like "tray," as shown in the photo below.

3. Place the Book-on-CD into the tray with the label facing up.

4. Press the button on the CD-ROM drive to close the tray, then proceed with Step 5 on the next page.

To use the Book-on-CD, your computer must have a CD-ROM drive. If you have any questions about its operation, check the manual that was supplied with your computer or check with your local technical support person.

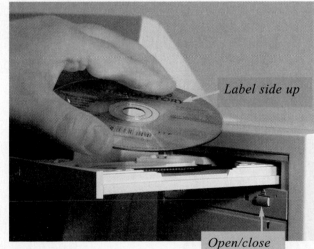

Label side up

Open/close tray button

5. Wait about 15 seconds. During this time, the light on your CD-ROM drive should flicker. Soon you should see *The Practical Office XP* Welcome screen.

If the Welcome screen does not appear, try the instructions in the Manual Start figure below.

Manual Start: *Follow the instructions in this figure only if the Welcome screen did **not** appear automatically in Step 5.*

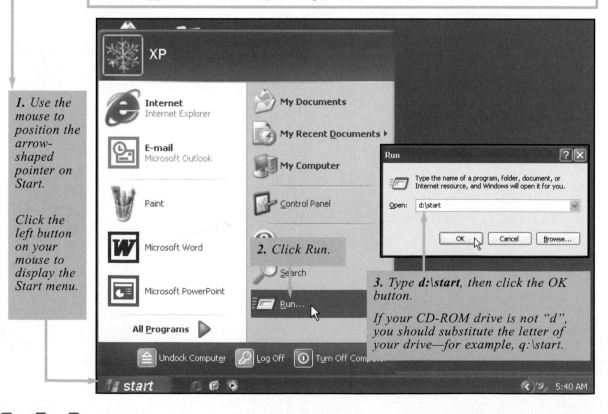

1. Use the mouse to position the arrow-shaped pointer on Start.

Click the left button on your mouse to display the Start menu.

2. Click Run.

*3. Type **d:\start**, then click the OK button.*

If your CD-ROM drive is not "d", you should substitute the letter of your drive—for example, q:\start.

■FAQ What do I do when the Welcome screen appears?

The Welcome screen is the home page for the Book-on-CD. Typically, you'll click **Open the electronic textbook** to start using the interactive Book-on-CD.

Other options on the Welcome screen allow you to jump directly to pages containing animations, to display your Tracking Disk data, and to turn the sound on or off.

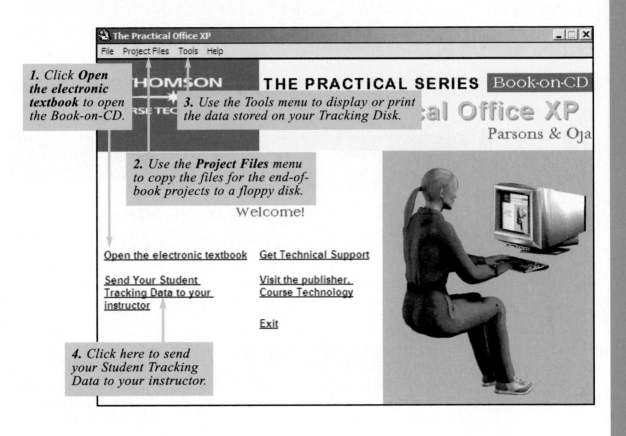

*1. Click **Open the electronic textbook** to open the Book-on-CD.*

3. Use the Tools menu to display or print the data stored on your Tracking Disk.

*2. Use the **Project Files** menu to copy the files for the end-of-book projects to a floppy disk.*

4. Click here to send your Student Tracking Data to your instructor.

Before You Begin

■FAQ How do I navigate through the Book-on-CD?

You can use either the mouse or the keyboard to navigate through the Book-on-CD.

To scroll up or down the page, press the Page Up or Page Down key or use the vertical scroll bar on the right side of the page. You'll know you've reached the bottom of a page when you see three red boxes.

If you scroll down past the end of a page, you'll move to the next page. If you scroll up past the top of a page, you'll move to the previous page. You can also use the Prev and Next buttons or press the left or right arrow keys to move to the previous or next page.

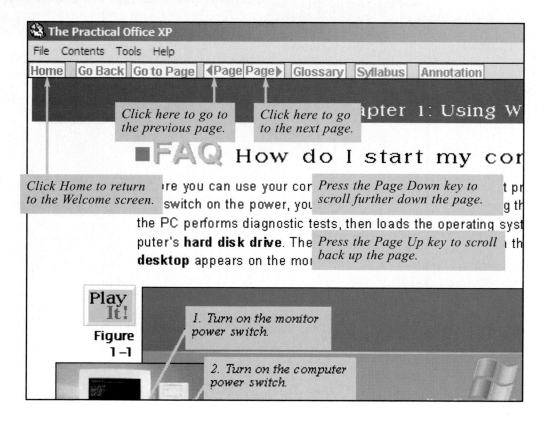

■FAQ How does the interactive Assessment page work?

Each chapter ends with an Assessment page containing interactive activities. You can use these activities to evaluate how well you've mastered the concepts and skills covered in the chapter. If you do well on the Assessment page QuickChecks and Skill Sets, then you'll know you're ready to move on to the next chapter. If you don't do well on the Assessment page, you might want to review the material before going on to the next chapter.

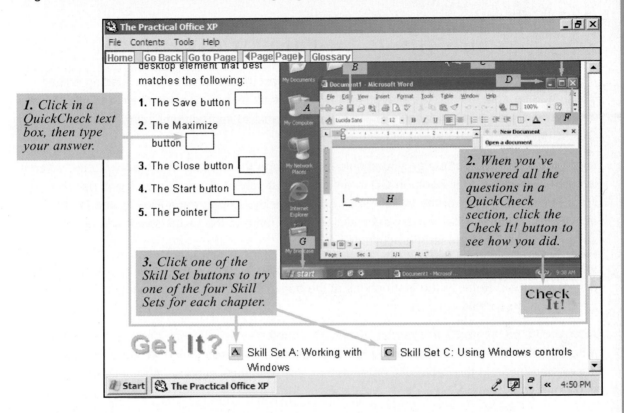

■FAQ What's a Tracking Disk?

A Tracking Disk records your progress by saving your scores on the Skill Sets. You can view or print a summary report of all your scores by using the Tracking Disk menu on the Welcome screen. In an academic setting, your instructor might request your Tracking Disk data to monitor your progress. Your instuctor will tell you if you should submit your Tracking Data using the WebTrack system, if you should hand in your entire Tracking Disk, or if you should send the tracking file as an e-mail attachment.

When you start a Skill Set, the program will check in drive A: for a Tracking Disk. If you want to create a Tracking Disk, insert a formatted floppy disk, then click **Create Tracking File A:\TRACKING.TRK**. You'll be prompted to enter your name, student ID, and section number, all of which will be stored on the Tracking Disk. If you don't want to save your results, just click **Continue without a Tracking Disk**. This option allows you try a Skill Set review without saving your results.

You only need to create a Tracking Disk one time. Once you've created the Tracking Disk, just insert it into the floppy disk drive of your computer when you insert the Book-on-CD or when you are prompted to do so.

■　■　■

■FAQ How do I end a session?

You'll need to leave the Book-on-CD disk in the CD-ROM drive while you're using it, or you will encounter an error message. Before you remove the CD from the drive, you must exit the program by clicking the File menu at the top of the Welcome screen, then clicking Exit. You can also exit by clicking the Close button in the top-right corner of the window.

■FAQ How do I get the most out of the book and the Book-on-CD?

If you have your own computer, you might want to start the CD and do your reading online. You'll then be able to click the Play It! and Do It! buttons as you come to them and click bold-face terms to see pop-up definitions. Also, you'll be able to immediately interact with the QuickCheck section at the end of each chapter.

If you do not have a computer, you should read through the chapter in the book. Later, when it is convenient, take your Book-on-CD to a computer at school, home, or work and use the Media menu at the top of the Welcome screen to quickly jump to each Play It! and Do It! activity in a chapter. After you try each skill, you can jump to the QuickCheck and Get It? sections to complete those interactive activities.

When you have completed a chapter, you might want to try the corresponding projects at the end of the book. Refer to the instructions at the beginning of the Projects section for more information on completing projects.

After you've completed *The Practical Office XP* chapters, keep the book near your computer as a handy reference. When you have a question about a Microsoft Office XP task, find the appropriate page in the Table of Contents, then use the figure captions and bulleted list items to refresh your memory.

■FAQ What about sound?

If your computer is equipped for sound, you should hear the audio during the screen tours and interactive simulations. If you don't hear anything, check the volume control on your computer by clicking the speaker icon in the lower-right corner of your screen. If you're working in a lab or office where sound would be disruptive, consider using headphones. You can also use the Options menu on the Welcome screen to turn off the sound; captions will still explain what you are seeing on the screen.

▪FAQ Can I make the type appear larger on my screen?

If the type in the Book-on-CD appears small, your monitor is probably set at a high resolution. The type will appear larger if you reduce the resolution by following the instructions in the figure below. This setting is optional. You can view the Book-on-CD at most standard resolutions; however, your computer should be set to use Windows standard fonts, not large fonts.

If you would like to see larger type on the screen, you can change the Display setting for your monitor by following the numbered steps below. However, you don't have to change this setting to use the Book-on-CD.

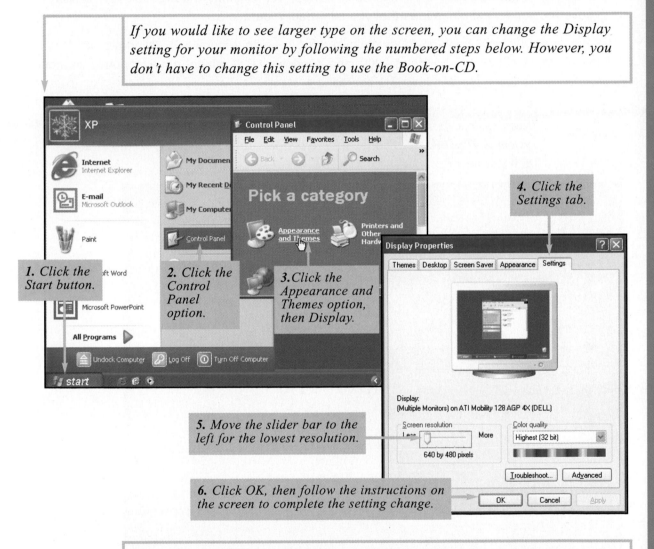

4. *Click the Settings tab.*

1. *Click the Start button.*

2. *Click the Control Panel option.*

3. *Click the Appearance and Themes option, then Display.*

5. *Move the slider bar to the left for the lowest resolution.*

6. *Click OK, then follow the instructions on the screen to complete the setting change.*

Note: You can skip Steps 1 through 3 if you right-click any empty space on the Windows desktop. On the shortcut menu that pops up, select Properties to open the Display Properties dialog box, then continue with Step 4 above.

Before You Begin

■FAQ Which version of Windows do I need?

Your PC's operating system sets the standard for the way all your software looks and works. Most of today's PCs use a version of the Microsoft Windows operating system—"Windows" for short. The most recent versions of Windows are called Windows 95, Windows 98, Windows Me, Windows NT, Windows 2000, and Windows XP. These versions of Windows look very similar and have a common set of features that you can readily learn to use.

The Practical Office XP Book-on-CD is optimized for use with Windows 95, Windows 98, Windows Me, Windows NT, Windows 2000, and Windows XP. It will not run acceptably on most older computers using the Windows 3.1 operating system.

If you see a screen similar to this one when you start your PC, your operating system is Windows 95, Windows 98, Windows Me, Windows NT, Windows 2000, or Windows XP.

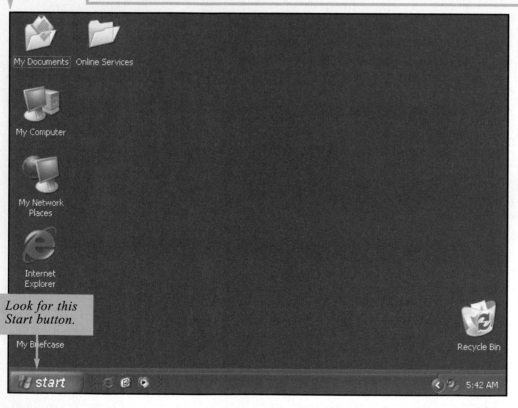

Look for this Start button.

The
Practical
Office XP

Chapter 1
Using Windows

What's Inside?

Microsoft Windows is an operating system with a graphical user interface. An operating system defines how you interact with your computer. The Windows graphical user interface includes rectangular areas on the screen called "windows" and small graphical objects called icons that you manipulate with a mouse.

Microsoft Office XP is a suite of programs that works with the Windows graphical user interface. In order to use the word processing, spreadsheet, database, and presentation software that's included in Microsoft Office XP, it's important to know how to use Windows.

In this chapter, you'll learn how to use Windows to start and manipulate programs, utilize Windows controls, and open and save files. This chapter is particularly important if you've never used a computer before or if you have never used the Windows operating system. If you are familiar with computers and Windows, skim through this chapter to make sure you remember these essential computer and Windows skills.

- **FAQs:**

How do I start my computer?	3
What's on the Windows desktop?	4
How do I start and stop an application program?	5
How do I change the size of a window?	6
How do I switch between programs?	7
How do menus work?	8
How do toolbars work?	9
How do Windows controls work?	10
How do I open a file?	12
How do I save files?	13
How do I turn off my computer?	14

- **Assessment**   15

■FAQ How do I start my computer?

Before you can use your computer, it must complete its boot process. As soon as you switch on the power, your PC starts to "boot up." During the **boot process**, the PC performs diagnostic tests, then loads the operating system from the computer's **hard disk drive**. The boot process is complete when the **Windows desktop** appears on the monitor.

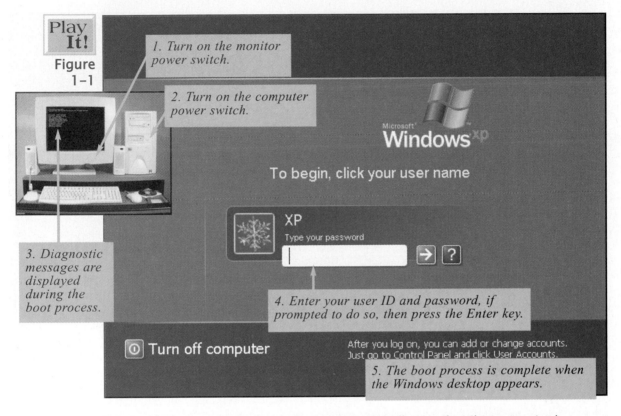

Play It!
Figure 1-1

1. Turn on the monitor power switch.

2. Turn on the computer power switch.

3. Diagnostic messages are displayed during the boot process.

4. Enter your user ID and password, if prompted to do so, then press the Enter key.

5. The boot process is complete when the Windows desktop appears.

Microsoft Windows xp

To begin, click your user name

XP
Type your password

After you log on, you can add or change accounts. Just go to Control Panel and click User Accounts.

⊙ Turn off computer

■ A small light on the computer's system unit indicates that the computer is turned on. A monitor light indicates that the monitor is turned on. If either light does not come on, check the power plugs and power source.

■ Many computers have a power-saving feature that turns off the monitor and, sometimes, the system unit as well, if they are not used for a period of time. You might have to press a key on the keyboard, press a power-save button, or click the mouse to turn the computer back on.

■ If the computer displays a "non-system disk" message, it probably means that a floppy disk has been left in the disk drive. Remove the disk and press any key to continue the boot process.

■ You might be prompted for your password near the end of the boot process. If your **user ID** is not displayed, type it in the user ID box. Then type your **password** in the password box. Press the Enter key to continue. You must use the correct upper-case and lowercase characters when typing your password. As you type your password, you will see an asterisk (*) or circle (•) for each character that you type. The asterisks or circles are a security feature that hides your password from an onlooker.

■ You can start using your computer when the Windows desktop appears.

■ ■ ■

■FAQ What's on the Windows desktop?

The **Windows desktop** is the gateway to all the tasks you perform with your PC. It is the screen you see when the boot process is complete, and it remains in the background as you use other software. You can use controls on the Windows desktop to start a **program**, to switch from one program to another, and to access information about your computer hardware.

Play It!

Figure 1-2

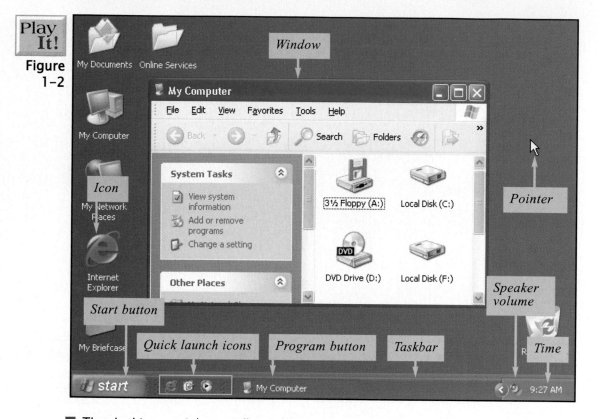

■ The desktop contains small graphics called **icons** that represent programs, hardware, and documents. Double-clicking an icon gives you access to the computer component that it represents.

■ A **window** is a rectangular area on the screen. Each program is displayed in its own window that can be sized and moved independently.

■ The **pointer** is usually shaped like an arrow, but it can change shape when it's positioned over different objects on the screen or while an action is in progress. For example, you might see an hourglass icon during the boot process. This icon signals that you must wait until Windows is ready to accept further commands.

■ The **taskbar** at the bottom of the screen displays buttons and icons that inform you of the status of your computer system. Status information includes the program that you are presently using and the current time.

■ The **Start button** is the main control on the Windows desktop. When you click it, Windows displays the **Start menu**. This menu is used to start programs, to change your hardware settings, to get help, and to install software.

■ **Quick launch icons** provide one-click access to Internet Explorer, e-mail, the desktop, and channels.

■FAQ How do I start and stop an application program?

The Windows operating system provides several ways to start an **application program** ("application" or "program" for short), but you'll typically use the Start button. Although Windows allows you to run several programs at the same time, it's best to close a program when you're finished using it. Closing unused programs frees up memory and helps your computer run more efficiently.

Do It!

Figure 1-3

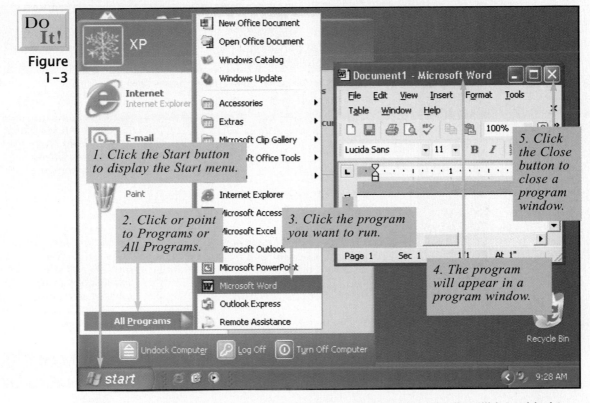

■ When you install a new program on your computer, it typically will be added to the Programs or All Programs menu during the installation process. Then you can just click the name of the program on the Programs or All Programs menu to start the program.

■ Some programs are installed in a submenu under the Programs or All Programs menu. A menu option that leads to a submenu will display ▶ to the right of the menu item's name. Click or point to the menu entry, then click the item on the submenu to run the program.

■ In addition to appearing in the Programs or All Programs menu, some programs, such as Internet Explorer, are represented by an icon on the Windows desktop (shown in the figure on page 4). To use one of these icons to start a program, just double-click it.

■ It's good practice to close a program when you're finished working with it. Closing unused programs frees up resources and allows your computer to operate more efficiently.

■   ■   ■

■FAQ How do I change the size of a window?

Each application program is contained in its own window. Typically, you'll want to maximize a program window so that it fills the screen and provides the largest amount of working space. However, you can resize windows to view more than one program at a time, or you can minimize a window while you work on another program.

Do It!

Figure 1-4

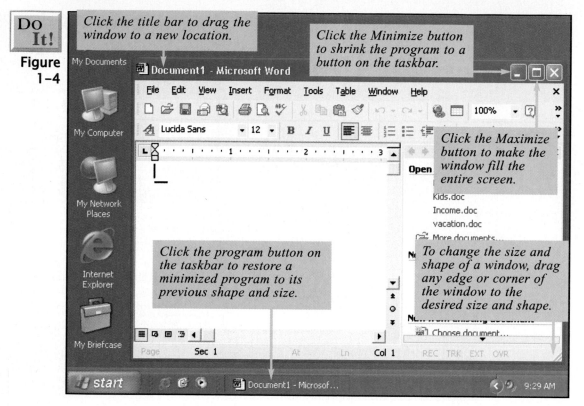

Click the title bar to drag the window to a new location.

Click the Minimize button to shrink the program to a button on the taskbar.

Click the Maximize button to make the window fill the entire screen.

Click the program button on the taskbar to restore a minimized program to its previous shape and size.

To change the size and shape of a window, drag any edge or corner of the window to the desired size and shape.

■ You'll probably find it convenient to maximize a program window to fill the entire screen. This gives you the largest working area for that particular program.

■ When a window is minimized, the program is still running. To close a minimized program, first click the program button on the taskbar to open the window, then click the Close button to close the program. A shortcut to close a minimized program is to right-click the program button on the taskbar. When you do so, a **shortcut menu** appears. You can click Close on this menu to close the program.

■ When a window is maximized, the middle button in the top-right corner changes to the Restore button. When the window is open, but not maximized, the middle button in the top-right corner changes to the Maximize button.

■ To **drag** a window to a new location, hold down the left mouse button over the window's title bar, then slide the mouse slightly on your desk. You can resize a window by dragging its edges. Move the pointer to the edge of the window. When the pointer changes to a double-headed arrow, hold down the left mouse button as you drag the edge to the desired window size.

■ You cannot move or resize a maximized window. Use the Restore button to return the window to its former size before you try to drag it or change its shape.

■FAQ How do I switch between programs?

You can have more than one window open on the desktop at a time. Each open window is represented by a button on the taskbar. Use the buttons on the taskbar to switch from one open program to another. If you need to work with two programs at the same time, you can use the taskbar shortcut menu to automatically size and position the windows so that you can see both at the same time.

Do It!

Figure 1-5

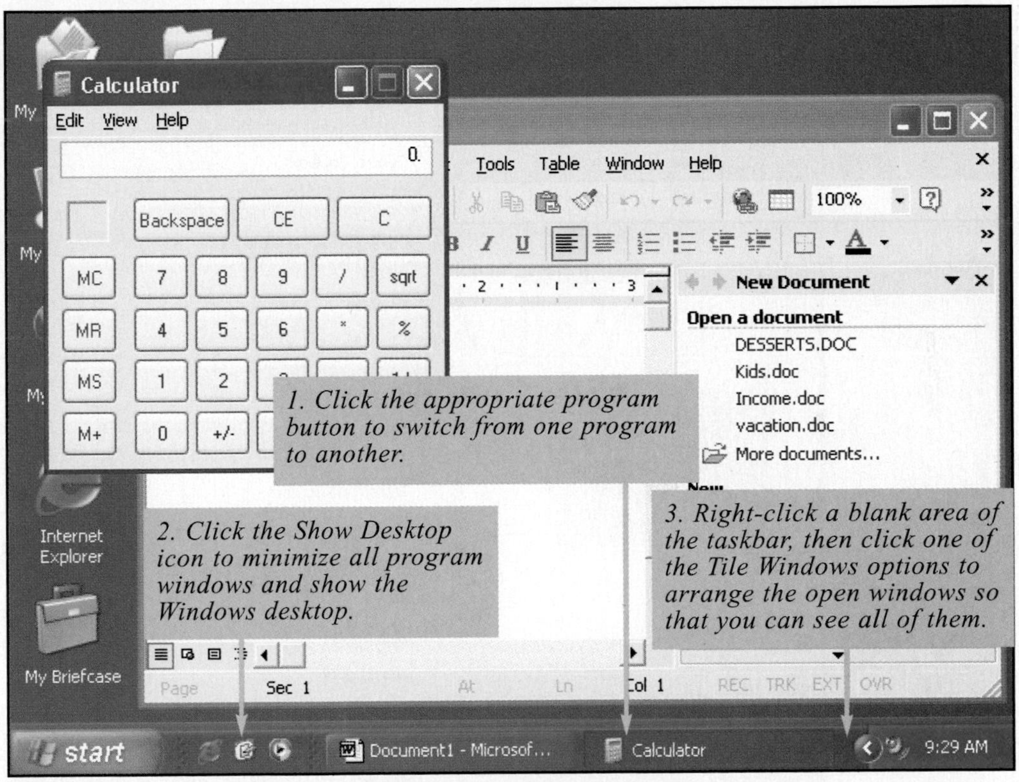

1. Click the appropriate program button to switch from one program to another.

2. Click the Show Desktop icon to minimize all program windows and show the Windows desktop.

3. Right-click a blank area of the taskbar, then click one of the Tile Windows options to arrange the open windows so that you can see all of them.

■ If a program window is minimized, clicking the program button on the taskbar will restore the window to its previous size and location.

■ If a program window is open, but hidden underneath another program window, clicking the program button on the taskbar will bring that window to the top, overlapping the other window on the desktop. You can also click on any visible part of the hidden window to make it active. The active window's title bar will be highlighted, either with a darker shade or a different color. In the above figure, it is dark blue, so you know that Calculator is the active window.

■ When you pause the pointer over an icon on the taskbar, a **ToolTip** shows you the name of the program. If you have more than one window open, you can use the ToolTips to identify all the programs that you have running. In Microsoft Office XP, a similar feature called a **ScreenTip** identifies the toolbar buttons.

■ Sometimes, the taskbar is set to disappear when it is not in use. To reveal it, you pass the mouse pointer off the bottom edge of the monitor display. You can also drag the taskbar up and down to make it larger or smaller to display many program buttons.

■ ■ ■

▪FAQ How do menus work?

Most application programs include a menu bar located below the title bar near the top of the program window. A menu provides a set of commands that you can use to tell the computer how you want to complete a task.

Typically, menus provide access to all the features of a program. If you don't remember how to access one of these features, you can browse through the menu options to find out how to do it.

Do It!

Figure 1-6

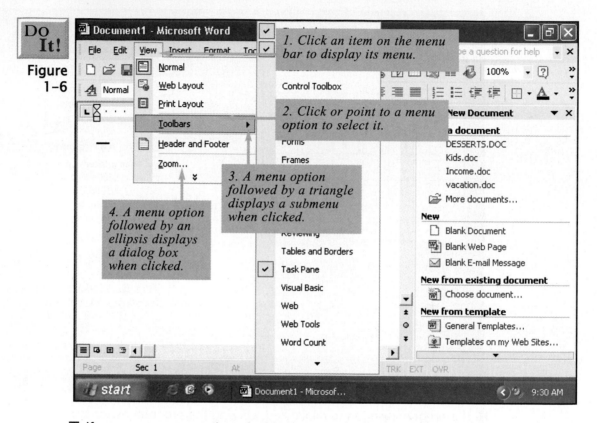

■ If you open a menu, then decide that you don't want to select an option after all, click the menu title again or press the Esc key to close the menu.

■ You can use your keyboard for fast access to commonly used menu items. Hold down the Alt key and press the underlined letter to display a menu. Press the underlined letter to select a menu option.

■ Menus that have more options that are not displayed will show ⌄ arrows at the bottom. Click the arrows to display hidden menu options. After a hidden option has been used, the next time the menu is displayed, the option will be displayed. A menu option will become hidden if it is not used frequently.

■FAQ How do toolbars work?

Most application programs display one or more **toolbars**, typically located below the menu bar near the top of the program window. Toolbars contain a number of buttons, sometimes called "tools," that provide a single-click shortcut for the most commonly used menu options.

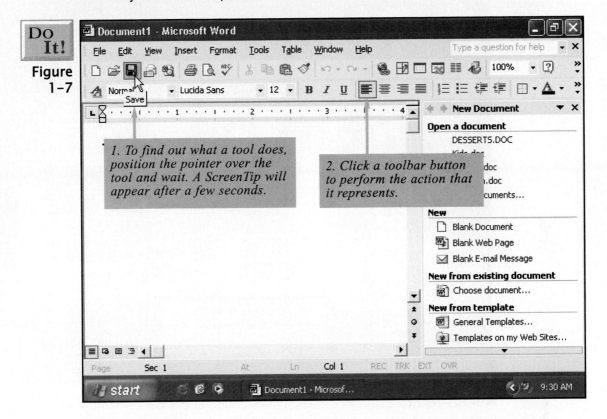

Do It!

Figure 1-7

■ Microsoft Office applications use similar toolbars and toolbar buttons. This consistency helps users to become familiar with program functions more quickly.

■ Some programs allow you to select the toolbars that you want to display. In Microsoft Office XP programs, click View, then click Toolbars to display a list of available toolbars. Click to place a check mark in front of any toolbar that you want to display. Click again to remove the check mark from any toolbar that you don't want to display.

■ You can move and position the toolbars in Microsoft Office programs. Click one of the toolbar borders, then drag the toolbar to a new location. If you drop the toolbar in the middle of the window, it will be placed in a separate window. If you drop the toolbar near the top, bottom, left, or right side of the window, it will attach itself to that edge of the window.

■ In Microsoft Office programs, the Standard and Formatting toolbars can be displayed as one or two rows of buttons. Unless you're working with a large monitor, you might prefer to display these toolbars as two rows. To change this setting, click Tools, then click Customize to display the Customize dialog box. Place a check mark in the *Show Standard and Formatting toolbars on two rows* check box.

■FAQ How do Windows controls work?

There are a variety of controls that work the same in almost all Windows programs, including Office XP programs. After you learn how to use these Windows controls, you'll find that you can easily use most Windows programs.

Do It!

Figure 1-8

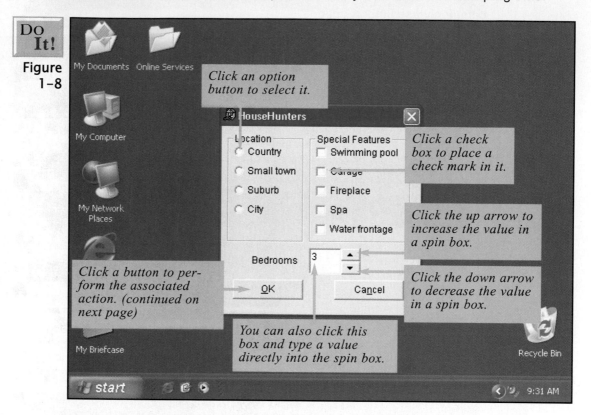

■ A **dialog box** usually contains an OK button and a Cancel button. Click the OK button to apply your selections and close the dialog box. Click the Cancel button to cancel your selections and close the dialog box without making any changes.

■ An **option button** is a circular-shaped control, which might appear with several others in a set. You can select only one option button at a time from each set. If you select a new option button, the old button will be deselected. Typically, at least one option button will always be selected.

■ A **check box** signals that more than one option can be selected at a time. You can place a check mark in one, some, none, or all the check boxes.

■ When you click an empty check box, a check mark appears in it. If you click a check box with a check mark in it, the check mark disappears.

■ A **spin box** allows you to click up and down arrows in order to increase or decrease a value. Alternatively, you can type a number in the spin box.

■How do Windows controls work? (continued)

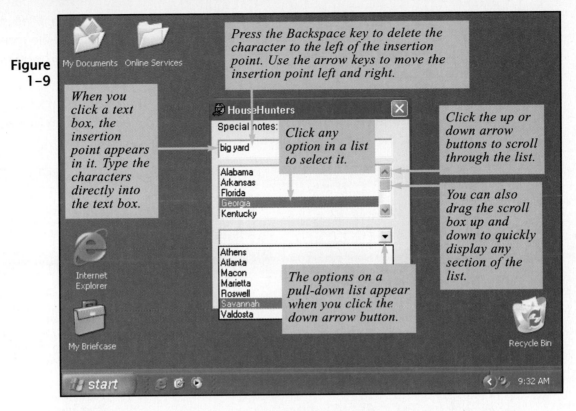

Figure
1-9

To delete the contents of a text box, double-click the text box to select the contents, then press the Delete key to delete the selected text.

Click any option on a standard **list** to select it. Click the up and down arrow buttons to scroll up and down the list. You can also drag the scroll box up and down to quickly display any section of the list.

The options on a **pull-down list** are displayed when you click the down arrow button. After the list is displayed, it works much like a standard list. Click any option to select it. Use the up and down arrow buttons or drag the scroll box to view other sections of the list.

Some pull-down lists allow you to type directly into the box at the top of the list or select an option from the list.

■FAQ How do I open a file?

Data is stored in files on the disks and CDs in your computer system. Files may be referred to in different ways in different programs. For example, a file created with Microsoft Word is usually called a document, while a Microsoft PowerPoint file is usually called a presentation.

Before you can work with a file, you need to open it. The programs in Microsoft Office XP use a standardized Open dialog box, which means opening files works pretty much the same way in Word, Excel, Access, and PowerPoint.

Do It!

Figure 1-10

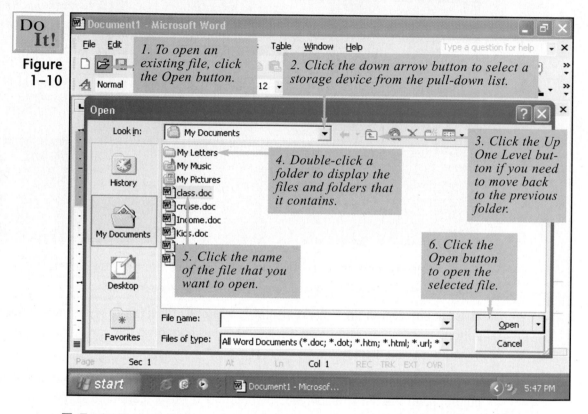

1. To open an existing file, click the Open button.

2. Click the down arrow button to select a storage device from the pull-down list.

3. Click the Up One Level button if you need to move back to the previous folder.

4. Double-click a folder to display the files and folders that it contains.

5. Click the name of the file that you want to open.

6. Click the Open button to open the selected file.

■ Each storage device on your computer is assigned a unique **device letter**. Most computers have at least three storage devices—a floppy disk drive called A, a hard disk drive called C, and a CD-ROM drive called D. Sometimes the CD-ROM drive, as well as other storage devices, might be assigned letters such as E or F.

■ **Folders**, sometimes called subdirectories, allow you to group and organize files for easy retrieval. Folders can contain both files and other folders, the latter of which can contain more files and folders.

■ Microsoft Office XP stores files in the My Documents folder on drive C if no other drive or folder is specified. If you saved a file but don't know where it went, check to see if it was saved in the My Documents folder.

■FAQ How do I save files?

When you create a file on your computer, you must save it if you want to be able to use it again in the future. When you save a file, you specify the drive letter, folder, and file name under which the file will be saved.

Do It!

Figure 1-11

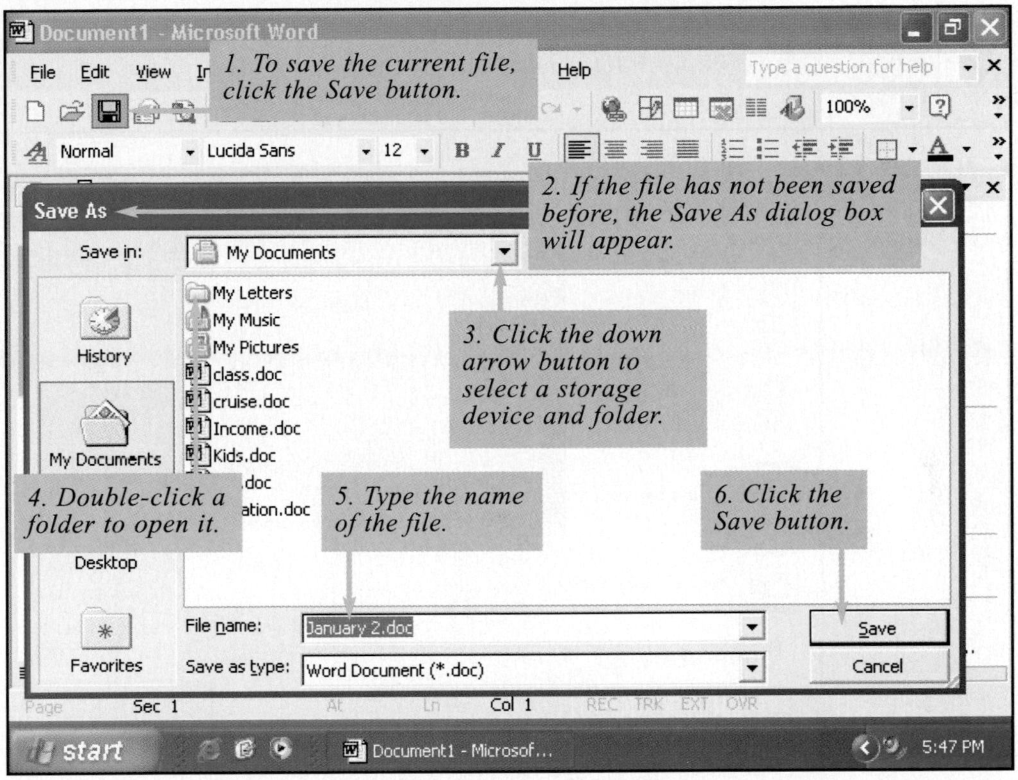

1. To save the current file, click the Save button.

2. If the file has not been saved before, the Save As dialog box will appear.

3. Click the down arrow button to select a storage device and folder.

4. Double-click a folder to open it.

5. Type the name of the file.

6. Click the Save button.

■ Each folder can contain only one file with a particular file name. However, different documents with the same name can be stored in different folders.

■ The file is assigned a name when it is saved. File names can consist of letters, spaces, numbers, and certain punctuation symbols. File names cannot include the characters / ? : = < > | and must not be longer than 255 characters.

■ A **file extension** is a set of up to three characters that indicates the file type. A file extension is separated from the file name by a period. Windows programs add the appropriate extension automatically, so you don't have to type it when saving a file.

■ The Save button works differently, depending on whether the file was previously saved. Clicking the Save button will automatically store the file using the original name on the drive and folder where it was previously stored. If the file hasn't been saved before, clicking the Save button will open the Save As dialog box. Select the drive and folder where you want to save the file, enter a file name, then click the Save button.

■ If you've modified an existing file and want to save the new version under a different name, click File, then click Save As to display the Save As dialog box. Enter a new name and select the drive and folder in which to store the file. The modified version of the file will be saved under the new name, leaving the original version of the file unchanged under the original name.

■ ■ ■

■FAQ How do I turn off my computer?

You should issue the **Shut Down** or **Turn Off Computer** command before you turn off your computer. The process ensures that your work for this computing session is saved, and it cleans out any temporary "scratchpad" data that the operating system created but doesn't need to save.

Do It!

Figure 1–12

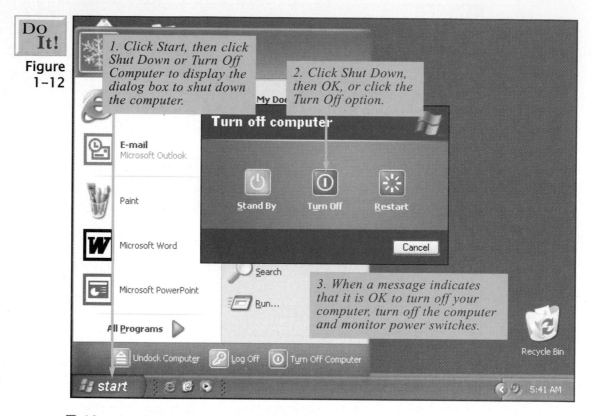

1. Click Start, then click Shut Down or Turn Off Computer to display the dialog box to shut down the computer.

2. Click Shut Down, then OK, or click the Turn Off option.

3. When a message indicates that it is OK to turn off your computer, turn off the computer and monitor power switches.

■ After the shut down process is complete, your computer will either display a message indicating that it is safe to turn off your computer, or it might turn off by itself. If the shut down message appears, and your computer doesn't turn off by itself, use the power switch to turn it off.

■ If occasionally you forget to use the Shut Down or Turn Off Computer command before switching off the power, you probably won't damage anything. However, you should make it a habit to do things the right way just to avoid potential problems.

■ If your computer was turned off without being shut down, you will be prompted to run a short disk test, called **ScanDisk**, the next time you start your computer. Just follow the instructions on the screen to continue the boot process.

■ Computer programs have "bugs" or errors that sometimes cause your computer to "freeze up" or "hang" so that it won't respond to your mouse clicks or keyboard commands. If this situation occurs, you won't be able to issue the regular Shut Down or Turn Off Computer command. Before you press the power switch, hold down the Ctrl, Alt, and Del keys at the same time. Then follow the directions in any dialog box that appears. If only one program has frozen, you'll be able to end that program without closing other programs that you are still using.

QuickCheck A

1. When the Windows desktop appears on the monitor, the [＿＿＿＿＿＿] process is complete and your computer is ready for use.

2. A(n) [＿＿＿＿＿＿] is a rectangular area on the screen that can be moved and sized independently.

3. To start a program, click the [＿＿＿＿＿＿], point to Programs or All Programs, then click the program you want to run.

4. True or false? To view the name of a toolbar button or taskbar icon, click the left mouse button. [＿＿＿＿]

5. True or false? The Save button works differently depending on whether the file has previously been saved. [＿＿＿＿]

Check It!

QuickCheck B

Indicate the letter of the desktop element that best matches the following:

1. The Save button [＿＿＿]

2. The Maximize button [＿＿＿]

3. The Close button [＿＿＿]

4. The Start button [＿＿＿]

5. The Pointer [＿＿＿]

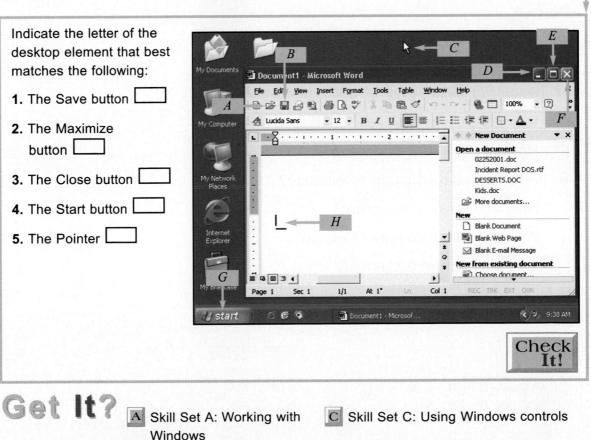

Check It!

Get It?

- **A** Skill Set A: Working with Windows
- **B** Skill Set B: Using menus and toolbars
- **C** Skill Set C: Using Windows controls
- **D** Skill Set D: Opening and saving files

Chapter 2
Creating a Document

What's Inside?

Microsoft Word is the component of the Microsoft Office suite best suited for creating documents such as letters and reports. As **word processing software**, Microsoft Word provides a set of tools for entering and revising text, adding graphical elements such as color and tables, then formatting and printing the completed documents.

Most people use Microsoft Word more frequently than any other component of Microsoft Office. Almost everyone needs to create documents, from personal letters to business proposals, and Microsoft Word is the best tool for creating these documents.

In Chapter 2, you'll learn how to create documents using Microsoft Word. Then you'll learn how to select and edit text. You'll also learn how to use document templates and document wizards to quickly generate common documents.

- FAQs:

What's in the Word program window?	17
How do I create a document?	18
How do I select text for editing?	19
How do I move, copy, and delete text?	20
How can I undo a command?	21
How do I use a document template?	22
How do I save a document?	23
How do I use a document wizard?	24
How do I print a document?	26

- Assessment   27

■FAQ what's in the Word program window?

The Word program window is the window that appears when you start Microsoft Word. To start Word, click Start, point to Programs or All Programs, then click Microsoft Word. The Word program window contains objects such as the title bar, the menu bar, the toolbars, the task pane, and the document window. You'll use these objects to create, edit, save, print, and format your documents.

Play It!

Figure 2-1

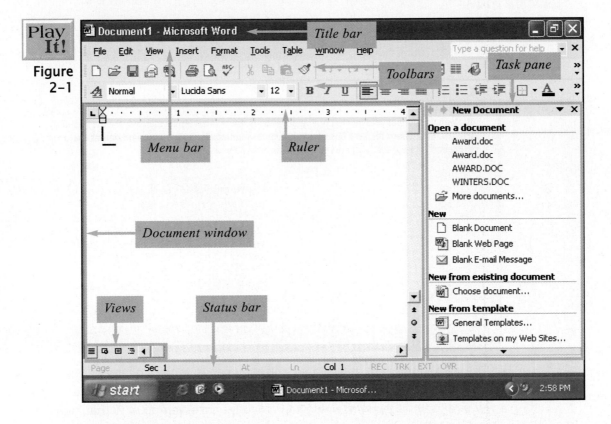

■ The **document window** represents a blank piece of paper. Characters that you type on the keyboard appear in the document window. The **title bar** indicates the name of the current document. If the current document has never been saved, the title bar displays the generic title "Document1". Word's **menu bar** and **toolbar** contain commands and tools that you'll use to create and edit your document. You'll learn more about toolbars and menu commands in other FAQs.

■ There are different ways to view your document. The **Normal View** allows quick text editing and formatting. The **Web Layout View** shows how your document would look in a Web browser. The **Print Layout View** shows how the content will look on the page, including margins as well as headers and footers. You can work in **Outline View** to look at the structure of a document.

■ The **status bar** provides information, such as the page number and total number of pages, about the document you are viewing in the window.

■ The **task pane** allows you to have quick access to commonly used features in Word. You can open a new document, view the clipboard, search for a document, and apply formatting quickly and easily.

■   ■   ■

■FAQ How do I create a document?

To create a new document, just click the blank document window and start typing. When typing the document, don't worry too much about spelling, formatting, or arranging the document. You'll find it's very easy to edit and format the document after you've entered the text.

Do It!

Figure 2-2

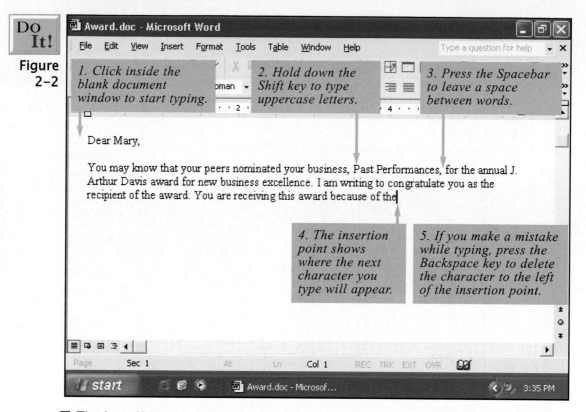

■ The **insertion point** shows your current location in the document. As you type, the insertion points moves to show where the next character will appear. Click anywhere in the document window to move the insertion point to that location. To add a blank line, press the Enter key.

■ Through a feature known as **word wrap**, the insertion point automatically jumps down to the beginning of the next line when you reach the right margin of the current line. If the last word on the line is too long for the line, it will be moved down to the beginning of the next line. You do not have to press the **Enter key** at the end of every line. Press the Enter key only when you complete a paragraph. Press Enter a second time to create a blank line before the next paragraph.

■ Press the **Backspace key** to delete the character to the left of the insertion point. You can also press the **Delete key** to delete the character to the right of the insertion point. These keys also work to erase spaces and blank lines.

■ If you need to add text in the middle of a line or word, use the mouse or arrow keys to move the insertion point to the desired location, then type the text you need to add. To make room for the new text, everything to the right of the insertion point will be pushed to the right and down as you type.

■FAQ How do I select text for editing?

Many word processing features require you to select a section of text before you edit, change, or format it. When you **select text**, you mark it to indicate the section of text that you want to modify in a later operation. Selecting text doesn't do anything useful by itself, but combined with other commands, it enables you to use many of the other important features of Word. Selected text is "highlighted," typically by displaying it as light text on a dark background. Word provides several ways to select text.

Do It!

Figure 2–3

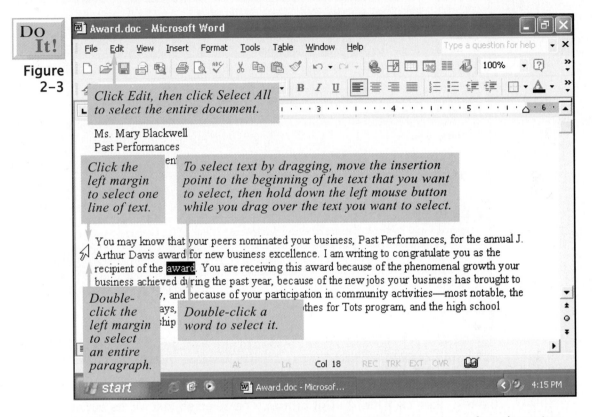

Click Edit, then click Select All to select the entire document.

Click the left margin to select one line of text.

To select text by dragging, move the insertion point to the beginning of the text that you want to select, then hold down the left mouse button while you drag over the text you want to select.

Double-click the left margin to select an entire paragraph.

Double-click a word to select it.

■ Use the drag method to select short sections of text, such as a few characters or several words. Use one of the other selection methods when you need to select a single word, a line, a paragraph, or the entire document.

■ When you point to a word, you can double-click to select only that word. You can **triple-click** to select the current paragraph.

■ When you point to the left margin, the pointer will change to a white arrow. You can click once to select a line of text or double-click to select a paragraph.

■ If you have trouble using the mouse, you can also use the keyboard to select text. Use the mouse or arrow keys to move the insertion point to the beginning of the text that you want to select. Hold the Shift key down while you use the arrow keys to select text.

■ To deselect text, you should click away from the text that is currently selected. You can also press one of the arrow keys to deselect text.

■FAQ How do I move, copy, and delete text?

As you create a document, you'll need to move or copy sections of text—words, paragraphs, or even entire pages—from one part of the document to another. To copy or move text, you'll use the **Clipboard**, a special memory location that can temporarily hold sections of your document.

Do It!

Figure 2-4

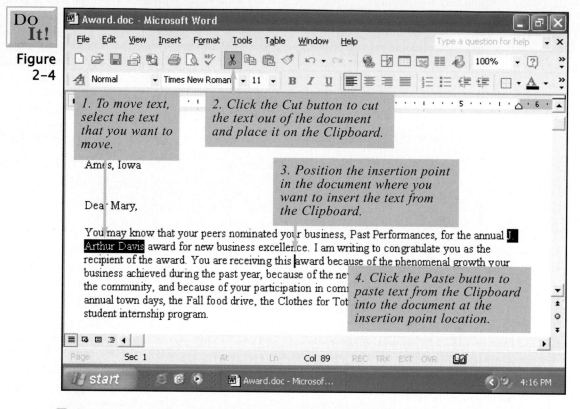

■ To move a section of text from one part of your document to another, first select the text, then click the ✂ **Cut button**. The selected text will be cut out of the document and placed on the Clipboard. To paste that text back into the document, move the insertion point to the place where you want to position the text, then click the 📋 **Paste button**. The text is copied from the Clipboard and placed into the document. This operation is known as **cut and paste**.

■ **Copy and paste** works much the same way as cut and paste, except that the text is not removed from its original location. Select the text you want to copy, then click the 📄 **Copy button**. The selected text is copied to the Clipboard, but the original text is not removed from the document. Move the insertion point to the place where you want to place the copy, then click the Paste button.

■ After you cut or copy, the copied text remains on the Clipboard. You can use this feature when you need to put several copies of the same text into your document. Just move the insertion point to the location where you want to place the next copy and click the Paste button. You can paste as many copies of the text as you like.

■FAQ How can I undo a command?

If you perform an action then change your mind, you might be able to use the Undo button to undo the action. The Undo button has a counterpart—the Redo button—that allows you to repeat an action that you mistakenly undid.

Do It!

Figure 2-5

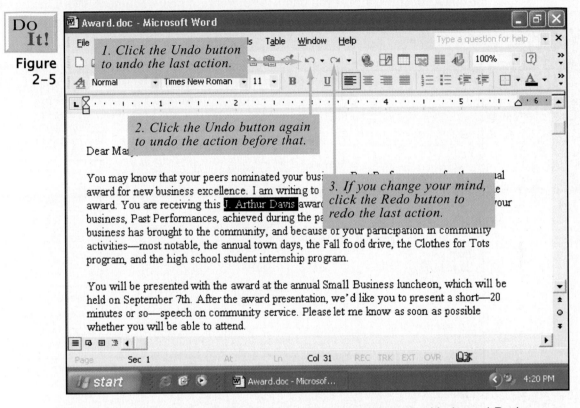

■ If there are no actions that can be undone or redone, the Undo and Redo buttons will be disabled—they will appear "grayed out" and nothing will happen if you click them.

■ The Undo button works best when undoing an editing or formatting command. Actions such as saving and printing files cannot be undone.

■ If you need to undo or redo a number of actions, click the ▼ down arrow button on the right side of the Undo or Redo buttons to display a list of actions that can be undone or redone. Drag to highlight down the list to select the actions that you want to undo or redo. You can also click on a specific action to select it, but all the actions prior to that one will also be performed.

■FAQ How do I use a document template?

You can create a document "from scratch" by typing in a blank, new document window. As an alternative, you can use a **document template**, which is a pre-formatted document that you can use to create a new document. Word includes templates for many basic documents, including letters, faxes, mailing labels, envelopes, and resumes.

Do It!

Figure 2-6

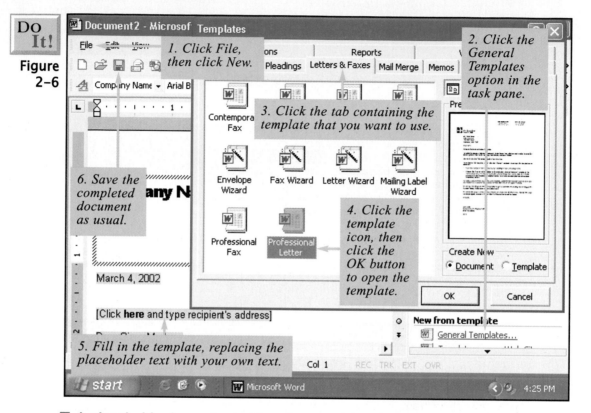

1. Click File, then click New.

2. Click the General Templates option in the task pane.

3. Click the tab containing the template that you want to use.

6. Save the completed document as usual.

4. Click the template icon, then click the OK button to open the template.

5. Fill in the template, replacing the placeholder text with your own text.

■ A **placeholder** is an element in a document template in which you enter text that will personalize your document. You click inside the placeholder and type your own text. The placeholder disappears and your text is displayed.

■ Word allows users to create their own custom document templates. After you're more familiar with Word, you might want to explore the template feature to create templates for documents that you need to create on a regular basis. You can find more information on creating templates in Microsoft Word Help and in the program documentation.

■ If you work in a large business or organization, someone else may have already created templates for the most commonly created documents. Some examples of document templates used in business are letterheads, fax cover sheets, memos, and reports.

■FAQ How do I save a document?

After you select a document template and personalize it with your own text, it's important to save the document properly so that you can find and use it again. The first time you save your document, be sure to store it in the correct location and as the appropriate file type.

Do It!

Figure 2-7

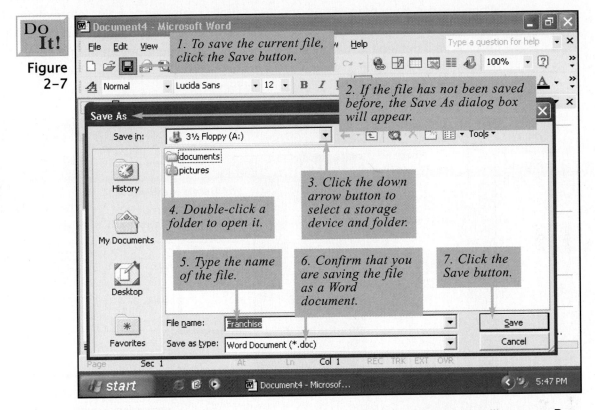

1. To save the current file, click the Save button.

2. If the file has not been saved before, the Save As dialog box will appear.

3. Click the down arrow button to select a storage device and folder.

4. Double-click a folder to open it.

5. Type the name of the file.

6. Confirm that you are saving the file as a Word document.

7. Click the Save button.

■ The first time you save your document, the Save As dialog box will appear. By default, Word will save your file as a Word document in the My Documents folder. You can save the document in another location by selecting a different drive and folder.

■ You can save your document as a different file type if you click the down arrow button to the right of the Save as type text box. For instance, you might want to save the document as an earlier version of Word in order to open the document on another computer that doesn't have Microsoft Office XP installed.

■ After you save the document the first time, you can save it more quickly by using the Save button. This action will automatically save the document using the original file name in the drive and folder where it was previously stored.

■   ■   ■

■FAQ How do I use a document wizard?

A **document wizard** provides yet another way for you to create a document. Like a document template, a document wizard provides you with a pre-formatted document. However, a document wizard differs from a template in several ways. When using a document wizard, you are usually prompted to enter information into the document wizard dialog boxes. This information is automatically incorporated into the final document. Wizards also typically allow you to select from a number of formatting options. For example, the resume wizard allows you to select contemporary, professional, or elegant formats.

Do It!

Figure 2-8

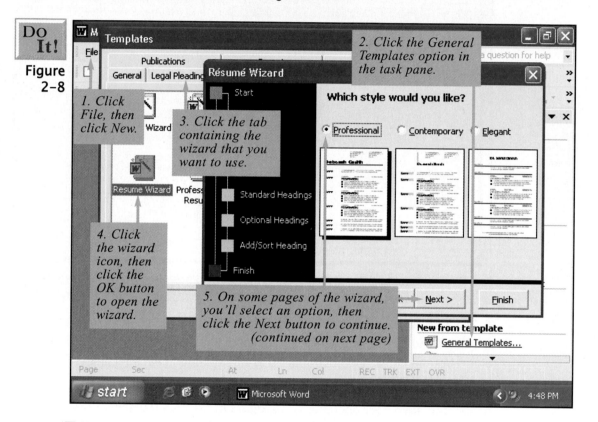

■ Wizards provide more options and generate a more complete document than templates. However, you cannot create your own wizards.

■ Wizards are mixed in the Templates dialog box along with templates. The wizards are labeled as wizards and are marked with a magic wand icon.

■ As you proceed through the wizard, you'll select options and enter information needed to generate the document.

■ After you complete each page of the wizard, click the Next button to go to the next page.

■How do I use a document wizard? (continued)

Figure 2–9

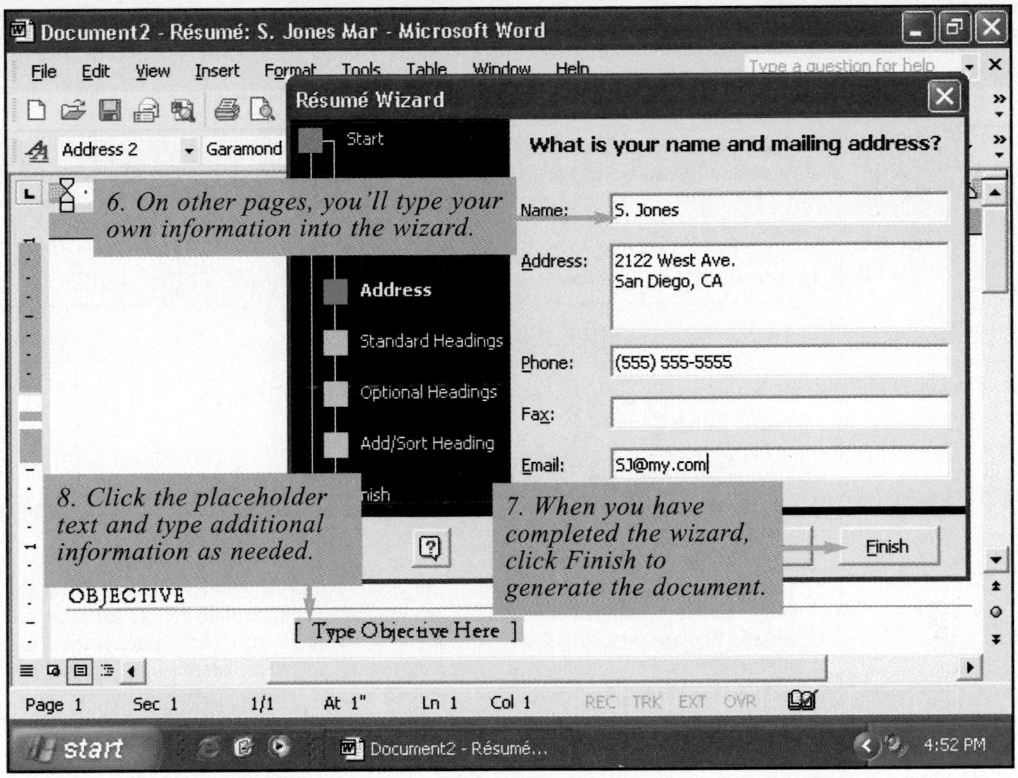

■ The final document will reflect the choices you made with the wizard and will include the information that you entered. However, the document will not be complete. You'll need to click the placeholder text and replace it with your own information. Edit the document as needed to add and delete text.

■ When the document is complete, save it as you would save any new document.

■FAQ How do I print a document?

Before you print your document, you can see how it will look on the page by using **Print Preview**. When the document is ready, you can print it using the Print button or the Print option on the File menu.

Do It!

Figure 2-10

Award.doc - Microsoft Word

File   Edit   View   Insert   Format   Tools

Type a question for help

Click Print Preview to view the document before you print it.

103%

Normal + Botto ▾   Times New Roman ▾

Click Print to print one copy of the document.

Ms. Mary Black
Past Performanc
10 Old Town Center
Ames, Iowa

Click File, click Send to, then click Mail Recipient (as attachment) to send the document electronically without printing it.

You may know that your peers nominated your business, Past Performances, for the annual award for new business excellence. I am writing to congratulate you as the recipient of the award. You are receiving this J. Arthur Davis award because of the phenomenal growth your business, Past Performances, achieved during the past year, because of the new jobs your business has brought to the community, and because of your participation in community activities—most notable, the annual town days, the Fall food drive, the Clothes for Tots program, and the high school student internship program.

Page   Sec 1   At   Ln   Col 1   REC TRK EXT OVR

start   Award.doc - Microsof...   4:53 PM

■ Print Preview allows you to see how the document will look when printed. Click the Print button on the toolbar to print the document. To exit Print Preview without printing, click Close on the toolbar.

■ The Print button sends one copy of the entire document to your default printer. If you want to print more than one copy, print a specific page, or switch to a different printer, you must click File, then click Print to open the Print dialog box. The Print dialog box is discussed in more detail on page 44.

■ In order to send the document as an e-mail attachment, you must have an account that gives you access to the Internet. Another requirement is to have a compatible e-mail program, such as Microsoft Outlook. You can find more information on using Word for sending e-mail in Microsoft Word Help.

QuickCheck A

1. When creating a document in Word, characters that you type appear in the _____ window.

2. Press the _____ key to delete the character to the right of the insertion point.

3. When you _____ text, the selected text is removed from the original location and placed on the Clipboard.

4. True or false? If you accidentally delete the wrong text, you can click the Redo button to cancel the deletion and display the original text. _____

5. A document _____ typically allows you to choose from a selection of formatting options as you are creating a new document.

Check It!

QuickCheck B

Indicate the letter of the desktop element that best matches the following:

1. Selected text _____

2. The Copy button _____

3. The Paste button _____

4. The Cut button _____

5. The end of a line of text where the Enter key was pressed _____

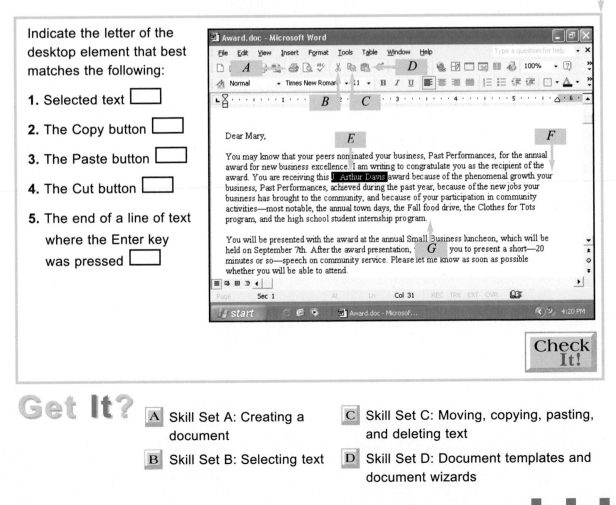

Check It!

Get It?

A Skill Set A: Creating a document

B Skill Set B: Selecting text

C Skill Set C: Moving, copying, pasting, and deleting text

D Skill Set D: Document templates and document wizards

Chapter 3

Formatting a Document

What's Inside?

In Chapter 3, you'll learn how to format your documents using features such as bold and italic text, different fonts and font sizes, paragraph alignment, and bulleted and numbered lists.

Experienced word processing users find that it's useful to apply formatting after writing the document. The idea is to focus initially on the content of the document, while adding, deleting, and moving text as needed. After you're satisfied with the content and order of the document, you can go back and format the document as needed.

Appropriate formatting can greatly increase the attractiveness and readability of your documents. However, it's important not to get carried away with formatting. Use different fonts, font sizes, and colors only where they add to the appearance or readability of the document. After all, you wouldn't want your documents to look like a ransom note pasted together with letters from a variety of newspaper stories!

■ FAQs:

How do I select different fonts, font sizes, and text colors?	29
How do I apply bold, italic, and underlining attributes?	30
How do I use the Font dialog box?	31
How do I center and align text?	32
How do I add numbering and bullets to a list?	33
How do I adjust the line spacing?	34
How do I use tabs?	35
How do I indent text?	36

■ Assessment   37

■FAQ How do I select different fonts, font sizes, and text colors?

You can use menus or tools on the Formatting toolbar to select different text attributes for letters, words, sentences, or paragraphs. The term **font** refers to the design or typeface of each character. Don't use too many different fonts—your documents will look more professional if you limit yourself to one or two basic fonts for each document.

Do It!

Figure 3-1

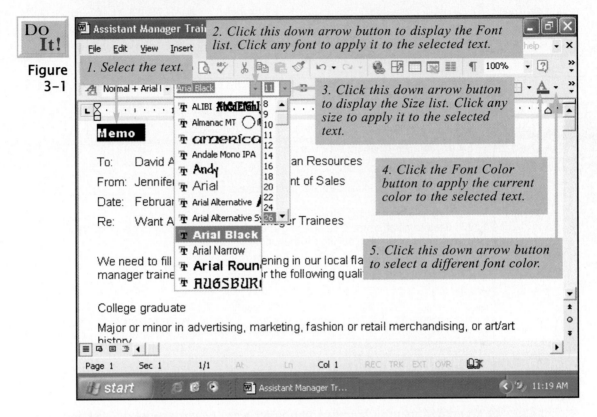

■ **Text attributes** include font, font size, bold, italic, underline, and text color. Font size is normally 9–12 points, but you can select any font size up to 72 points, which is equal to one inch. You can make text even larger by typing in a number larger than 72. This feature is useful for making signs and posters.

■ Once you've selected text, you can change the font, font size, and color without reselecting the text. As long as the text remains selected, you can apply additional formatting options to it. After you've formatted the text, click anywhere outside of the highlighted area to deselect it.

■ If you want to change the font or font size for the entire document, click Edit, then click Select All to select the entire document. Using this feature, you can apply any text attributes to all the text in a document, even to multiple pages.

▪FAQ How do I apply bold, italic, and underlining attributes?

You can use menu options and toolbar buttons to apply text attributes such as bold, italic, and underlining to text within your document.

Do It!

Figure 3-2

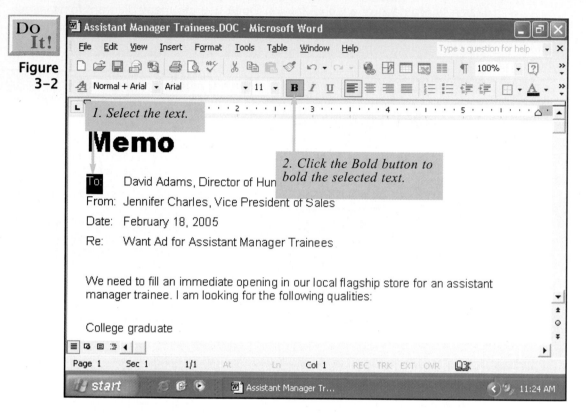

▪ Typically, you'll apply text attributes to text that you've already typed. Just select the text, then use the toolbar button to apply the text attribute.

▪ You can apply the bold text attribute before typing new text. Click the **Bold button**, then type the text. Click the Bold button again to discontinue bold and continue typing normal text.

▪ Toolbar buttons both apply and remove attributes. For instance, if you applied the bold attribute, but then changed your mind and wanted to display the text as normal, you would select the text, and then click the Bold button to remove the bold attribute. The selected text will be displayed as normal text.

▪ The **Italic button** and the **Underline button** work the same way as the Bold button, but they apply different text attributes.

▪ You can combine the bold, italic, and underline text attributes by clicking any combination of buttons. To display bold, underlined text, select the text, click the Bold button, then click the Underline button. You can freely mix and match bold, underlined, and italic text.

▪ If you select a section of text that includes both normal and bold text, the first time you click the Bold button, all the selected text will be displayed as bold. Click the Bold button again to display all the selected text as normal text.

▪ ▪ ▪

■FAQ How do I use the Font dialog box?

As you've already learned, you can apply some text attributes—such as bold, italic, and underlining—using the Formatting toolbar. But other text attribute options, such as the styles of underlines and the character spacing options, are only available from the Font dialog box.

You can also use the Font dialog box if you need to apply multiple formatting options to selected text. It's faster to use the Font dialog box to apply all the attributes in one operation than to apply the attributes one at a time using the toolbar buttons.

Do It!

Figure 3-3

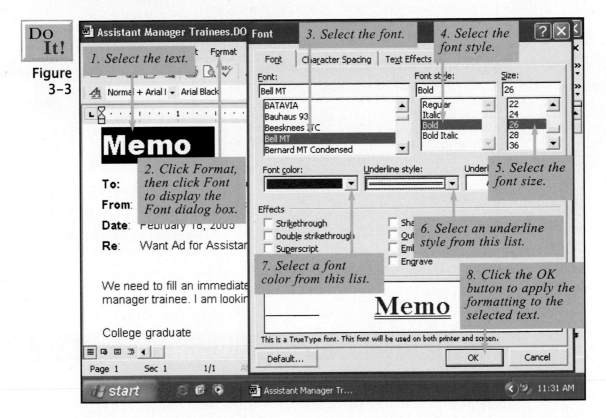

■ Use the Character Spacing tab in the Font dialog box if you need to change the size, spacing, vertical position, or kerning of selected text. Changing the kerning—the space between each letter—can be particularly useful when you need to make text fit into a limited space.

■ The Text Effects tab of the Font dialog box allows you to apply animation effects to selected text. Be careful not to overuse these effects; they can be very distracting to the reader.

■ The Preview area of the Font dialog box shows how your selections affect the selected text. You'll see the selected font, font styles, colors, and effects before you click the OK button to accept your changes. If you don't like what you see there, you can change your selections in the Font dialog box or click the Cancel button to keep the text as it was before it was selected.

■FAQ How do I center and align text?

The Format menu and the Formatting toolbar provide options for centering, right aligning, left aligning, and justifying text.

Most text is aligned along the left margin. Centering is typically used for titles. You might want to justify the text in the body of a formal document to give it a more professional look with both left and right margins aligned. Right-aligned text is rarely used, but can be useful for headings in a paper, for example, or for the return address in a letter.

Do It!

Figure 3-4

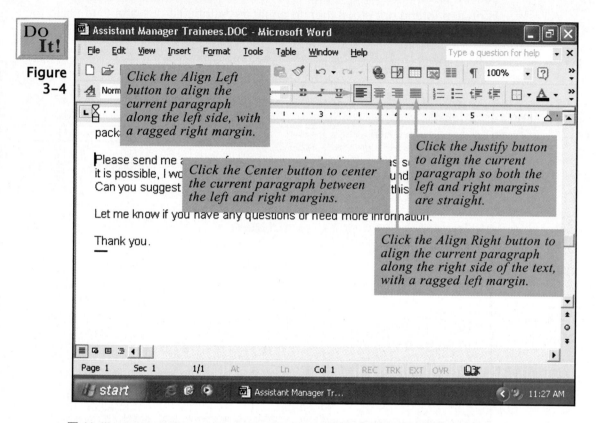

Click the Align Left button to align the current paragraph along the left side, with a ragged right margin.

Click the Center button to center the current paragraph between the left and right margins.

Click the Justify button to align the current paragraph so both the left and right margins are straight.

Click the Align Right button to align the current paragraph along the right side of the text, with a ragged left margin.

■ Unlike bold, italic, and underlining, alignment options apply to an entire paragraph. You don't have to select the text to align it—just click in the paragraph that you want to align then click the appropriate alignment button. All the lines of text in that paragraph will be aligned.

■ To center a title, press the Enter key at the end of the title so it becomes a separate paragraph. Click anywhere in the title, then click the Center button. If the text is a single line such as a title, it will be centered between the left and right margins. If the paragraph consists of multiple lines, every line in the paragraph will be centered.

■ To return a centered paragraph to left alignment, click in the paragraph, then click the Align Left button.

■ ■ ■

■FAQ How do I add numbering and bullets to a list?

Word's Formatting toolbar contains buttons to format a list with bullets or numbers. A **bullet** is a symbol placed before each item in a list. You can use bullets when you want to set off the items in a list but don't want to imply a specific order. A numbered list is a list with a number in front of each item on the list, which implies the items are listed in order.

Do It!

Figure 3-5

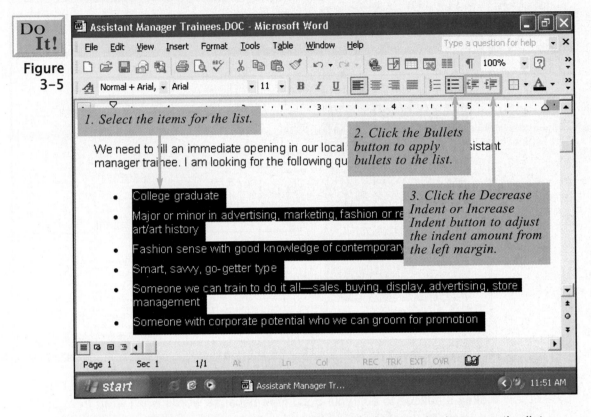

■ Numbered lists work the same as bulleted lists. Select the items on the list, then click the ⁞☰ Numbering button to add numbers to the list.

■ If you haven't typed the list yet, click the Numbering or Bullets button, then type the items on the list. Each time you press Enter, a new number or bullet will be inserted before that item on the list. At the end of the list, press Enter and click the Numbering or Bullets button to discontinue the numbering for the next line of text.

■ To remove numbering or bullets from a list, select the list, then click the Numbering or Bullets button to turn off the feature.

■ If you add, delete, or move the items on a numbered list, Word will renumber the list for you. If the numbering is incorrect, select the list, then click the Numbering button twice. This procedure removes and then reapplies the number- ing, which usually corrects any problem with the numbers on the list.

■ To change the numbered or bulleted list style, select the list, then right-click the list to display the shortcut menu. Click Bullets and Numbering to display the Bullets and Numbering dialog box. Select the Bulleted or Numbered tab, select a style, then click the OK button to apply the style to the list.

■ ■ ■

■FAQ How do I adjust the line spacing?

Your Word document will be single-spaced unless you specify another spacing option, such as double- or triple-spacing. You can apply line-spacing options to a single paragraph, to a group of paragraphs, or to the entire document.

Do It!

Figure 3-6

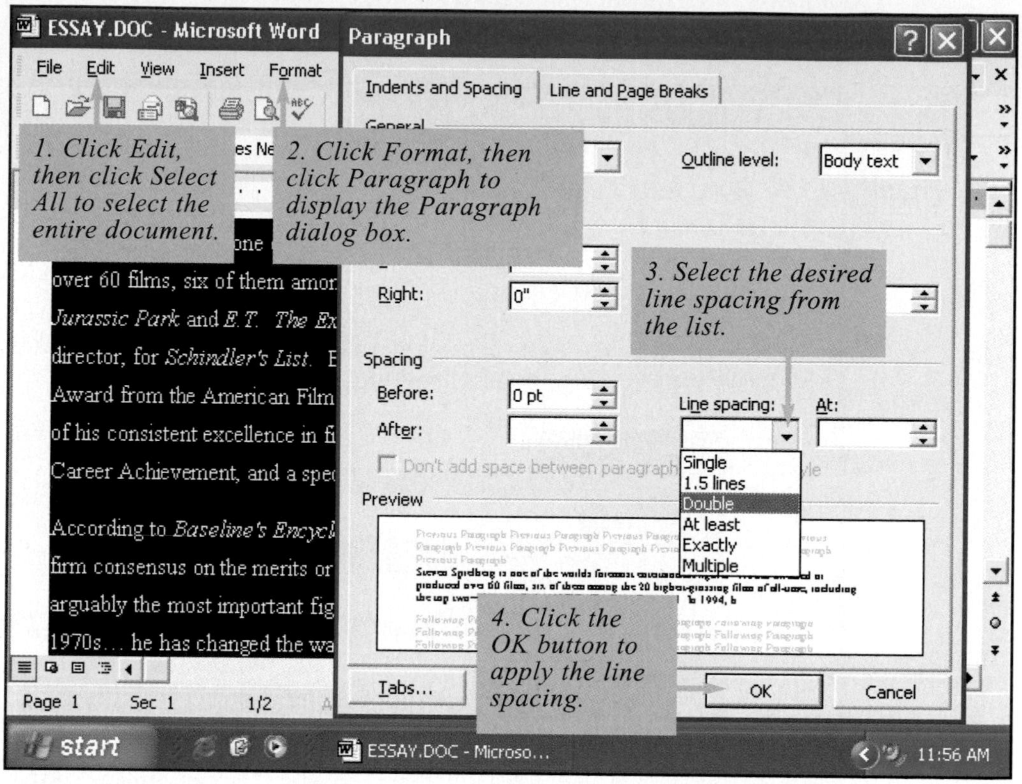

Figure 3-6 callouts:

1. Click Edit, then click Select All to select the entire document.

2. Click Format, then click Paragraph to display the Paragraph dialog box.

3. Select the desired line spacing from the list.

4. Click the OK button to apply the line spacing.

■ Do not press Enter at the end of each line to create double-spaced text. This makes it difficult to edit your document because words won't wrap from one line to the next. The preferred way to double-space a document is to type the document as regular single-spaced text, then set the line spacing to double.

■ To adjust the line spacing for one paragraph of text, position the insertion point in the paragraph, click Format, then click Paragraph to display the Paragraph dialog box. Select the desired spacing from the *Line spacing* drop-down list on the Indents and Spacing tab. Single- and double-spacing are the most commonly used spacing settings.

■ To adjust the line spacing for more than one paragraph, select the paragraphs, then adjust the line spacing as described above.

■ You can set the line spacing for the entire document before you begin typing. Click Edit, then click Select All. Click Format, then click Paragraph. Select the desired line spacing, then click OK. As you type, the text will appear on the screen with the selected line spacing.

■FAQ How do I use tabs?

Setting a **tab** provides an easy way to align text in columns. Word provides default tab stops every 1/2", but you can change the default tab settings and add your own tab stops. The position of a tab stop is measured from the left margin.

Do It!

Figure 3-7

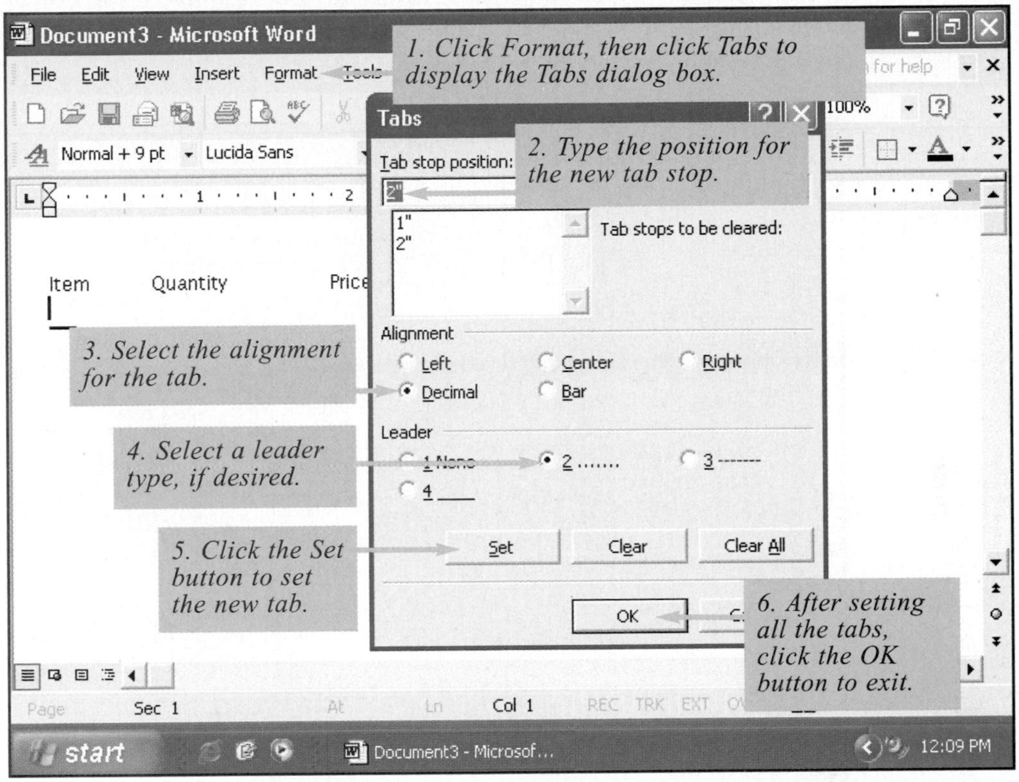

- There are many types of tab stops. A left tab stop means that text will be aligned on the left side of the tab. A right tab stop means that text will be aligned on the right side of the tab. A center tab stop centers text at that location, while a decimal tab stop aligns numbers with the decimal at the tab location. A bar tab stop places a vertical bar at the tab location.

- A **leader** is a line of punctuation characters, such as periods, that fills the area between text and a tab stop. Leaders are typically used in a table of contents to associate a page number with the appropriate chapter or heading. To add a leader to a tab stop, click the option button to select the leader type. When you tab to that tab stop, the leader character—usually a series of periods—will fill the area to the tab stop.

- To clear one tab stop, click that tab stop in the Tab stop position box, then click the Clear button. To clear all tab stops, click the Clear All button in the Tabs dialog box.

- On the Word ruler bar, tab stops are represented by these small icons:

  L Left tab   **↓** Decimal tab
  ↓ Right tab   **I** Bar tab
  ↓ Center tab

To set tabs using the ruler, select the type of tab stop by clicking the icon at the left end of the ruler. Click a location on the ruler to set the tab stop. You can move a tab stop by selecting it, then sliding it right or left on the ruler bar.

■   ■   ■

■FAQ How do I indent text?

You can indent text from the left margin, from the right margin, or from both margins. You can also indent the first line of text differently from the rest of a paragraph. Normally, the first line is indented farther to the right than the rest of the paragraph, but you can use a **hanging indent** to move the first line of text more to the left than the rest of the paragraph. Word's Format menu provides several options for indenting text.

Do It!

Figure 3-8

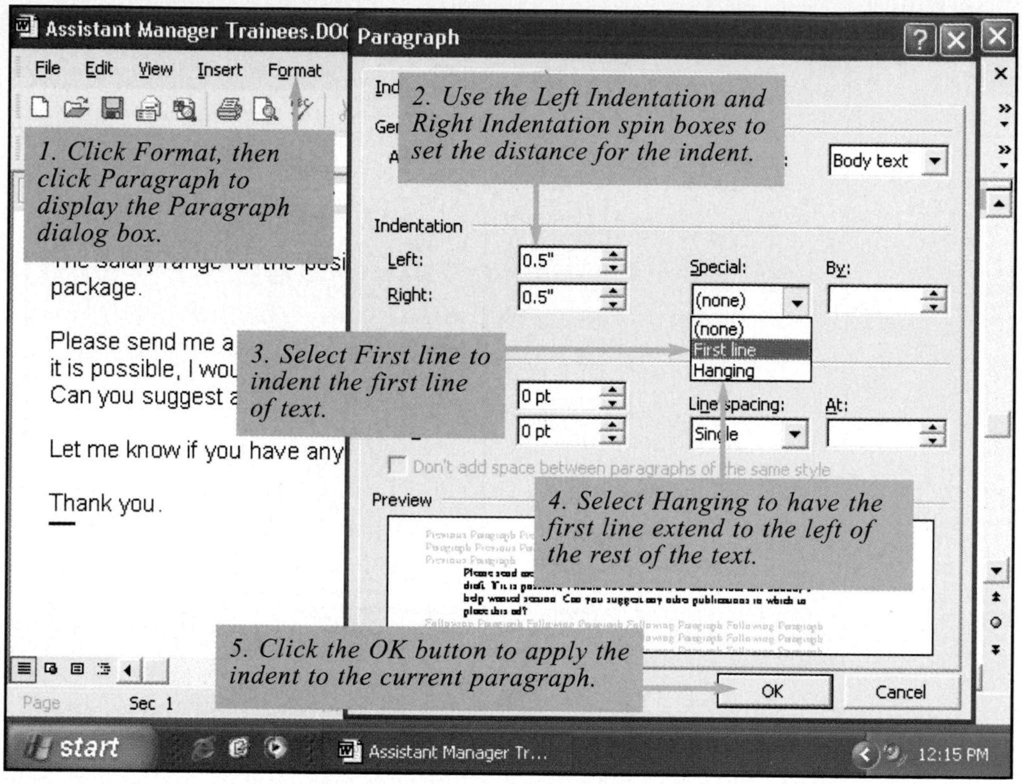

1. Click Format, then click Paragraph to display the Paragraph dialog box.

2. Use the Left Indentation and Right Indentation spin boxes to set the distance for the indent.

3. Select First line to indent the first line of text.

4. Select Hanging to have the first line extend to the left of the rest of the text.

5. Click the OK button to apply the indent to the current paragraph.

■ To indent an entire paragraph from the left, click the spin box buttons in the Left Indentation box to increase or decrease the left indentation. Use the same process with the Right Indentation box to increase or decrease the right indentation.

■ The Preview section shows an example of how the paragraph will look after it is indented. As you change your selections, the Preview will be updated.

■ To indent the first line of text, select First line from the Special pull-down list. Select the amount of indentation for the first line of the paragraph from the By spin box. A first line indent by a negative number will move the indent to the left of the left margin.

■ To create a hanging indent in which the first line of text extends more to the left than the rest of the text, select Hanging from the Special pull-down list. Select the amount of negative indent for the first line of the paragraph from the By spin box.

■ The indent settings apply to the paragraph that contains the insertion point. To apply an indent to more than one paragraph, select the paragraphs, then use the Paragraph dialog box to set the indent.

■ ■ ■

QuickCheck A

1. To select an entire document for editing, click Edit, then click _____. Whatever text attribute you then select will be applied to the entire document.

2. The centering and the alignment options apply to an entire _____ of text.

3. You should use the _____ dialog box to apply multiple formatting options in a single operation.

4. A(n) _____ is a symbol, such as a square or circle, placed before an item in a list.

5. True or false? To double-space a document, you should press the Enter key two times at the end of every line of text. _____

Check It!

QuickCheck B

Indicate the letter of the desktop element that best matches the following:

1. The Underline button _____

2. The Font list _____

3. The Center button _____

4. The Bullets button _____

5. A paragraph containing a hanging indent _____

Assistant Manager Trainees.DOC - Microsoft Word

File   Edit   View   Insert   Format   Tools   Table   Window   Help   Type a question for help

Norma + Arial, ▾ Arial   ▾ 11 ▾   B   I   U

A   B   C   D   E   F   G

H   The salary range for the position is $20,000 to $25,000 with the standard benefits package.

Please send me a copy of your proposed advertisement as soon as you have a draft. If it is possible, I would like to see this ad make it into this Sunday's help wanted section. Can you suggest any other publications in which to place this ad?

Let me know if you have any questions or need more information.

Thank you.

Page   Sec 1   At   Ln   Col 1   REC TRK EXT OVR

start   Assistant Manager Tr...   12:17 PM

Check It!

Get It?

A Skill Set A: Using text attributes and fonts

C Skill Set C: Creating lists and setting line spacing

B Skill Set B: Centering and aligning text

D Skill Set D: Indenting and setting tabs

Chapter 4

Finalizing a Document

What's Inside?

In the previous chapters, you've learned how to use Microsoft Word to create and then format a document. In Chapter 4, you'll learn how to add the finishing touches to your document to prepare your document for printing or to use as a Web page.

Important features covered in this chapter include spelling and grammar checking, using the thesaurus to find more suitable words, creating tables, adding headers and footers, and setting margins. You'll also learn how to use the Print dialog box to print multiple copies or selected pages of your document. Finally, you'll learn how to save your document as a Web page so it can be posted on the World Wide Web.

■ FAQs:

How do I check spelling and grammar?	39
How do I use the thesaurus?	40
How do I create headers and footers?	41
How do I set the margins?	42
How do I create a table?	43
How do I use the Print dialog box?	44
How do I use styles?	45
How do I save my document as a Web page?	46

■ Assessment   47

■FAQ How do I check spelling and grammar?

Microsoft Word provides tools to help you check the spelling and grammar of your documents. You should use these tools to check the spelling and grammar of all documents before you print them—it only takes a few minutes and can help you catch embarrassing mistakes. However, you'll still need to proofread your documents by reading them carefully yourself. You can't depend on the spelling and grammar checker to identify all mistakes or to make sure that your document says what you really mean it to say.

Do

Figure 4-1

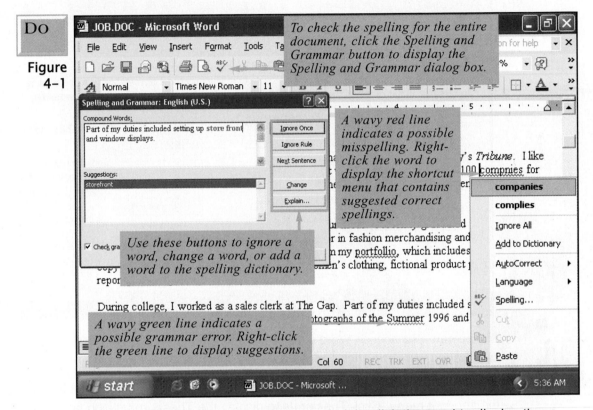

To check the spelling for the entire document, click the Spelling and Grammar button to display the Spelling and Grammar dialog box.

A wavy red line indicates a possible misspelling. Right-click the word to display the shortcut menu that contains suggested correct spellings.

Use these buttons to ignore a word, change a word, or add a word to the spelling dictionary.

A wavy green line indicates a possible grammar error. Right-click the green line to display suggestions.

■ If a wavy red line appears under a word, right-click the word to display the shortcut menu. If the correct spelling appears on the list, click it to correct the spelling of the word. If you want to add the word to the dictionary, click Add to Dictionary. The word will be added to the dictionary and will not be flagged as a misspelled word in the future.

■ If a wavy green line appears under a phrase or sentence, right-click it to display the shortcut menu. If you like one of the suggestions on the list, click it to change the wording of your sentence. If you like the sentence as it is and want to get rid of the green line, click Ignore Once.

■ If you don't see any wavy lines, this feature may be turned off. Click Tools, then click Options to open the Options dialog box. On the Spelling & Grammar tab, select *Check spelling as you type*.

■ You can also check the spelling and grammar of a complete document by clicking the Spelling and Grammar button. Words that might be misspelled are shown in red. Possible grammar mistakes are shown in green. You can click the appropriate buttons to ignore or replace each word or phrase.

■ ■ ■

■FAQ How do I use the thesaurus?

A thesaurus contains synonyms for words and some common phrases. When you are composing a document and can't think of just the "right" word, you can type the closest word that comes to mind, then use Word's thesaurus to search for words with a similar meaning.

Do It!

Figure 4-2

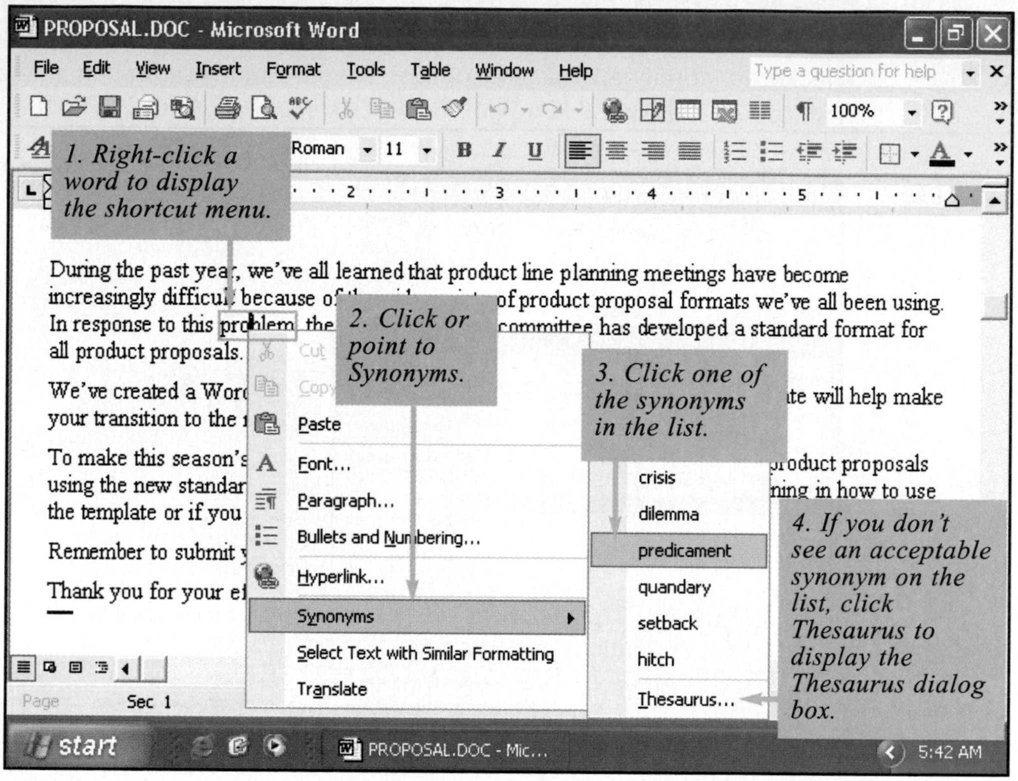

1. Right-click a word to display the shortcut menu.

2. Click or point to Synonyms.

3. Click one of the synonyms in the list.

4. If you don't see an acceptable synonym on the list, click Thesaurus to display the Thesaurus dialog box.

■ You can also access Word's thesaurus through the Tools menu. Click Tools, click Language, then click Thesaurus.

■ To find a synonym for a phrase, select the phrase, then right-click it to display the shortcut menu. Click Thesaurus to display the Thesaurus dialog box. A list of phrases appears. Sometimes you'll find an acceptable alternate phrase, but beware—some of the phrases listed may not be appropriate substitutes.

■FAQ How do I create headers and footers?

A **header** is text that appears at the top of every page of a document. A **footer** is text that appears at the bottom of every page. Headers and footers typically contain information such as the title of the document, the date, the name of the author, and the current page number.

Do It!

Figure 4-3

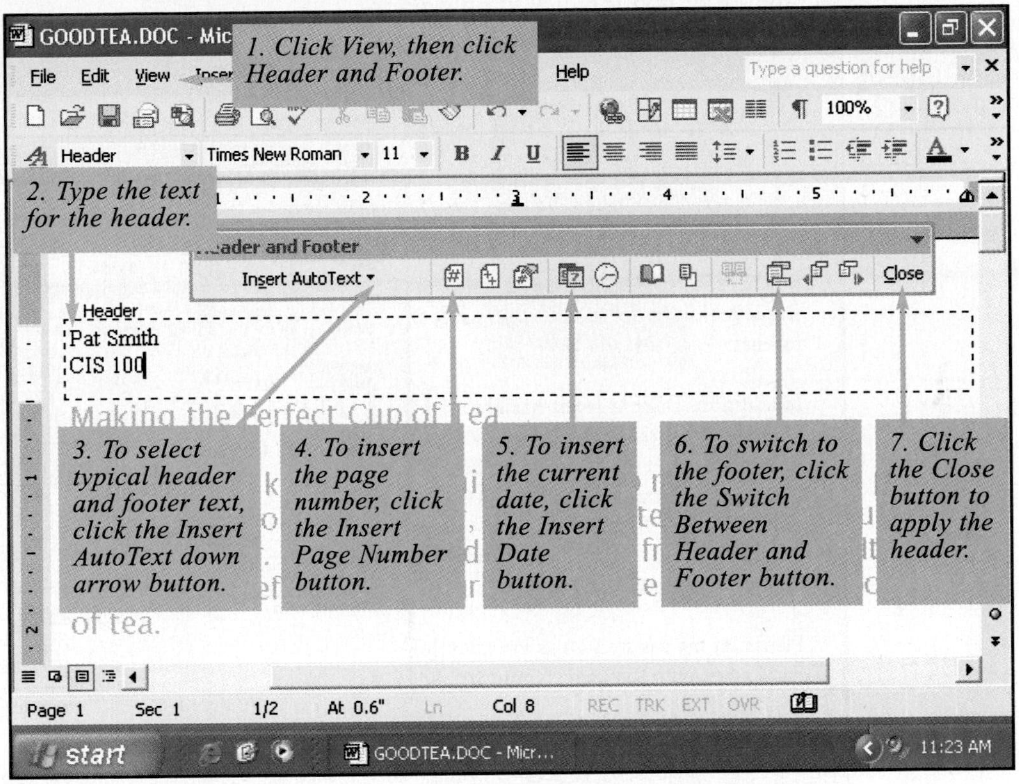

1. Click View, then click Header and Footer.

2. Type the text for the header.

3. To select typical header and footer text, click the Insert AutoText down arrow button.

4. To insert the page number, click the Insert Page Number button.

5. To insert the current date, click the Insert Date button.

6. To switch to the footer, click the Switch Between Header and Footer button.

7. Click the Close button to apply the header.

■ Headers and footers are only displayed in ▣ Print Layout View, in ▣ Print Preview, and on printed pages.

■ The header and footer have preset tabs—a center tab in the middle of the page, and a right tab near the right margin. Press the Tab key to move the insertion point to the next tab to enter text at that location.

■ To insert typical header text, click Insert AutoText, then select the text that you want to include in the header.

■ If you want to include text such as "Page 6" in your header or footer, type the word Page in the header or footer, press the Spacebar, then click the ▦ Insert Page Number button. Page numbers will be automatically updated when page content changes during editing.

■ To insert the current date and time, click the ▦ Insert Date or ◔ Insert Time buttons. The date and time will be automatically updated each time you open the document.

■ Click the ▤ Switch Between Header and Footer button to switch between the header and footer. You can edit the header or the footer, but not both at one time.

■ ■ ■

■FAQ How do I set the margins?

Margin settings typically apply to an entire document and are changed using the Page Setup option on the File menu.

In a Word document, the default margins are 1" on the top and bottom and 1.25" on the left and right. The margin setting affects the amount of text that you can fit on a page. Smaller margins allow for more text, whereas larger margins reduce the amount of text that will fit on a page.

Do It!

Figure 4-4

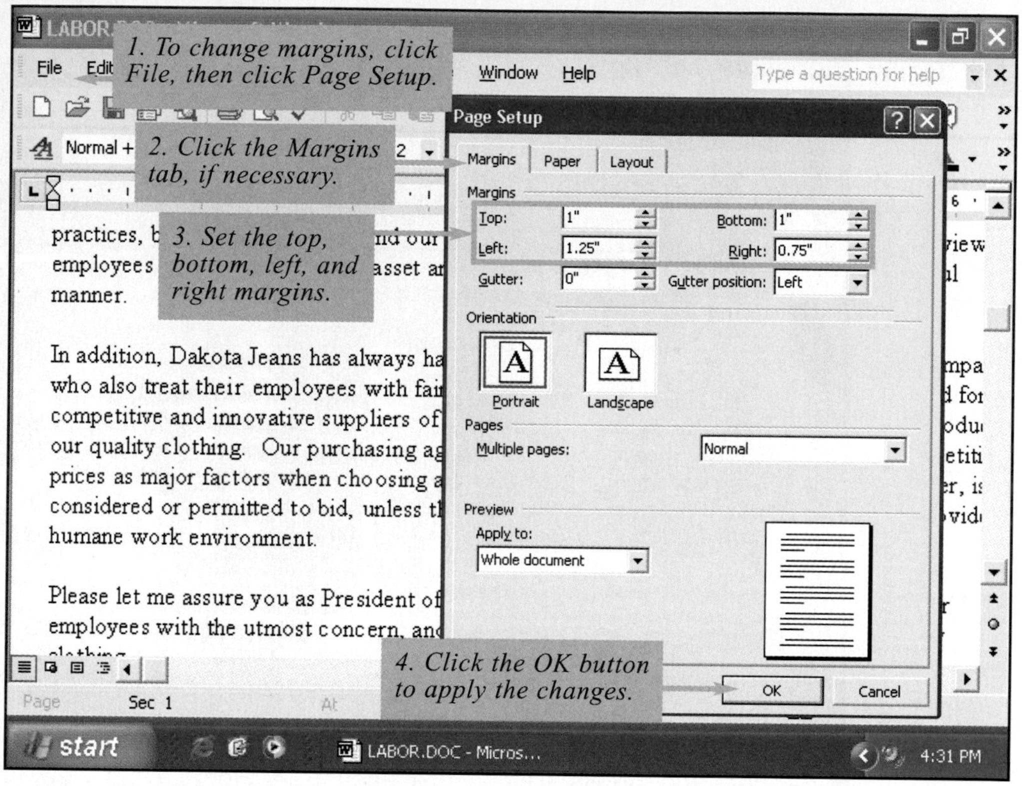

1. To change margins, click File, then click Page Setup.

2. Click the Margins tab, if necessary.

3. Set the top, bottom, left, and right margins.

4. Click the OK button to apply the changes.

■ Don't set the top and bottom margins too small if you're using headers and footers. The header and footer will not print correctly if there isn't enough room in the top or bottom margin.

■ Select Portrait orientation to print the page vertically. If you have a wide document, select Landscape orientation to print the page sideways.

■ You can use the Paper tab to set the paper size and to control how paper feeds into your default printer. Select the appropriate paper size from the Paper size list. You can find more information about your printer options in the printer documentation.

■ The Layout tab is useful for creating different headers and footers for odd and even pages. Other layout options allow you to center text vertically on the page, insert line numbers, and add graphical elements, such as borders, to the document.

■ All these formatting options can apply to the whole document, to selected sections of the document, or to the rest of the document that follows the current location of the insertion point. You can find more information about page setup options in Microsoft Word Help and in the program documentation.

■ ■ ■

■FAQ How do I create a table?

A **table** is a grid consisting of rows and columns. The intersection of each row and column is called a **cell**. You can enter text into each cell of the table and format the entire table or each cell separately.

Do It!

Figure 4-5

1. Put the insertion point where you want to insert the table.

2. Click Table, click Insert, then click Table.

Insert Table

Table size

Number of columns: 4

Number of rows: 5

3. Set the number of columns and rows.

AutoFit behavior

- Fixed column width: Auto
- AutoFit to contents
- AutoFit to window

Table style: Table Grid   AutoFormat...

5. The table appears in the document.

Remember dimensions for new tables

OK   Cancel

4. Click the OK button to create the table.

The following is a list of the remainin

If you would like to place an order fo

start   UNIFORMS.DOC - Mic...   4:34 PM

■ To create a table, place the insertion point where you want to insert the table. Click Table, click Insert, then click Table to display the Insert Table dialog box. Set the number of columns and rows, then click the OK button to create the table.

■ To add text to the table, click any cell in the table, then type the text in that cell. The word wrap feature moves text down while you are typing and expands the size of the cell to make room for all of your text. To move to another cell, press the arrow keys, press the Tab key, or click in the desired cell.

■ To quickly format the table, make sure the insertion point is in the table, click Table, then click Table AutoFormat to display the Table AutoFormat dialog box. Select a format from the list, then click the OK button to apply the format to the table. You can then modify the format to change, for instance, the font.

■ To insert new rows or columns, place the insertion point in the cell closest to where you want them to appear. Click Table, click Insert, then choose from among the options to place the new row or column.

■ To delete unused rows or columns, position the insertion point in the column or row that you want to delete. Click Table, click Delete, then click Columns or Rows.

■ To adjust the width of a column, position the pointer over the dividing line between the columns. When the pointer changes to a ◄║► shape, press the left mouse button and drag the column to the correct width.

■   ■   ■

▪FAQ How do I use the Print dialog box?

When you click the Print button on the Word toolbar, one copy of the current document is printed using the default print settings. If you want to print multiple copies of the document, print selected pages, or select an alternate printer, you must click File, then click Print to display the Print dialog box.

Do It!

Figure 4-6

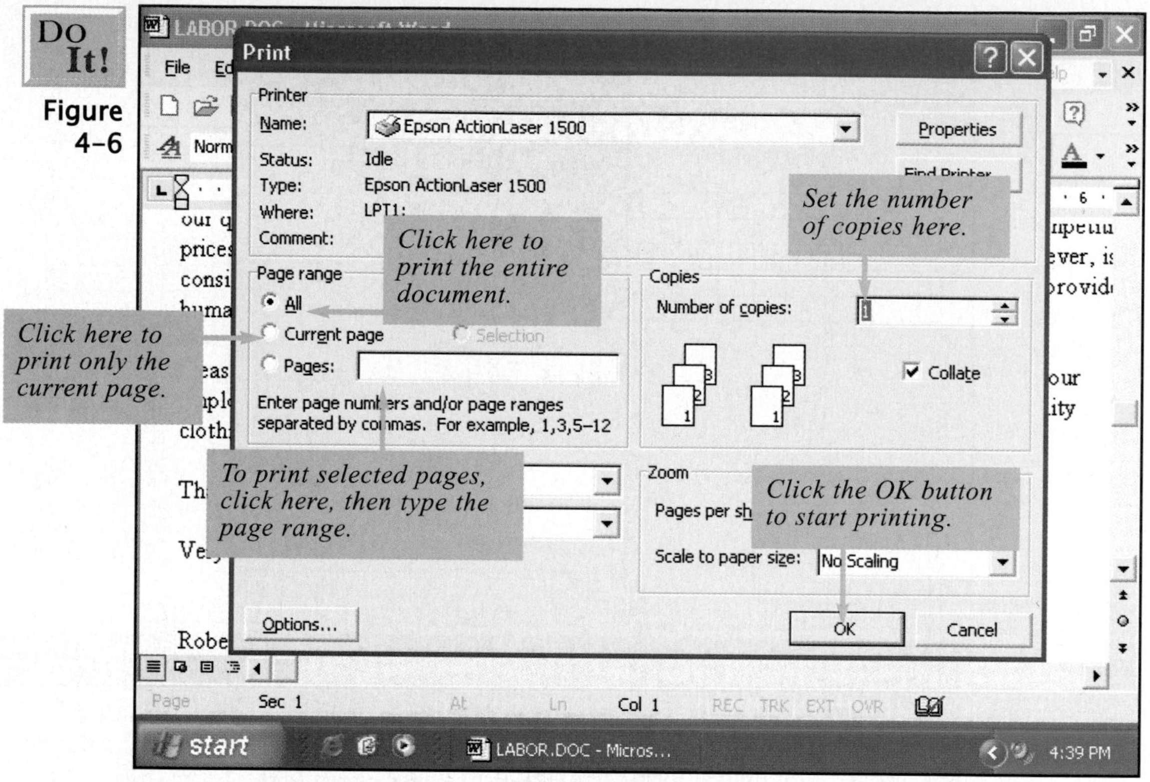

Click here to print only the current page.

Click here to print the entire document.

Set the number of copies here.

To print selected pages, click here, then type the page range.

Click the OK button to start printing.

▪ To print more than one copy of a document, use the *Number of copies* spin box.

▪ To print the entire document, make sure the *All* option button is selected in the Page range section.

▪ To print only the current page, click the *Current page* option button in the Page range section.

▪ To print a range of pages, enter the first page, a hyphen, then the last page in the range. For example, to print pages 13 through 28, you would enter 13-28.

▪ To print specific pages that are not in a sequence, click the Pages option button, then enter the page numbers in the Pages text box, separated by commas. For example, to print pages 3, 7, 11, and 38, you would enter 3, 7, 11, 38.

■FAQ How do I use styles?

A **style** consists of predefined formatting that you can apply to selected text. Word comes with several predefined styles, such as Heading 1, which is Arial, 16 point, bold.

Do It!

Figure 4-7

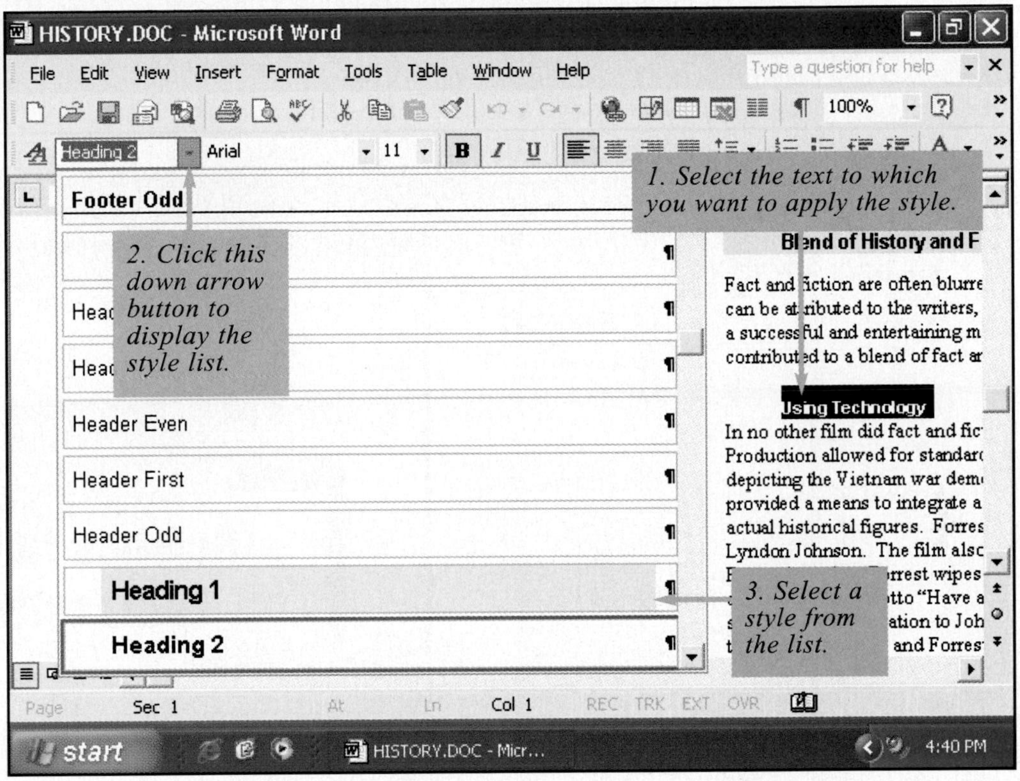

■ One advantage of using styles is that they allow you to be consistent in formatting text throughout a document. If you find yourself regularly applying multiple format settings to sections of text, you can save time by defining your own style, then applying it as needed.

■ To create a style, format a section of text using the desired font, font size, and font styles. Click Format on the menu bar, then click Styles and Formatting to display the Styles and Formatting task pane. Click the New Style button to display the New Style dialog box. Click the Name text box, then type the name for your new style. Click OK to close the New Style dialog box. Click the Close button to close the Styles and Formatting task pane. Your new style is added to the Style pull-down list. To apply the style to other text, select the text, then select your style from the Style pull-down list.

■ To remove a style from a section of text, select the text, click the down arrow button on the Style pull-down list, then select the Normal style.

■ To delete a style so that it no longer appears in the Style list, click Format, then click Styles and Formatting to display the Styles and Formatting task pane. Click the style you want to delete, click the down arrow button, then click Delete. Click Yes, then click the Close button to close the Styles and Formatting task pane.

■ Another advantage of styles is that they are recognized by many desktop publishing programs and Web authoring tools. Consequently, a document retains its formats and styles even if you import it into a different software package.

■ ■ ■

■FAQ How do I save my document as a Web page?

Instead of printing a document, you might want to post it on the Internet as a Web page. As with other Web pages, your document must be in HTML (Hypertext Markup Language) format to be accessible to Web browsers such as Internet Explorer and Netscape Navigator. You can use the Save As Web Page option on Word's File menu to save a document in HTML format.

Do It!

Figure 4-8

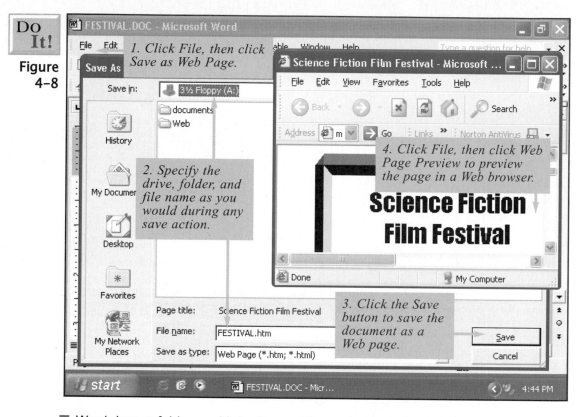

1. Click File, then click Save as Web Page.

2. Specify the drive, folder, and file name as you would during any save action.

3. Click the Save button to save the document as a Web page.

4. Click File, then click Web Page Preview to preview the page in a Web browser.

■ Word does a fairly good job of converting a document to HTML, but several formatting options available in Word cannot be duplicated in HTML documents. If a document contains formatting that cannot be duplicated in HTML, Word will display a message during the conversion process that describes the problem areas. You will then have the option of canceling or continuing with the save.

■ To see how the document will look when viewed in a Web browser, click File, then click Web Page Preview. Close the Web browser to return to Word.

■ When you save a long document as a Web page, it will be displayed as a single long page—sort of like a papyrus scroll—even though it may have been divided into separate pages as a Word document. When you view it in a Web browser, you'll use the vertical scroll bar to move through the document.

■ Contact your Internet Service Provider (ISP) or technical support person if you need instructions for posting your Web pages on the Internet.

QuickCheck A

1. You can use Word's [_____] feature to find synonyms.

2. A(n) [_____] is a grid consisting of rows, columns, and cells.

3. A(n) [_____] is text placed at the bottom of every page of a Word document.

4. To print pages 3 through 46 of a document, you would enter [_____] in the Pages text box in the Print dialog box.

5. When you save a Word document as a Web page, it is converted to [_____] markup language format.

Check It!

QuickCheck B

Indicate the letter of the desktop element that best matches the following:

1. A possible spelling error [____]

2. A possible grammatical error [____]

3. The Switch Between Header and Footer button [____]

4. The Insert Page Number button [____]

5. The Insert Date button [____]

Check It!

Get It?

A Skill Set A: Checking spelling and grammar

B Skill Set B: Creating a table

C Skill Set C: Styles, headers, and footers

D Skill Set D: Margins, printing, and Web pages

Chapter 5
Creating a Worksheet

What's Inside?

In Chapter 5, you'll learn the essentials of creating a worksheet with Microsoft Excel.

Microsoft Excel is the component of the Microsoft Office suite best suited for working with numbers and formulas. As **spreadsheet software**, Microsoft Excel provides a set of tools for simple or complex calculations such as creating a budget, estimating expenses, and creating an income and expense projection.

An electronic spreadsheet, often referred to as a worksheet, functions much like a visual calculator. You place each number needed for a calculation into a cell of the grid. You then enter formulas to add, subtract, or otherwise manipulate these numbers. The spreadsheet software automatically performs the calculations and displays the results.

■ FAQs:

What's in the Excel window?	49
How do I enter labels?	50
How do I enter values?	51
How do I enter formulas?	52
How do I create complex formulas?	53
How do I use functions?	54
How do I use the AutoSum button?	56

■ Assessment   57

■FAQ What's in the Excel window?

To start Excel, click Start, point to Programs or All Programs, then click Microsoft Excel. You should notice that many of the menus and toolbar buttons are similar to those you learned to use in Microsoft Word. In this chapter, you will learn some of the important features of Excel that are different from the features of Word.

Play It!

Figure 5-1

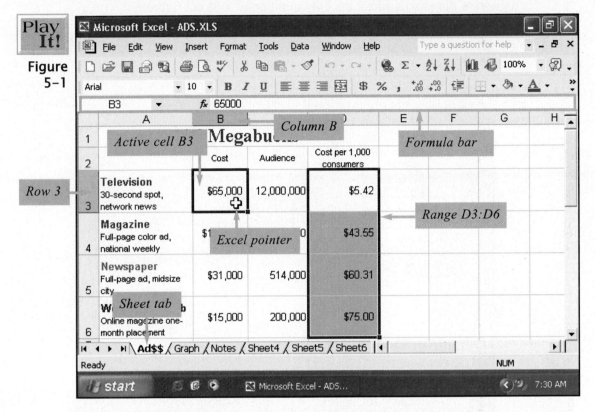

■ A **worksheet** consists of a grid of columns and rows. The columns are typically labeled with letters, starting with A as the column farthest to the left. The rows are typically labeled with numbers, starting with 1 as the top row.

■ Excel worksheets are saved in a **workbook**. A workbook contains one or more worksheets, each represented by a tab at the bottom of the Excel window. When you save or open a workbook, all worksheets in that workbook are automatically saved or opened. To switch to a different worksheet in the current workbook, click its sheet tab. Right-click a sheet tab to rename, insert, or delete a worksheet.

■ A **cell** is the rectangle formed by the intersection of a column and row. Each cell has a unique name consisting of the column letter and row number. For example, cell B3 is located in the second column of the third row.

■ The **active cell** is the cell that you can currently edit or modify, and it is marked with a black outline. You can change which cell is the active cell by clicking any other cell with the mouse. You can also change which cell is the active cell by pressing the arrow keys to move the black outline up, down, left, or right.

■ A **range** is a series of cells. For example, D3:D6 is a range that contains all cells from D3 through D6, inclusive. To select a range of cells, click the cell in the top-left corner of the range, then drag the mouse to the bottom-right cell in the range.

■ ■ ■

■FAQ How do I enter labels?

A **label** is any text entered into a cell of the worksheet. You can use labels for a worksheet title, to describe the numbers that you've entered in other cells, and for text data, such as the names of people or cities. Any "number" data that you do not intend to calculate should be entered as a label. This data might be a telephone number, a social security number, or a street address.

Do It!

Figure 5-2

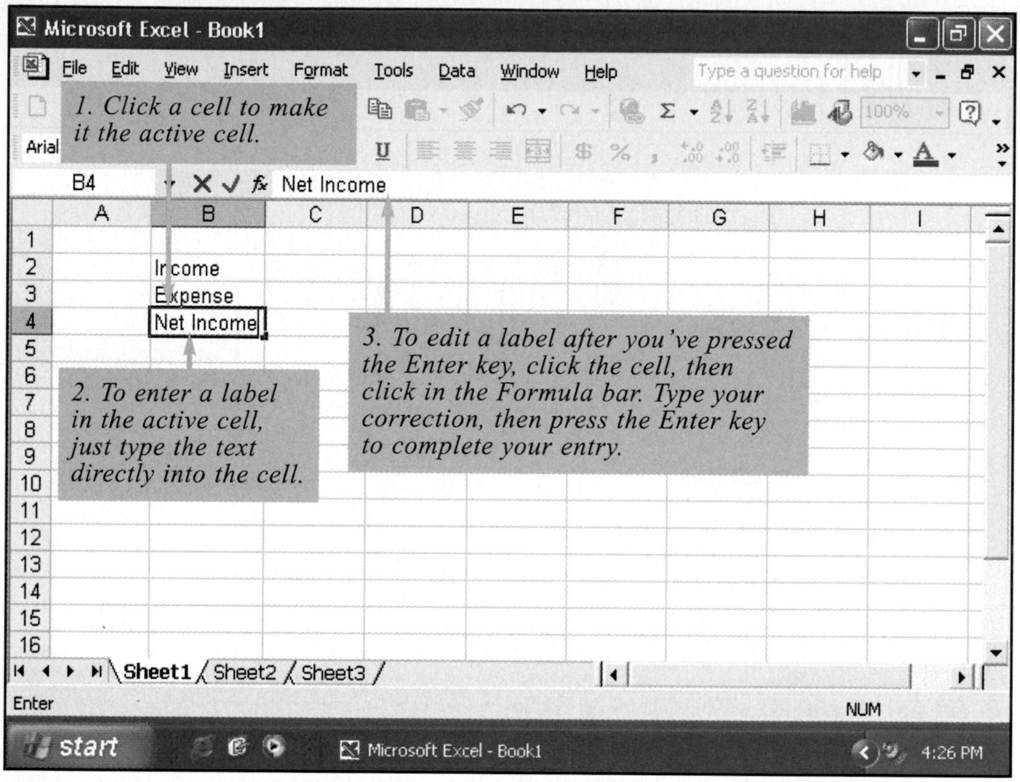

1. Click a cell to make it the active cell.

2. To enter a label in the active cell, just type the text directly into the cell.

3. To edit a label after you've pressed the Enter key, click the cell, then click in the Formula bar. Type your correction, then press the Enter key to complete your entry.

■ If a label is too long to fit in the current cell, it will extend into the cells to the right, if they are empty. If the cells on the right are not empty, part of the label will be truncated, which means it will be hidden behind the adjacent cell's content.

■ It's possible to make a long label "wrap" so that it is displayed in two or more lines of text inside the same cell. Select the cell or cells, click Format, then click Cells on the menu bar to display the Format Cells dialog box. Click the Alignment tab, then click the Wrap text check box. Click OK to apply the change.

■ To edit a label after you've pressed the Enter key, click the cell, then click in the Formula bar. Use the left and right arrow keys to move the insertion point in the Formula bar, and use the Backspace and Delete keys to delete characters. Press the Enter key when you have finished editing the label. You can also press the ✓ Enter button on the Formula bar to complete your entry. Press the ✗ Cancel button to exit the Formula bar without keeping any changes.

■ It's possible to edit a label inside a cell. Double-click the cell to activate it, then edit the contents using the arrow, Backspace, and Delete keys. Press the Enter key when you have finished editing the label.

■FAQ How do I enter values?

A **value** is a number that you intend to use in a calculation and that is entered into a cell of a worksheet. Cells containing values can be used in formulas to calculate results. It's important for you to recognize when a number should be entered as a value and when a number should be entered as a label.

Do It!

Figure 5–3

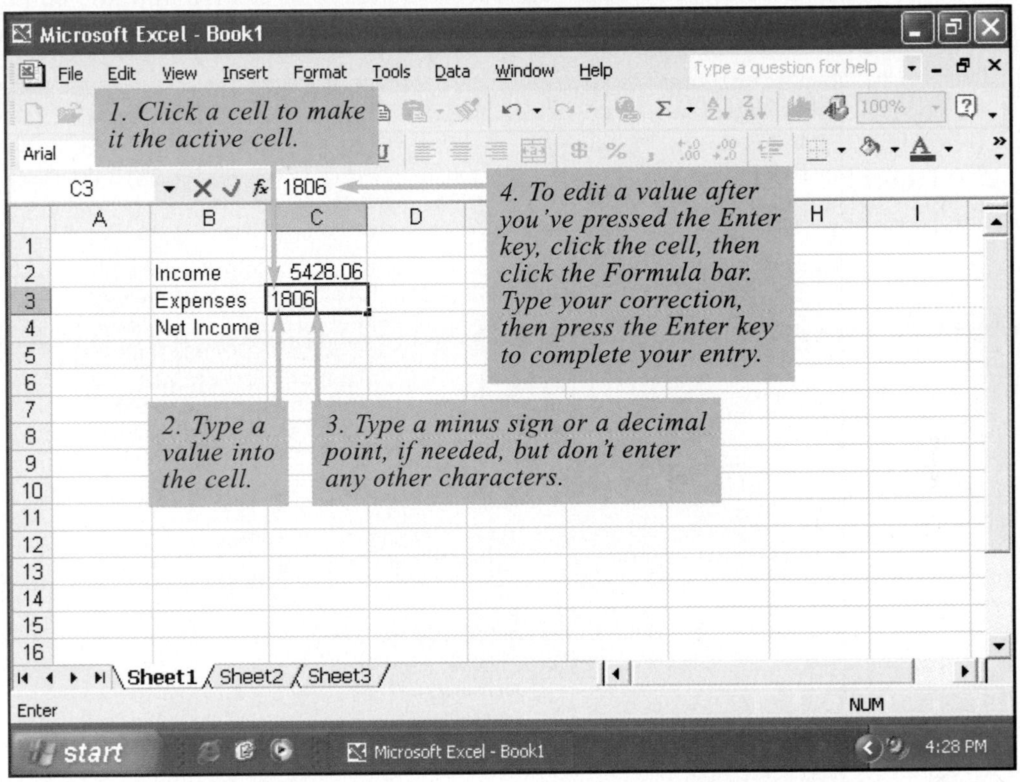

1. Click a cell to make it the active cell.

2. Type a value into the cell.

3. Type a minus sign or a decimal point, if needed, but don't enter any other characters.

4. To edit a value after you've pressed the Enter key, click the cell, then click the Formula bar. Type your correction, then press the Enter key to complete your entry.

■ Type a minus sign (-) before the number to enter a negative value. Although you can include the dollar sign and comma in values, it's best to just enter the unformatted number into a cell. You will learn to format values in the next chapter.

■ After you've pressed the Enter key, you can edit a value just as you would edit a label—in the cell or in the Formula bar.

■ Excel will make assumptions about your entry while you are typing and will recognize common combinations of numbers and punctuation as label data rather than as value data. If you want to specifically enter a number as a label, you can type an apostrophe (') before the number. For instance, type '555-1234 to enter 555-1234 as a telephone number.

■ Values can be entered automatically using the Fill handle and a technique called **drag-and-fill**. Enter a number in a cell, then point to the bottom-right corner of the cell. The pointer will change to a black cross ⬛ shape when you are in the right spot. Drag that pointer across or down several other cells. Excel will fill the new cells with the same number.

■ There are several other ways to drag-and-fill data, and you can use the Fill option on the Edit menu. You can find more information about automatically filling cells in the Microsoft Excel Help and program documentation.

■ ■ ■

■FAQ How do I enter formulas?

A **formula** specifies how to add, subtract, multiply, divide, or otherwise calculate the values in the cells of a worksheet. A formula always begins with an equal sign (=) and can use cell references that point to the contents of other cells. A **cell reference** is the column and row location of a cell. In the example below, the formula =C2-C3 would subtract the contents of cell C3 from the contents of cell C2 and display the results in cell C4.

Do It!

Figure 5-4

Screen callouts:

1. Click the cell where you want the results of the formula to appear.

2. Type = then click the first cell to be referenced in the formula.

3. Type an arithmetic operator, then click the next cell you want to reference in the formula.

4. Press Enter when the formula is complete.

5. To edit a formula after you've pressed the Enter key, click the cell, then click the Formula bar. Type your correction, then press the Enter key to complete your entry.

	A	B	C	D
2		Income	5428.06	
3		Expenses	1802	
4		Net income	=C2-C3	

■ The most common arithmetic operators are - (subtraction), + (addition), * (multiplication), and / (division). Note that an asterisk (*) instead of the letter X is used for multiplication.

■ The easiest way to create a formula is to use the "pointer method." Basically, this means that you click the cell where the results of the formula should appear, type the equal sign (=), and click the first cell referenced in the formula. You will see a rectangle of dashes around the cell you just clicked. This is a **marquee**, which indicates the cell you selected. If it is not the correct cell, click on another cell to place the correct cell reference into your formula. To continue creating your formula, type an arithmetic operator (+, -, *, /), then click the next cell referenced in the formula. Continue until the formula is complete, then press Enter to end the formula.

■ You can also type a formula directly into a cell. For example, you could type =B2*B3, then press the Enter key to complete the formula. The problem with this method is that it's easy to make a mistake and type an incorrect cell reference.

■ You can edit a formula after you've pressed the Enter key in the same way that you would edit labels or values—in the cell or in the Formula bar.

■ ■ ■

■FAQ How do I create complex formulas?

A worksheet can be used for more than simple calculations. You can build complex formulas to calculate statistical, financial, and mathematical equations by using the usual arithmetic operators, parentheses, and a mixture of both values and cell references. The most commonly used arithmetic operators are +, -, *, /, and %.

Do It!

Figure 5-5

Microsoft Excel - Dealer.XLS

File   Edit   View   Insert   Format   Tools   Data

Arial   10   B   I   U

D3   ƒx   =(B3+C3)*1.2

Operations within parentheses are completed first. In this formula, the contents of cell B3 will be added to the contents of cell C3 before their sum will be multiplied by 1.2.

	A	B	C		G
1	*Honest Ernie's Used Cars*				
2	Car	Dealer Cost	Dealer Prep	Sale Price	
3	2000 Jetta	$ 14,283.00	$ 275.00	$ 17,469.60	
4					
5					
6					
7					
8					
9					

Click a cell to display the formula in the Formula bar.

Ernie / Source / Sheet3 / Sheet4 / Sheet5 / Sheet

Ready   NUM

start   Dealer.XLS   6:36 AM

■ Use parentheses to make sure that arithmetic operations in a complex formula are executed in the correct order. If you don't use parentheses, Excel calculates the result using the standard mathematical order of operations—multiplication and division, then addition and subtraction. For example, if you enter the formula =B3+C3*1.2, Excel will first multiply the contents of cell C3 by 1.2, then add the result of the calculation to the value in cell B3. By using parentheses, you can specify a different order for a calculation. For example, if you would like to add the contents of B3 and C3 before multiplying by 1.2, you would enter this formula: =(B3+C3)*1.2.

■ Formulas can include values, cell references, or both. For example, if the total price of an item was displayed in cell C18, you could calculate a 6% sales tax using the formula =C18*.06. Or, you could put the sales tax percentage in cell C19, then calculate the sales tax using the formula =C18*C19. The result would be the same either way.

■ You should be aware that cell references in formulas can lead to unexpected results when you copy or move the formulas. You'll learn more about this topic in the next chapter.

■ ■ ■

■FAQ How do I use functions?

In addition to writing your own formula, you can use a predefined formula called a **function**. Excel includes many financial functions such as payments and net present value, mathematical and trigonometric functions such as absolute value and arctangent, and statistical functions such as average and normal distribution.

Do It!

Figure 5-6

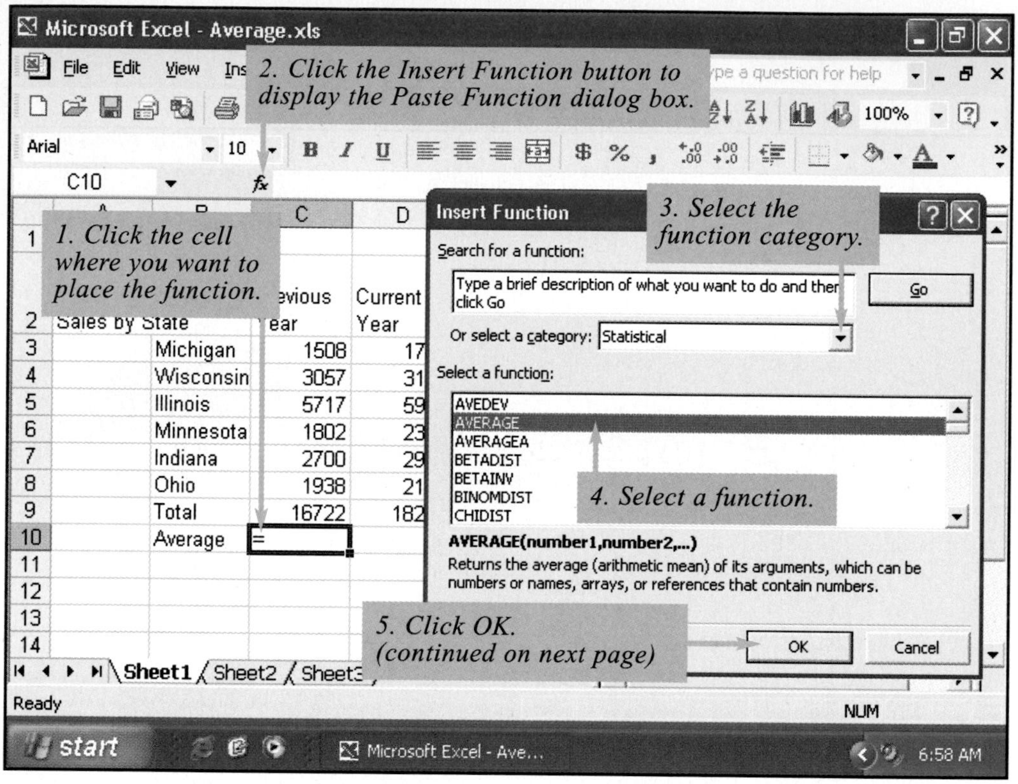

■ You can use the Insert Function button to select a function from a list. Excel includes more than 250 functions from which you can choose. Aside from the Sum function, the most common functions are the Average, Minimum, and Maximum functions located in the Statistical category.

■ Another useful function is the Payment or PMT function, which calculates the payments for a loan. You can use the PMT function to calculate all types of loan payments, such as those for a car or for a house. Unfortunately, the PMT function is one of the more difficult functions to use, which is why it's covered in the Do It! on this page.

■How do I use functions? (continued)

After you select a function, you'll have to specify the **arguments**—either values or cell references—used to calculate the result of the function. For example, the Average function requires an argument consisting of a series of numbers or a series of cells. When you complete the Average function, the result is calculated as an average of the values in the cells that you specified.

Figure 5-7

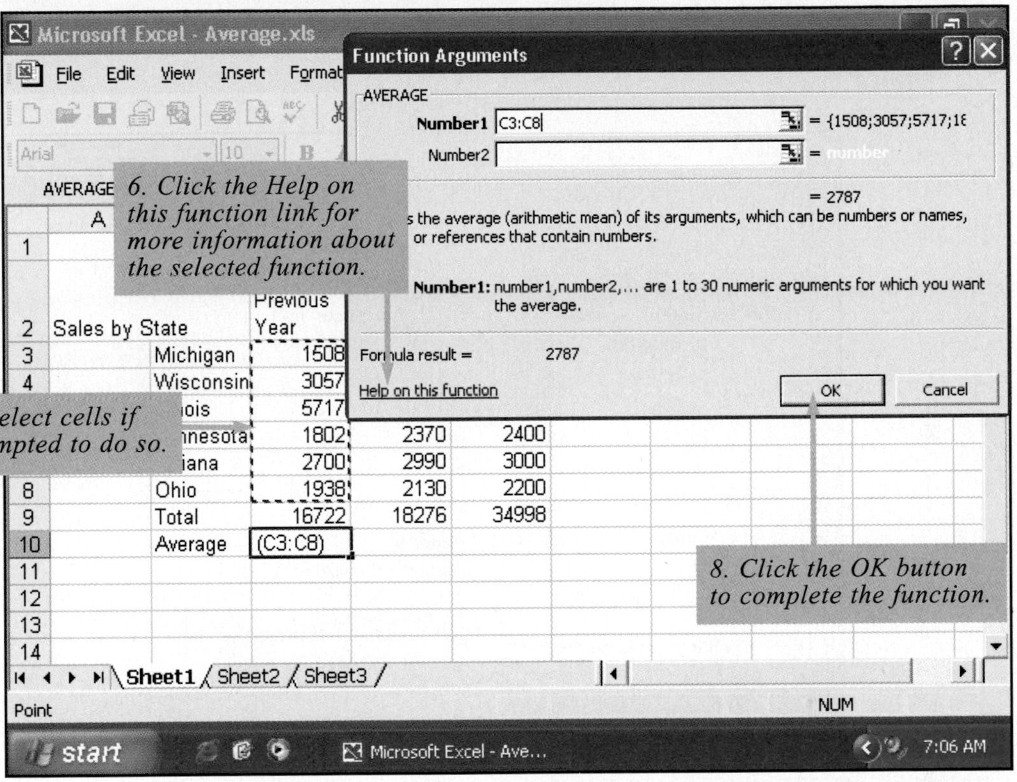

■ To select a range of cells for use as arguments in a function, click the top-left cell that contains data that you want to use in the function, then drag down to the bottom-right cell. When you release the mouse, the selected range of cells will be displayed in the dialog box. Click OK to calculate the function.

■ Some functions use more than one argument and those arguments can be required or optional. The Payment (or PMT) function, for example, has three required arguments (Rate, Nper, and Pv) and two optional arguments (Fv and Type).

■ It can be difficult to determine how to enter the arguments for a function. For the PMT function, you have to divide the annual interest rate by 12 if you're using monthly payments. If you need help with the arguments for a function, click the *Help on this function* link.

■ Be careful about using functions that you don't fully understand. If you're not sure how a function works, use the Microsoft Excel Help system to find out more about it. When you use a new function, you should check the results with a calculator to make sure that the function is working as you expected.

■FAQ How do I use the AutoSum button?

Use the AutoSum button to quickly create a function to calculate the total of a column or row of cells. Excel will examine the cells to the left of and above the current cell to determine which cells should be included in the total.

Do It!

Figure 5-8

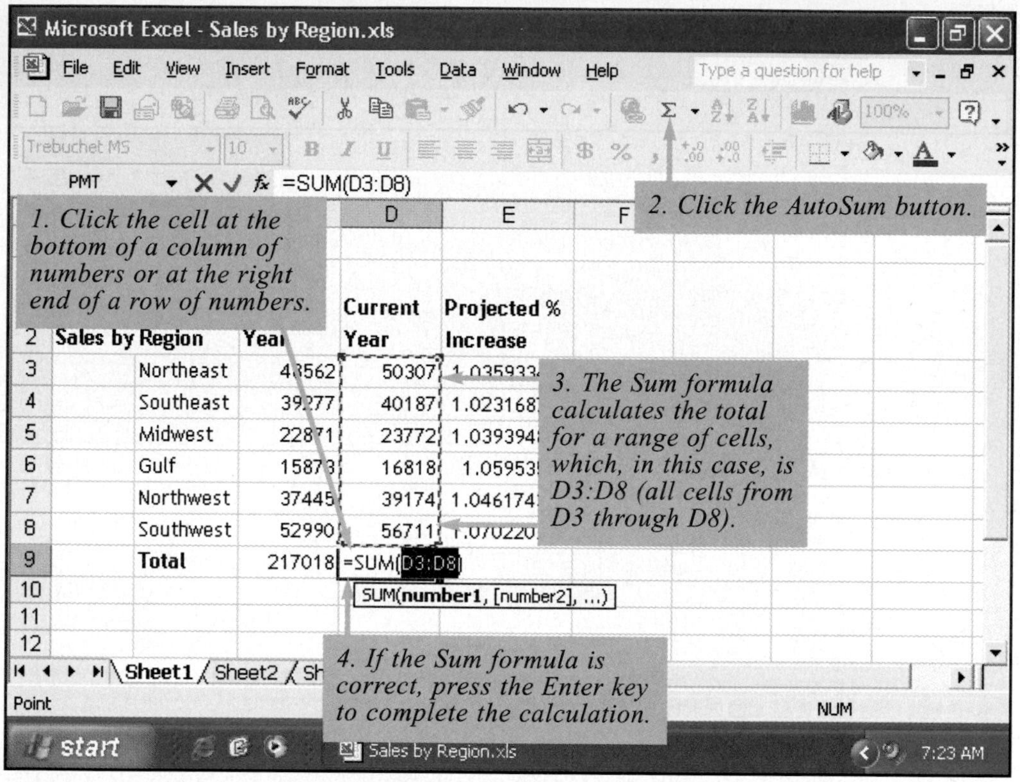

1. Click the cell at the bottom of a column of numbers or at the right end of a row of numbers.

2. Click the AutoSum button.

3. The Sum formula calculates the total for a range of cells, which, in this case, is D3:D8 (all cells from D3 through D8).

4. If the Sum formula is correct, press the Enter key to complete the calculation.

■ The cells included in the Sum function are displayed as a range or as a series of adjacent cells. A range consists of two cells and all cells located between them. A range is written with the first cell reference, a colon, and then the last cell reference. For example, the range C2:C5 includes cells C2, C3, C4, and C5.

■ The AutoSum button usually does a good job of selecting the cells to be included in the function, but a blank cell or a cell containing a label can produce an incorrect answer. AutoSum works best if every cell in the row or column of cells contains a value.

■ Be careful if you use the AutoSum button to calculate the sum of a column of cells with a number—such as 2003—as a column heading. If the heading has not been specifically formatted as a date, Excel will include it in the sum. Watch the marquee to be sure the correct range of cells is selected before you press the Enter key.

■ If the AutoSum button does not automatically select the correct cells, press the Esc key to remove the function and create the Sum function manually. You can also drag across the correct range of cells, or hold down the Shift key while you use the arrow keys to select the correct range of cells. When the correct cells are selected, press the Enter key to complete the function.

QuickCheck A

1. The _____ cell is the cell that you can currently edit or modify.

2. B3:B12 is an example of a(n) _____ of cells.

3. To edit a label, value, or formula after you've pressed the Enter key, click the cell, then click the _____ bar.

4. The formula to subtract the contents of cell C3 from the contents of cell C2 is _____.

5. A(n) _____ is a value or cell reference that is used to calculate the result of a function.

Check It!

QuickCheck B

Indicate the letter of the desktop element that best matches the following:

1. A cell containing a label _____

2. A cell containing a value _____

3. A cell containing a formula _____

4. The AutoSum button _____

5. The Insert Function button _____

Check It!

Get It?

A Skill Set A: The Excel window	**C** Skill Set C: Formulas
B Skill Set B: Labels and values	**D** Skill Set D: Functions

Chapter 6

Formatting a Worksheet

What's Inside?

In Chapter 6, you'll learn how to format worksheets created with Microsoft Excel.

Formatting is not just for looks—an effectively formatted worksheet is more readable and helps the reader understand the purpose and meaning of the values and formulas that the worksheet contains. For instance, an accountant might use a red font color for negative values in a large worksheet so possible losses are easier to spot. A quarterly banking statement might use a different colored border for each month to help the reader recognize which transactions were made in a particular month.

You learned in Chapter 5 that there is an important difference between label and value data. In this chapter, you will learn that each type of data has special formatting characteristics, which help to identify its purpose. Rather than typing in dollar signs to identify financial values, for example, you will learn to format the values as currency data.

One of the most powerful advantages of using spreadsheet software for calculations is that you can easily make changes to the data in order to see how the results are affected by the changes. You will learn how to copy and move data in a worksheet, and how the new location might change formulas and produce different results. Most importantly, this chapter explains how to avoid making incorrect modifications to value data in a worksheet.

■ FAQs:

How do I add borders and background colors?	59
How do I format worksheet data?	60
How do I use the Format Cells dialog box?	61
How do I adjust the width of a column?	62
How do I center and align cell contents?	63
What happens when I copy and move cells?	64
How do I know when to use absolute references?	65
How do I delete and insert rows and columns?	66

■ Assessment   67

■FAQ How do I add borders and background colors?

Borders and background colors define areas of a worksheet and call attention to important information. You can use Excel's Format menu to add borders and a colored background to one or more cells.

Do It!

Figure 6-1

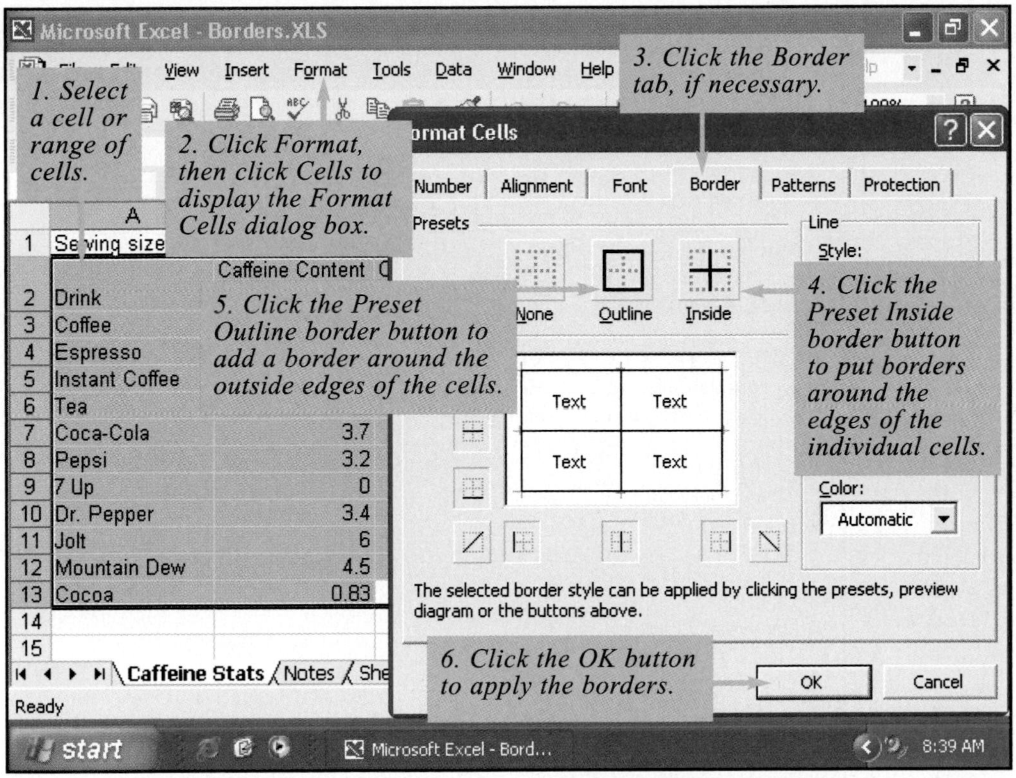

1. Select a cell or range of cells.

2. Click Format, then click Cells to display the Format Cells dialog box.

3. Click the Border tab, if necessary.

4. Click the Preset Inside border button to put borders around the edges of the individual cells.

5. Click the Preset Outline border button to add a border around the outside edges of the cells.

6. Click the OK button to apply the borders.

■ To add borders around the outside and inside edges of the selected cells, click both the Outline Preset and Inside Preset border buttons, as shown in the above figure. The Outline Preset puts a border around the outside edges of the selected cells. The Inside Preset adds borders between individual cells.

■ You can add and remove border lines by pressing the border option buttons in the Border section of the dialog box. These buttons control all the lines in the selected range of cells:

- Top of range
- Left of range
- Inside horizontal lines
- Inside vertical lines
- Bottom of range
- Right of range

■ The Line area allows you to select a decorative line style or to make all the border lines appear in a selected color.

■ To add a colored background to the selected cell or cells, click the Patterns tab. Select a color, then click the OK button to apply the background color.

■ You can quickly add borders using the Borders button on the Formatting toolbar. However, this shortcut doesn't allow you to use the options in the Format Cells dialog box.

■ ■ ■

■FAQ How do I format worksheet data?

You can use buttons on the Formatting toolbar to select different font attributes for any data in worksheet cells. Values, including numbers as well as the results of formulas in cells, can be formatted with the same font attributes used to enhance the appearance of labels.

Do It!

Figure 6-2

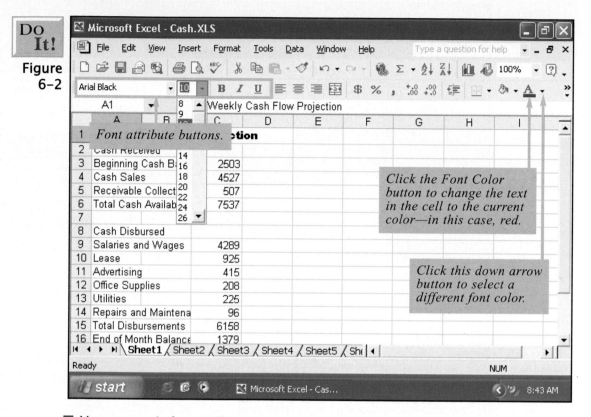

■ You can apply font attributes to any worksheet data—a single character, a single cell, a range of cells, or the entire worksheet. Click in the cell you want to format, then click as many font attribute buttons as you want. Click outside the cell to complete the process.

■ To change the font for a range of cells, click the top-left cell, then drag the mouse to select the range of cells. Release the mouse button, then apply the font formatting option to the selected cells.

■ Font attributes are typically applied to the entire contents of a cell, but it is possible to change the font attributes for selected text inside a cell. For example, to display one of the words in a cell in bold text, type the contents of the cell, then click the Formula bar. Use the mouse or the arrow keys to select one word within the cell, then click the Bold button. You can use the same process to apply different fonts and attributes such as italics, underline, and font sizing.

■ For more formatting options, select a cell to format. Click Format, then click Cells to display the Format Cells dialog box. Click the Font tab if necessary. Select the formatting options, then click the OK button to apply them.

■FAQ How do I use the Format Cells dialog box?

In addition to font attributes, you can also apply number formats—currency, percent, commas, and decimals—to cells that contain values. The most commonly used number formats are available as buttons on the Excel Formatting toolbar. In addition, the Format Cells dialog box provides some special format options for number data to improve the readability of a worksheet.

Do It!

Figure 6-3

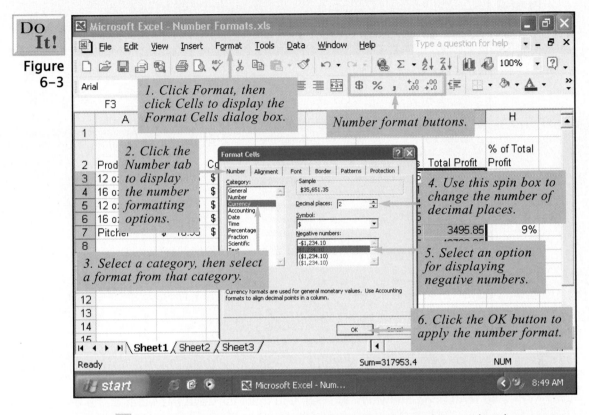

■ The **$** Currency Style button displays the cell contents in your local currency format. For example, if your copy of Windows is configured for use in the U.S., the currency button displays the cell contents as dollars and cents with a leading $ sign and two digits to the right of the decimal point.

■ The **%** Percent Style button displays the cell contents as a percentage, which means .35 will be displayed as 35%.

■ The **,** Comma Style button adds a comma to the values displayed in the cell. If your computer is configured for use in the U.S., the Comma Style button adds a comma every three digits to the left of the decimal place and displays two digits to the right of the decimal point.

■ When you click the Decrease Decimal button, one less digit is displayed after the decimal point. When you click the Increase Decimal button, one more digit is displayed after the decimal point.

■ To apply number formats to more than one cell, select a range of cells before you click any of the number format buttons or before you open the Format Cells dialog box.

■ ■ ■

■FAQ How do I adjust the width of a column?

If a column is too narrow, labels might be cut off and numbers might be displayed as #####. Narrow columns allow you to fit more information on the screen or on the printed page, but you may need to adjust the width of columns in your worksheet to make all of your worksheet data visible.

Do It!

Figure 6-4

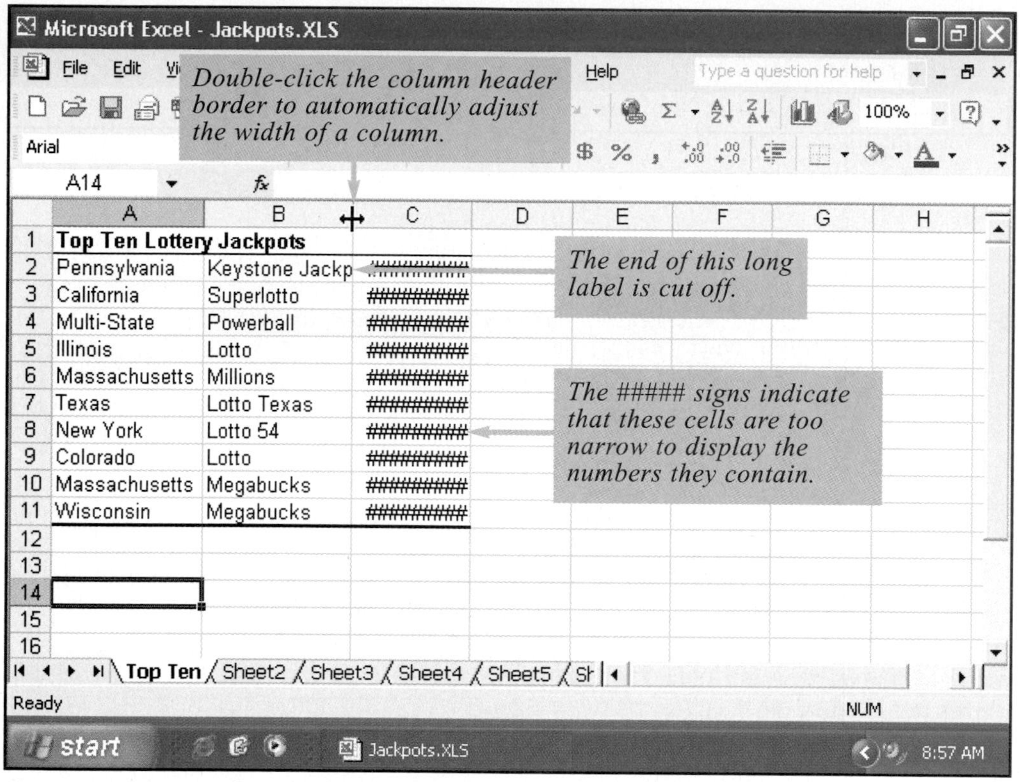

Double-click the column header border to automatically adjust the width of a column.

The end of this long label is cut off.

The ##### signs indicate that these cells are too narrow to display the numbers they contain.

■ To change the width of a cell, you must increase the width of the entire column. You can't make one cell in a column wider without affecting the other cells in that column.

■ To manually adjust the width of a column, position the pointer over the vertical line between two column headings so that the pointer changes to a ✛ shape. Press and hold the left mouse button while you drag the vertical line left or right to manually adjust the width of the column.

■ If a label is too long to fit into a cell, it will extend into the next cell on the right, if that cell is empty. If the cell on the right contains data, the end of the label will be cut off.

■ If a value is too long to fit into a cell, Excel displays a series of # characters in the cell. This is a signal that the cell contains a value that cannot fit in the current cell, which means that you will need to increase the width of that cell.

■ If the result of a formula is too long to fit into a cell, Excel will display the result in **scientific notation**—something like 6.79E+09. Make the column wider so that the formatted result can be displayed in the cell.

■FAQ How do I center and align cell contents?

By default, labels are aligned on the left edge of the cell while values and formulas are aligned on the right edge of the cell. Unfortunately, this means that a label at the top of a column of numbers is not aligned with the numbers in the column. Typically, you'll want to center or right-align a label when it is a column heading.

Do It!

Figure 6-5

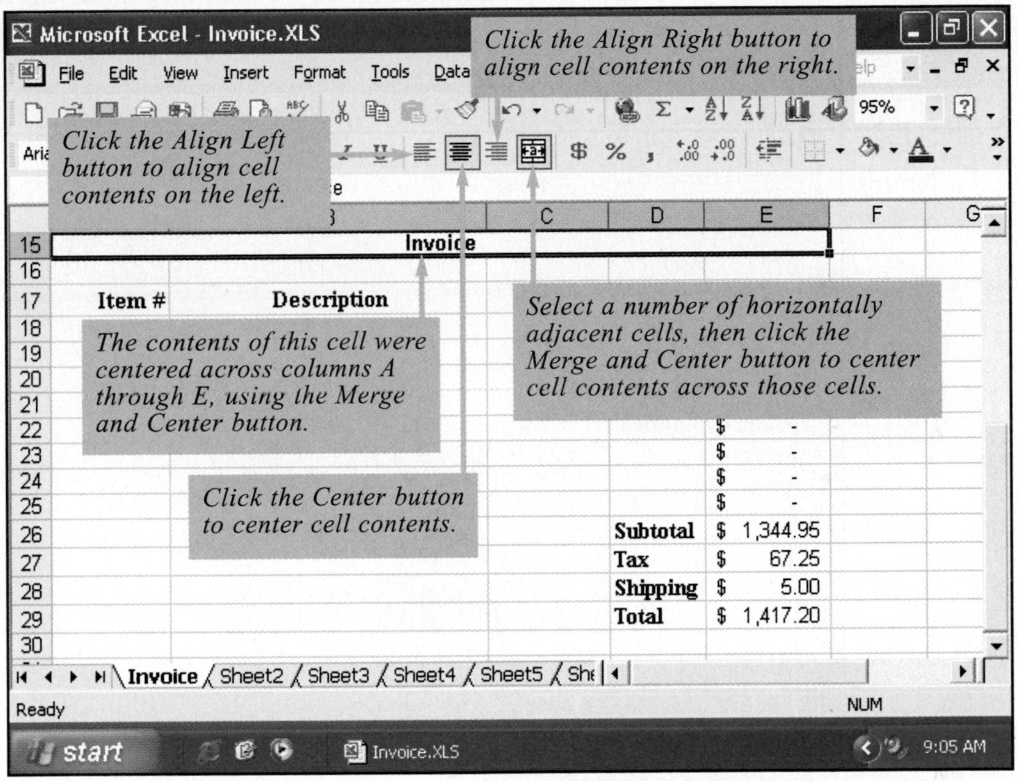

■ If a cell that contains label data is a column heading, select the cell and click the Align Right button to move the label to the right side of the cell so that it aligns with the column of numbers.

■ To change the alignment of a range of cells at one time, select the range of cells, then click the Align Left, Center, or Align Right button.

■ To quickly select all cells in a column, click the gray column header at the top of the column. To quickly select all cells in a row, click the gray box on the left side of the row.

■ Sometimes you'll need to center a label across a number of columns. In the figure above, the title "Invoice" is centered across columns A through E. To center text across columns, select the range of cells to be merged, then click the Merge and Center button.

■ To merge a range of cells in a column, select the range of cells, then click Cells on the Format menu. Click the Alignment tab, then select the Merge cells check box. You can also center text vertically or move cell contents up or down in the merged cell.

■ ■ ■

■FAQ What happens when I copy and move cells?

You can use the Cut, Copy, and Paste buttons on Excel's Standard toolbar to copy and move cells contents to a different worksheet location. Label data is copied or moved without changing. If you copy and paste cells that contain a formula, the copied formula is modified to work in the new location. A cell reference that changes when a formula is copied or moved is called a **relative reference**. Excel treats all cell references as relative references unless you specify otherwise.

Do It!

Figure 6–6

1. To copy the contents of cells to a new location, select a cell or range of cells.

2. Click the Copy button to copy the cell data to the Clipboard.

3. Click the cell where you want to paste the Clipboard data.

4. Click the Paste button to paste the Clipboard data to the new location.

5. Press the Esc key to remove the marquee from the original cells.

	Central America	2003	2004	Change
3	Central America	2003	2004	Change
4	Guatemala	$14,250.00		
5	Honduras	$10,275.00		
6	El Salvador	$8,524.00		
7	Nicaragua	$9,872.00		
8	Costa Rica	$17,892.00	$19,758.00	
9	Panama	$12,252.00	$14,234.00	
10	Total	$73,065.00	$69,938.00	
12	Average	$12,177.50		

■ To move the data in cells, select the cells, then click the Cut button. Click the cell where you want to paste the data, then click the Paste button. The data is moved from the original location to the new location.

■ If you copy or move the data in a range of cells, the pasted data is positioned below and to the right of the active cell. In other words, click the cell in the top-left corner of where you want the data to be pasted.

■ A formula that contains a relative reference changes when the formula is copied or moved. For example, assume cell C4 contains the formula =C2+C3. You then copy and paste that formula to cell F4. The formula will be changed to =F2+F3. The references C2 and C3 in the original formula were relative references. When the formula was originally located in cell C4, they actually meant =(the contents of the cell two rows up)+(the contents of the cell one row up). When you copied the formula to cell F4, Excel adjusted the formula so that it retained the same relative references. When you pasted the formula into cell F4, it became =F2+F3.

■FAQ How do I know when to use absolute references?

Most of the time, you will want Excel to use relative references, but in some situations, cell references should not be modified when moved to a new location. An **absolute reference** will not change, but will always refer to the same cell, even after the formula is copied or moved.

Do It!

Figure 6-7

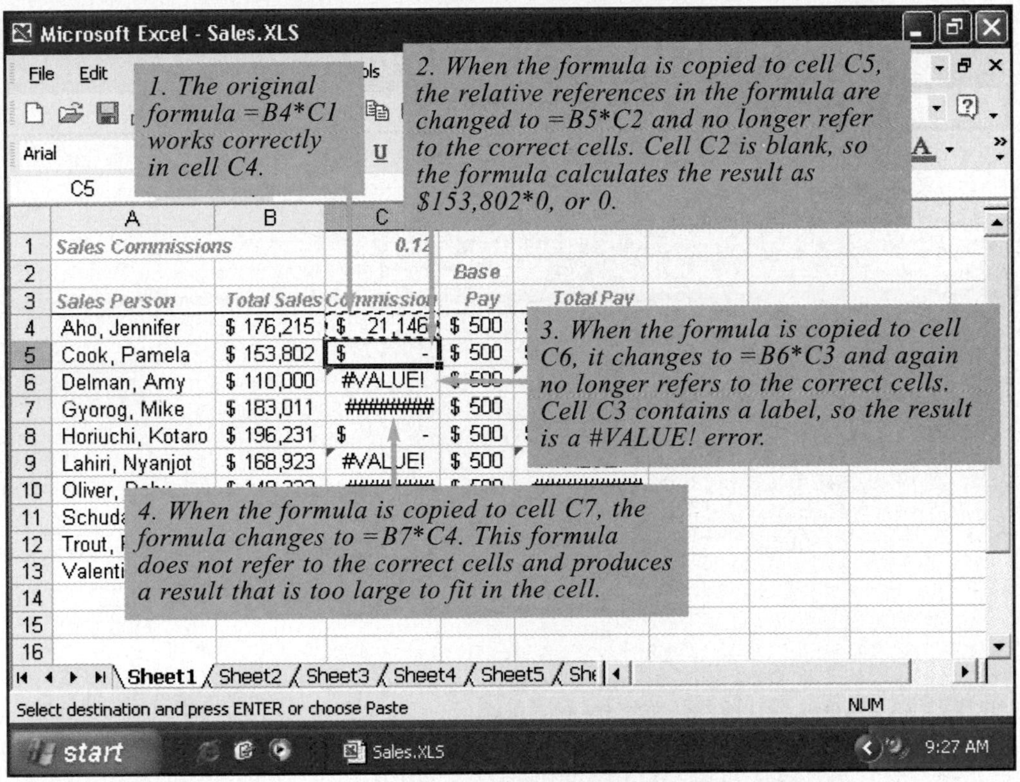

*1. The original formula =B4*C1 works correctly in cell C4.*

*2. When the formula is copied to cell C5, the relative references in the formula are changed to =B5*C2 and no longer refer to the correct cells. Cell C2 is blank, so the formula calculates the result as $153,802*0, or 0.*

*3. When the formula is copied to cell C6, it changes to =B6*C3 and again no longer refers to the correct cells. Cell C3 contains a label, so the result is a #VALUE! error.*

*4. When the formula is copied to cell C7, the formula changes to =B7*C4. This formula does not refer to the correct cells and produces a result that is too large to fit in the cell.*

■ In the example above, cell C1 contains a commission rate. When you copy the formula in cell C4 to cell C5, the original formula =B4*C1 is changed to =B5*C2. The B5 part is fine, but C2 is an empty cell. The formula should still refer to the commission rate in cell C1.

■ To create an absolute reference, insert a dollar sign ($) before the column reference and another dollar sign before the row reference. In the example above, you would modify the original formula to read =B4*C1. Now, no matter what you do to the worksheet, Excel must always refer to the contents of cell C1 for the second part of the formula. When you copy the formula =B4*C1 to cell C5, the formula is changed to =B5*C1. The absolute cell reference is "protected" by the $ sign and will not be modified or adjusted.

■ If you want to use an absolute reference in a formula, you can start typing, then press the F4 key after you click a cell to add it to the formula. Pressing the F4 key changes the current reference to an absolute reference.

■ You can also combine references so that only one of the column or row references is absolute. For example, $C1 creates an absolute column and a relative row reference; C$1 creates a relative column and an absolute row reference. The absolute identifier will not change, but the relative identifier will.

■ ■ ■

■FAQ How do I delete and insert rows and columns?

It's easy to delete a row or insert a blank row between rows that already contain data. You can also insert and delete columns. Excel will even modify your formulas as needed to make sure they refer to the correct cells each time you insert a new row.

Do It!

Figure 6-8

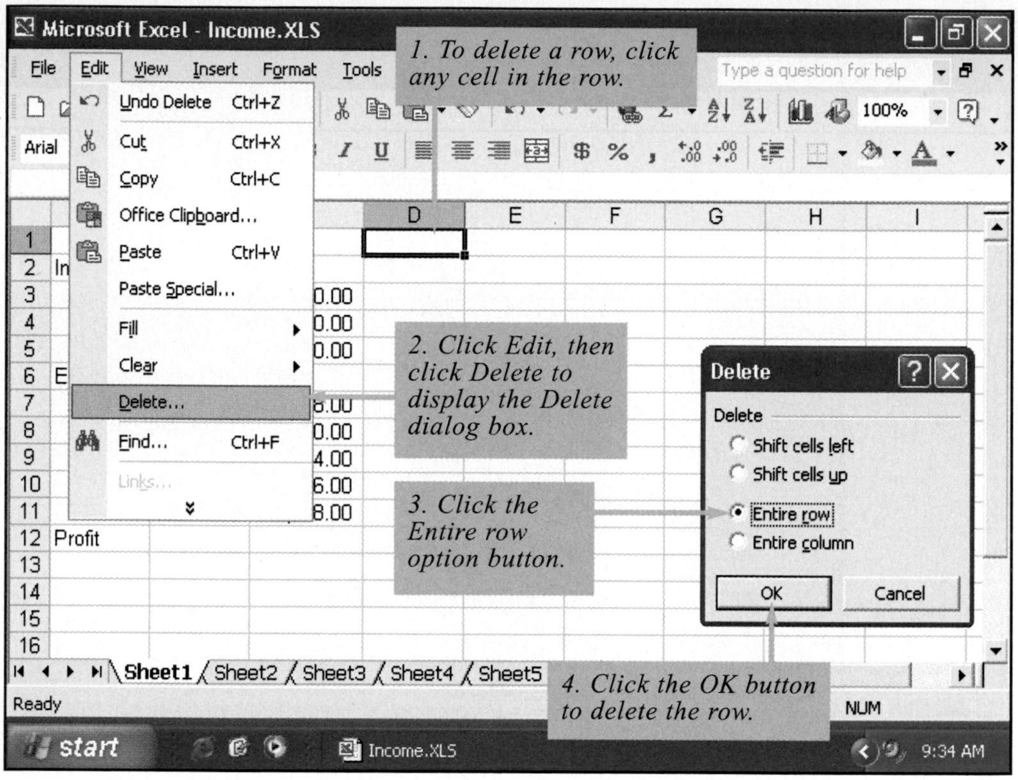

1. To delete a row, click any cell in the row.

2. Click Edit, then click Delete to display the Delete dialog box.

3. Click the Entire row option button.

4. Click the OK button to delete the row.

■ To insert a row, click any cell. You can also select a row by clicking the gray row identifier button on the left side of the window. Click Insert, then click Rows to insert the new row. The new row is inserted above the selected row.

■ To insert more than one row at a time, drag down over the number of rows that you want to insert. Click Insert, then click Rows to insert that number of new rows.

■ To delete more than one row at a time, drag down over the rows that you want to delete. Click Edit, then click Delete. Click the *Entire row* option button, then click the OK button to delete the rows.

■ Use the same procedures to insert and delete columns. To insert one or more columns, select the column or columns, click Insert, then click Columns. To delete one or more columns, select the column or columns, click Edit, click Delete, click the *Entire column* option button, then click the OK button.

■ As you insert and delete rows and columns, Excel will adjust the relative cell references in formulas to keep them accurate. For example, the formula =C8+E8 will change to =C8+D8 if the original column D is deleted. In the same way, the formula =C8+E8 will change to =C7+E7 if row 6 is deleted.

QuickCheck A

1. True or false? When the contents of a cell are displayed as #####, that cell contains a number that is too long to display in the cell. [____]

2. To center a label across a number of cells, select the horizontally adjacent cells, then click the [_____] and Center button.

3. A(n) [_____] reference is a cell reference that will be modified if the formula is copied or moved to a new cell.

4. A(n) [_____] reference is a cell reference that will not be modified if the formula is copied or moved to a new cell.

5. To write the formula =B2*D6 so that it always refers to cell D6 even when moved or copied, you would change the formula to [_____].

Check It!

QuickCheck B

Indicate the letter of the desktop element that best matches the following:

1. The Currency Style button [__]

2. The Merge and Center button [__]

3. A cell formatted in the Currency style [__]

4. A cell formatted in the Percent style [__]

5. The Decrease Decimal button [__]

Check It!

Get It?

A Skill Set A: Fonts and number formatting

C Skill Set C: Column width and aligning cell contents

B Skill Set B: Borders and background colors

D Skill Set D: Copying, moving, inserting, and deleting cells

Chapter 7

Finalizing a Worksheet

What's Inside?

In Chapter 7, you'll learn how to finalize your worksheets by checking spelling, sorting data, testing the data in worksheets, and inserting charts. Finally, you'll learn how to prepare your worksheets for printing, including the addition of headers and footers, and how to distribute worksheet data on the Internet.

■ FAQs:

How do I check the spelling in a worksheet? 69

How do I sort data in a worksheet? 70

How do I test my worksheet? 71

How do I create a chart? 72

How do I use the print preview and page setup options? 74

How do I add headers and footers to a worksheet? 76

How do I use the Print dialog box? 77

How do I save a worksheet as a Web page? 78

■ Assessment 79

■FAQ How do I check the spelling in a worksheet?

Excel provides a tool that allows you to check the spelling of all text entered into cells in a worksheet. Unlike Word, however, Excel doesn't show misspelled words with wavy red underlines. Excel also doesn't provide a grammar checker. So it's important for you to remember to check for both spelling and grammar errors.

Do It!

Figure 7-1

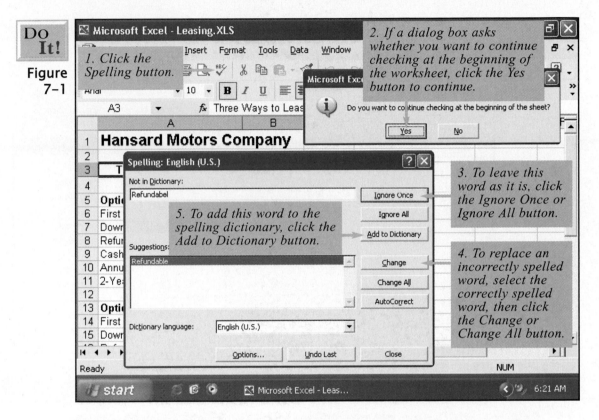

1. Click the Spelling button.

2. If a dialog box asks whether you want to continue checking at the beginning of the worksheet, click the Yes button to continue.

3. To leave this word as it is, click the Ignore Once or Ignore All button.

4. To replace an incorrectly spelled word, select the correctly spelled word, then click the Change or Change All button.

5. To add this word to the spelling dictionary, click the Add to Dictionary button.

■ You can begin to check the spelling with any cell selected. However, if you make cell A1 the active cell, you will avoid the question displayed in the above figure's Step 2.

■ If the correct spelling appears in the Suggestions list, click to select it, then click the Change button to correct the misspelled word.

■ If no suggested spellings are displayed, click the *Not in Dictionary* text box, then type the correct word. Click the Change button to replace the misspelled word.

■ If you're sure the word is spelled correctly, click the Ignore Once button to ignore this occurrence of the word. Sometimes a word—for example, a person's name—is not recognized by Excel. Click the Ignore All button if you want to ignore all other occurrences of this word throughout the entire worksheet.

■ If the word is one you use frequently, click the Add to Dictionary button to add the current word to the spelling dictionary. In the example above, adding the company name "Hansard" to the Excel dictionary stops the spelling tool from identifying it as a misspelled word.

■ ■ ■

■FAQ How do I sort data in a worksheet?

Excel provides tools that allow you to sort data in ascending or descending order. Data sorted in ascending order will be arranged in alphabetical order—labels that start with A will be positioned above those that start with B. Data sorted in descending order will be arranged in reverse alphabetical order—labels that start with Z will be positioned above those that start with Y.

Do It!

Figure 7-2

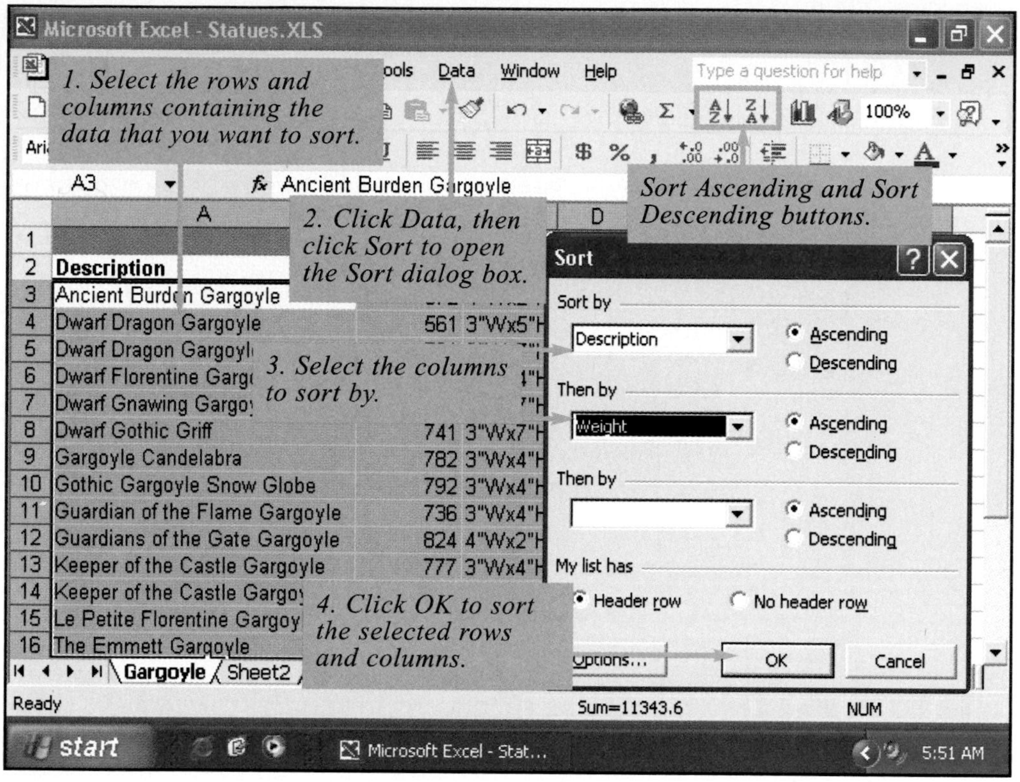

■ It's a good idea to save your worksheet before performing a sort, just in case you forget to select all the necessary columns and end up scrambling your data.

■ It is essential that you select all columns of related data. For example, if column A contains the names of sales people and column B contains the year-to-date sales for each person, you must select all cells in column A and column B before performing the sort.

■ If you forgot to select all columns before sorting, click the Undo button to undo the sort. Check the data carefully to make sure that each row still contains the correct data, then select all columns of data and try the sort again.

■ If you just want to sort by the data in the first column, you can use the ⬆ Sort Ascending or ⬇ Sort Descending buttons on the toolbar.

■ If you need to sort by a column other than the first column, or if you need to sort by several columns, use the procedure shown in the figure. If you need to perform a multi-level sort after you designate the first column for the sort order, designate the second and third columns from the *Then by* lists. You can set each level of the sort for either ascending or descending order. Click OK to apply the sort.

FAQ How do I test my worksheet?

You should always test your worksheets before relying on the results. Don't assume that the result is correct just because it's generated by a computer. Your computer is almost certainly returning the correct results for the formulas and data that you've entered, but it is possible that you might have entered the wrong value in a cell, used the wrong cell reference in a formula, or made some other mistake in a formula.

Do It!

Figure 7-3

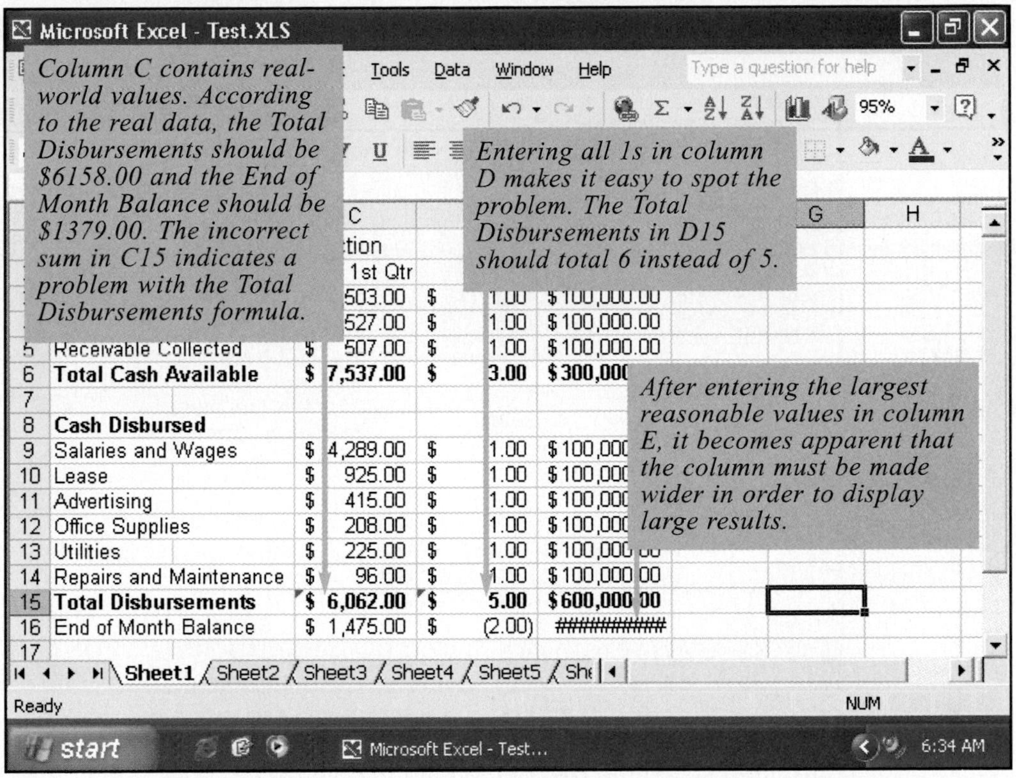
Microsoft Excel - Test.XLS
Column C contains real-world values. According to the real data, the Total Disbursements should be $6158.00 and the End of Month Balance should be $1379.00. The incorrect sum in C15 indicates a problem with the Total Disbursements formula.
Entering all 1s in column D makes it easy to spot the problem. The Total Disbursements in D15 should total 6 instead of 5.
After entering the largest reasonable values in column E, it becomes apparent that the column must be made wider in order to display large results.
Total Cash Available
Cash Disbursed
Salaries and Wages
Lease
Advertising
Office Supplies
Utilities
Repairs and Maintenance
Total Disbursements
End of Month Balance

■ It's a good idea to rename and save an extra copy of your worksheet before testing, just in case your test significantly changes the worksheet.

■ One way to test your worksheet is to enter a series of consistent and easily verified values, such as 1 or 10, into the data cells. If you enter all 1s, you can quickly check the calculated results "in your head" and spot potential formula errors.

■ Another way to test your worksheet is to enter a set of real-world values for which you already know the results. Compare the calculated result from the worksheet with the real-world result to make sure the worksheet is returning the correct results. Testing with real data will also help identify problems such as columns that are too narrow to hold calculated results.

■ It's also a good idea to test your worksheet by entering the largest and smallest values that would reasonably be expected in normal use of your worksheet. Small values, including zero, can lead to errors such as division by zero. The use of large values can lead to results that do not fit into the cell where the answer is to be displayed. In such a case, you'll need to make those columns wider.

∎FAQ How do I create a chart?

You can use the Excel Chart Wizard to create a chart or graph of the data in your worksheet. You should pick a chart type that suits the data. Line charts are used to show data that changes over time. Pie charts illustrate the proportion of parts to a whole. Bar charts are used to show comparisons.

Do It!

Figure 7-4

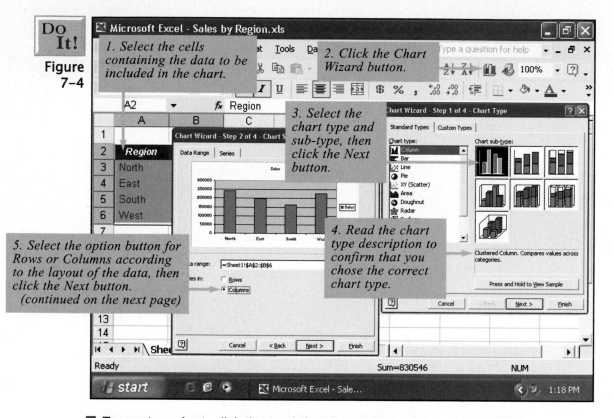

■ To create a chart, click the top-left cell containing data to be included in the chart, then select the rest of the data that you want to include in the chart. If the selected cells consist of a column of labels followed by one or more columns of data, the labels will be used to identify the data series.

■ Click the ▦ Chart Wizard button to start the Chart Wizard.

In Chart Wizard - Step 1 of 4:

■ Select the type of chart from the Chart type list. Select the chart sub-type, then click the Next button to go to the next step of the Wizard.

In Chart Wizard - Step 2 of 4:

■ The data range should be highlighted in Step 2 of the Chart Wizard. If the data to be charted is in rows (related cells are positioned in a row next to each other), click the Rows option in the *Series in* section. If the data to be charted is in columns (related cells are positioned in a column above or below each other), click the Columns option in the *Series in* section. Click the Next button to continue.

■How do I create a chart? (continued)

Figure
7–5

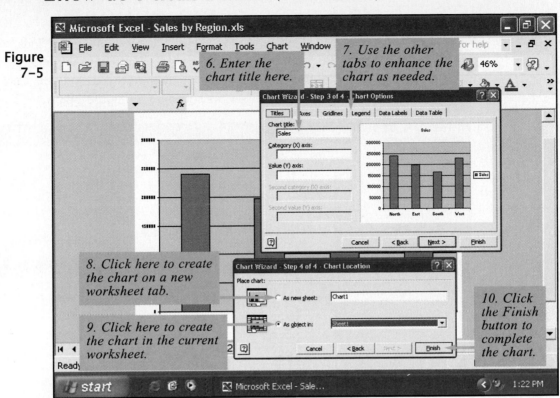

In Chart Wizard - Step 3 of 4:

■ Enter the chart title in the Chart title text box. The chart title usually prints above the chart, but you can move it after you have created the chart.

■ If you'd like to include labels for the X (horizontal) axis or the Y (vertical) axis, enter the appropriate labels in the text boxes.

■ You can use the other tabs in the *Chart Wizard Step 3 of 4* dialog box to modify titles, to add or remove axes and gridlines, to move or remove the legend, and to add or remove data labels and a data table.

■ Click the Next button to go to the last step of the Chart Wizard.

In Chart Wizard - Step 4 of 4:

■ If you want the chart to be inserted into the current worksheet, make sure that the *As object in* option button is selected, then click the Finish button.

■ If you want the chart to be placed in a new page of the worksheet, click the *As new sheet* option button, then click the Finish button.

■FAQ How do I use the print preview and page setup options?

Excel's Print Preview feature allows you to see how the worksheet will look when it is printed. To display the print preview, click the 🔍 Print Preview button on the Excel toolbar or click File, then click Print to display the Print dialog box. Click the Preview button to open the print preview, as shown in the figure below.

Do It!

Figure 7-6

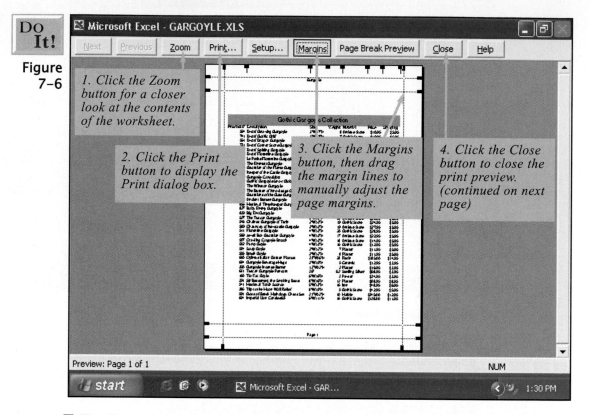

The Zoom button switches between a close-up and a normal view. Just click the Zoom button again to switch back to the previous view. It's a good idea to zoom in to look for cells that contain #####, which indicates a column that needs to be wider.

■ To manually adjust the margins, click the Margins button. Position the pointer over a margin line until it changes to a ↔ shape or a ↕ shape, drag that line to the new position, then release the mouse button. You can also set the margins using the Setup button as indicated on the next page.

■ Notice that there are two margin lines at the top and bottom of the page. The outside top and bottom lines control the location of the header and footer. The inside lines control the placement of the worksheet between the header and footer.

■ The print preview option is particularly important for worksheets that are too wide to fit on a single sheet of paper. From the print preview, you can adjust the page settings and margins so that the worksheet prints correctly.

■ If you're not satisfied with the appearance of the worksheet in print preview, click the Setup button to display the Page Setup dialog box. You will find more options there for changing the printed version.

■How do I use the print preview and page setup options?
(continued)

Figure 7-7

Microsoft Excel - GARGOYLE.XLS

5. Click the Setup button to display the Page Setup dialog box.

6. The Portrait option means the worksheet will print in the normal or vertical position.

Orientation

Portrait   Landscape

7. Click the Landscape option on the Page tab to print the worksheet sideways on the paper.

Scaling

Adjust to: 100 % normal size

Fit to: 1 page(s) wide by 1

8. Click the Fit to option button on the Page tab to make the worksheet print on a single page.

Paper size: Letter

Print quality: 300 dpi

First page number: Auto

9. Click the OK button to close the Page Setup dialog box.

OK   Cancel

Preview: Page 1 of 1   NUM

start   Microsoft Excel - GAR...   1:30 PM

■ Worksheets can easily become very large. To print a large worksheet on one page makes it easier to read. The Page tab controls help you to print a wide worksheet in a landscape orientation on the page. You can also use the Scaling options to adjust the worksheet's overall size or to force it to fit to the width of a single page. Be careful when using these scaling options because the font size can become so small that the data is no longer readable. To cancel scaling, click the *Adjust to* option button and change the corresponding value to 100% normal size.

■ Click the Margins tab if you'd prefer to specify the margin settings rather than drag the margin lines in the print preview.

■ Click the Header/Footer tab to change or add headers and footers. Detailed instructions on how to use these options are on page 76.

■ The options on the Sheet tab are less frequently used. Its most useful option is a check box that controls the printing of gridlines on the worksheet.

■ Page setup changes are saved when you save the worksheet. The next time you open the worksheet, settings such as landscape printing and margins will be loaded automatically.

■ When you close the Page Setup dialog box, you'll return to the print preview. Click the Print button if you want to print the worksheet. Click the Close button to close the print preview.

■FAQ How do I add headers and footers to a worksheet?

A header is text that appears at the top of every page of a document. A footer is text that appears at the bottom of every page. Headers and footers on worksheets typically contain information such as the title of the worksheet, the date, and the page number. You can also type your own header or footer text, just as you can in Word. However, the process for editing Excel headers and footers is quite different from the process for editing Word headers and footers.

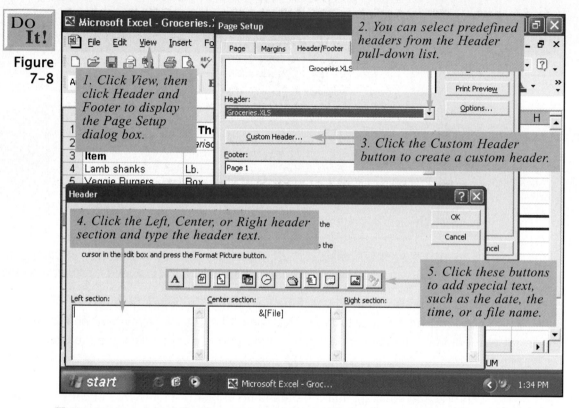

Do It!

Figure 7-8

1. Click View, then click Header and Footer to display the Page Setup dialog box.

2. You can select predefined headers from the Header pull-down list.

3. Click the Custom Header button to create a custom header.

4. Click the Left, Center, or Right header section and type the header text.

5. Click these buttons to add special text, such as the date, the time, or a file name.

■ Footers work just like headers—simply select the appropriate footer option. The custom Header and Footer dialog boxes contain buttons that insert commonly used elements in the header or footer. To use these buttons:

A Select the text, then click this button to display the Font dialog box to format the header text.

Click this button to insert the page number.

Click this button to insert the total number of pages.

Click this button to insert the current date.

Click this button to insert the current time.

Click this button to insert the name of the file.

Click this button to insert the name of the worksheet tab.

Click this button to insert the path of the file.

Click this button to insert a picture.

Click this button to format the picture that you have inserted.

■FAQ How do I use the Print dialog box?

You can click the Print button on the Excel toolbar if you want to print a single copy of the current worksheet. However, you'll need to use the Print dialog box if you want to print multiple copies, print selected pages, or use advanced print options. For instance, you can print all the worksheets that make up a workbook. The default setting prints only the current worksheet.

Do It!

Figure 7-9

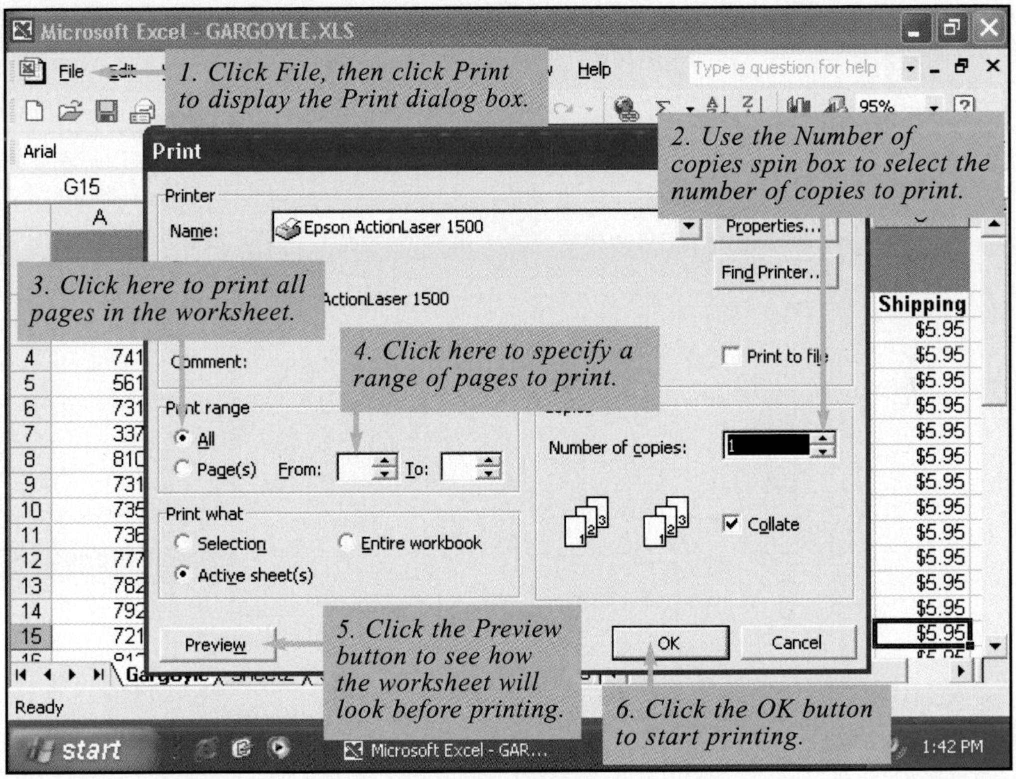

1. Click File, then click Print to display the Print dialog box.

2. Use the Number of copies spin box to select the number of copies to print.

3. Click here to print all pages in the worksheet.

4. Click here to specify a range of pages to print.

5. Click the Preview button to see how the worksheet will look before printing.

6. Click the OK button to start printing.

■ Determine what you want to print before opening the Print dialog box. By default, Excel will print all of the active worksheet. If you want to print only a section of the worksheet, select the range of cells before you click File. Then click Print. Finally, click the *Selection* option in the Print what section of the dialog box.

■ To print only the current worksheet, click the *Active sheet(s)* option in the Print what section of the dialog box.

■ To print all worksheets in the current workbook, click the *Entire workbook* option in the Print what section of the dialog box.

■ Click the Preview button to see how the worksheet or workbook will look when printed.

■FAQ How do I save a worksheet as a Web page?

You can save your worksheet as a Web page that you can then post on the Internet. This Excel feature provides an easy way to make your worksheet data accessible to a large number of people without having to send each person a printed copy of the worksheet. Excel's File menu contains a Save as Web Page option that converts a worksheet into HTML format.

Do It!

Figure 7-10

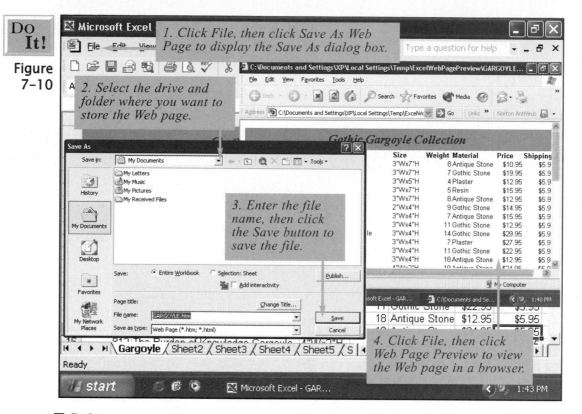

■ Before you save the worksheet as a Web page, it's a good idea to save it as a normal worksheet.

■ A worksheet that is saved as a Web page with the Add interactivity option can be accessed and modified by other users who have Microsoft Office XP and at least Internet Explorer 4.01. Users with older versions of Office and other Web browsers can view the worksheet, but only as a graphic—no modifications can be made.

■ Tables are a valuable formatting tool for creating Web pages. You can use Excel to create a table for this purpose. First, select the range of cells you want to include in the table, then follow the same steps to save as a Web page. In the Save As dialog box, click the Selection option, then name your file and click Save.

■ Some formatting options available in Excel cannot be duplicated in a Web page. If a worksheet contains formatting that isn't available in HTML, you'll be notified of the problem areas and will have the option of canceling or continuing with the save.

■ Not all worksheets convert successfully to Web pages, so you should preview your worksheet in a Web browser to make sure that the conversion is acceptable before you post your worksheet Web pages on the Internet.

■ ■ ■

QuickCheck A

1. True or false? Excel displays a wavy red underline under words that might be misspelled.

2. If the words apple, banana, and peach are sorted in descending order, which word would be at the top of the sorted list?

3. True or false? Spreadsheet software always calculates correctly, so it's not necessary to test your worksheets before using them.

4. Use a(n) [   ] chart to show proportions of a part to a whole.

5. True or false? Excel includes a feature that will make a worksheet fit on a single page of paper when printed.

Check It!

QuickCheck B

Indicate the letter of the desktop element that best matches the following:

1. The Spelling button

2. The Sort Ascending button

3. The Chart Wizard button

4. The Print Preview button

5. A column that is good for testing data because it contains easily verified values

Microsoft Excel - Test.XLS

	A	B	D	E	H
1	Weekly Cash Flow Projection				
2	Cash Received	1st Qtr	2nd Qtr	3rd Qtr	
3	Beginning Cash Balance	$ 2,503.00	$ 1.00	$100,000.00	
4	Cash Sales	$ 4,527.00	$ 1.00	$100,000.00	
5	Receivable Collected	$	$	$100,000.00	
6	Total Cash Available	$ F	$ G	$300,000.00	
7					
8	Cash Disbursed				
9	Salaries and Wages	$ 4,289.00	$ 1.00	$100,000.00	
10	Lease	$ 925.00	$ 1.00	$100,000.00	
11	Advertising	$ 415.00	$ 1.00	$100,000.00	
12	Office Supplies	$ 208.00	$ 1.00	$100,000.00	
13	Utilities	$ 225.00	$ 1.00	$100,000.00	
14	Repairs and Maintenance	$ 96.00	$ 1.00	$100,000.00	
15	Total Disbursements	$ 6,062.00	$ 5.00	$600,000.00	
16	End of Month Balance	$ 1,475.00	$ (2.00)	###########	
17					

Check It!

Get It?

A Skill Set A: Spelling, headers, and footers

C Skill Set C: Creating charts

B Skill Set B: Sorting data and testing worksheets

D Skill Set D: Print, print preview, and saving as a Web page

Chapter 8

Creating a Presentation

What's Inside?

In Chapter 8, you'll learn the essentials of creating presentations with Microsoft PowerPoint.

Microsoft PowerPoint is the component of the Microsoft Office suite that is best suited for creating a visual backdrop for a presentation. As **presentation software**, Microsoft PowerPoint provides a set of tools to help you script, organize, and display a presentation.

A Microsoft PowerPoint **presentation** consists of a number of slides. Each **slide** contains objects such as titles, items in a bulleted list, graphics, and charts. Slides usually are presented with a computer and a projection device and are used to accompany speeches and oral presentations. PowerPoint presentations can also be printed on transparent sheets for use with an overhead projector, printed on paper for handouts, or converted to Web pages for display on the Internet.

■ FAQs:

What's in the PowerPoint window?   81

How do I create a presentation?   82

How do I add a title slide?   83

How do I add a bulleted list?   84

How do I add a graphic?   85

How do I add a chart?   86

How do I add a table?   87

How do I view a slide show?   88

■ Assessment   89

■FAQ What's in the PowerPoint window?

Microsoft PowerPoint creates a slide show that can be presented with a computer and a projection device, printed on transparency film, or converted to HTML and viewed through a Web browser. To create useful handouts for distribution to an audience, the slides can be printed on paper in a variety of layouts.

To start PowerPoint, click Start, point to Programs or All Programs, then click Microsoft PowerPoint. The PowerPoint window includes several work areas, called "panes," as shown in the figure below.

Play It!

Figure 8-1

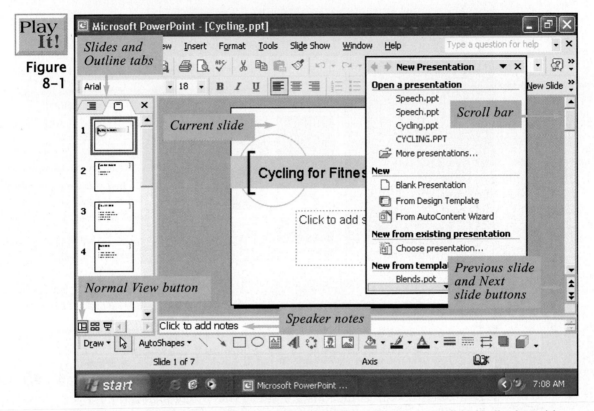

■ When a presentation is open in **Normal View**, the current slide is displayed in the right pane of the PowerPoint window, the Slides and Outline tabs are shown in the left pane of the window, and a pane in the lower-right corner of the window provides a place to type speaker notes.

■ Use the scroll bar or the ▲ Previous Slide and ▼ Next Slide buttons to move from one slide to another in Normal View.

■ When you create a presentation, you have the option to start with one of PowerPoint's design templates. A **design template** contains color schemes, custom formatting and fonts, and provides a professional look to the presentation. When you use a design template, each slide you add has the same custom look.

■ Another option for creating a presentation is to use the **AutoContent Wizard**, which opens a sample presentation that you can customize for your use.

■ ■ ■

■FAQ How do I create a presentation?

A PowerPoint presentation is a series of slides that can contain text, graphics, and charts. All the slides in a presentation will have a similar "look," or design. PowerPoint provides a collection of professionally designed templates with preselected color schemes, fonts, graphic accents, and background colors.

Do It!

Figure 8-2

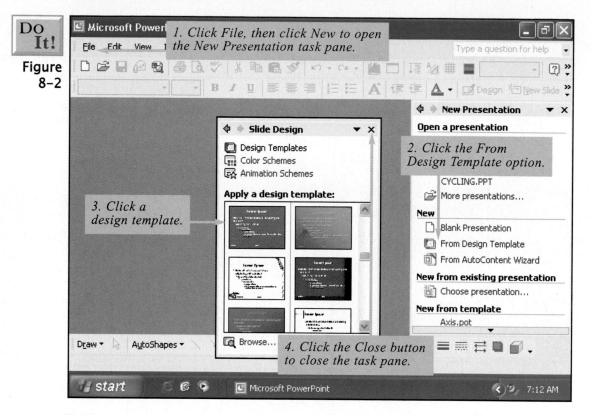

■ When you create a new presentation, a Title Slide is generated for you. There are other slide layouts available on the Slide Layout task pane.

■ It's a good idea to save your presentation as soon as you have created the first slide. PowerPoint presentations are saved with a .ppt extension. As you are building the presentation, you should save frequently. When you save a presentation, all slides in the presentation are saved in the same file.

■ If you change your mind about the template that you select for a presentation, you can change it by clicking the Design button on the Formatting toolbar. Click any template to apply the new design to all slides in the presentation. You can apply a template to just one slide or to a group of slides by selecting the slides, pointing to the design template in the Slide Design task pane, clicking the arrow that appears, then selecting Apply to Selected Slides. All formatting that you may have added before you changed your mind is replaced with the format that is part of the new template.

■FAQ How do I add a title slide?

When you create a presentation or add a slide to an existing presentation, PowerPoint gives you a choice of slide layouts. The **Title Slide layout** provides two areas, called **placeholders**, in which you can enter text. You can use the Title Slide layout for any slide in a presentation, not just for the first one.

Do It!

Figure 8-3

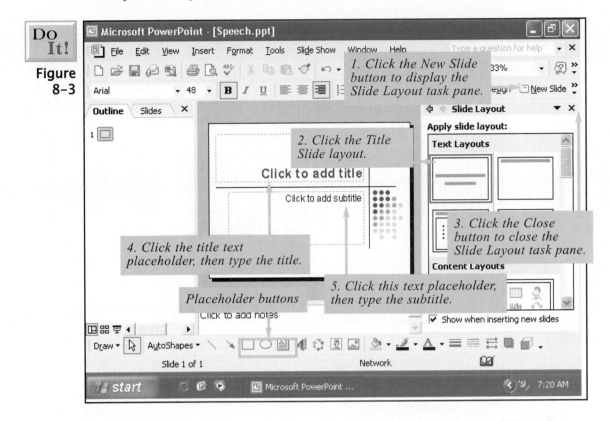

■ The Slide Layout task pane includes thumbnail sketches of each slide type. Hold your mouse over a slide layout to see its name.

■ Each design template has its own Title Slide layout. There is usually a graphic element, which you can delete or modify to customize your presentation.

■ If you don't like the Title Slide layout, you can use the **Title Only layout** or **Blank layout** for the first slide of your presentation. Use the buttons on the Drawing toolbar to add new placeholders. For example, click the ▤ Text box button, then drag across a section of the slide to create a text placeholder. Click inside the placeholder, then type your text.

■ You can resize any placeholder by using its sizing handles. When you select any object, **sizing handles** are the small squares that appear at the corners and along the edges. Drag the sizing handles to resize any type of object.

■ The process is the same for adding any slide layout. Click the New Slide button, select the slide layout that you want to add, then click the Close button to close the Slide Layout task pane.

■ ■ ■

■FAQ How do I add a bulleted list?

The most commonly used slide layout is the **Title and Text layout**. Use the Title and Text layout when you want to present a main point with one or more subpoints. PowerPoint features several types of title and text layouts—Title and Text, Title and 2-Column Text, Title and Text over Content, and Title and 2 Content over Text—just to name a few.

Do It!

Figure 8-4

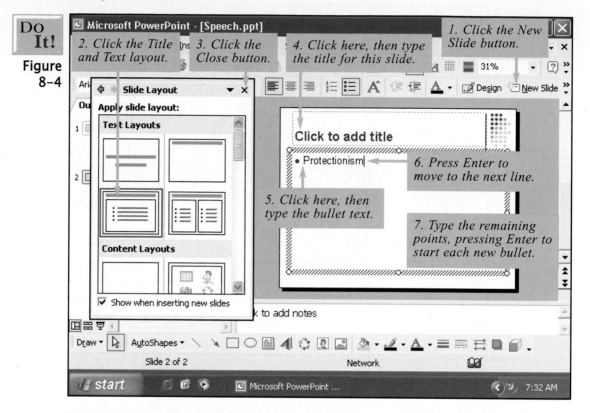

■ When you use the Title and Text layout, the text is formatted as a bulleted list. If you do not want the text bulleted, you can click the ▤ Bullets button on the Formatting toolbar to remove them.

■ Press Enter after typing each item in a bulleted list. Each time you press the Enter key, a new bullet is added to the list. After you type the last bulleted item, press Enter. Click the Bullets button on the Formatting toolbar to stop entering bulleted items. You can also press the backspace key to remove a bullet.

■ In a presentation, bulleted items focus the audience's attention on each point you are making. Each bullet should be a brief summary of what you are saying. For further emphases, you can use the ▤ Increase Indent button on the Formatting toolbar to indent a bulleted item, making it a sublevel of the previous bulleted item.

■ You can add animation effects to the bulleted list to make the bulleted items appear in sequence on the slide. You'll learn how to do this on page 95.

■ You might find it easier to type and edit bulleted items in the Outline tab on the left side of the Normal View window. To change the order of items on the list, select the text of the bulleted item that you want to move, then drag it to the desired location. You can also drag text in the slide pane to change the order of bullets.

■FAQ How do I add a graphic?

You can add visual interest to your slides with graphics. The easiest way to add a slide with a graphic is to select a slide from the Content Layouts or Text and Content Layouts sections in the **Slide Layout task pane**. After adding the slide, you'll replace the content placeholder with the graphic that you want to use.

Do It!

Figure 8-5

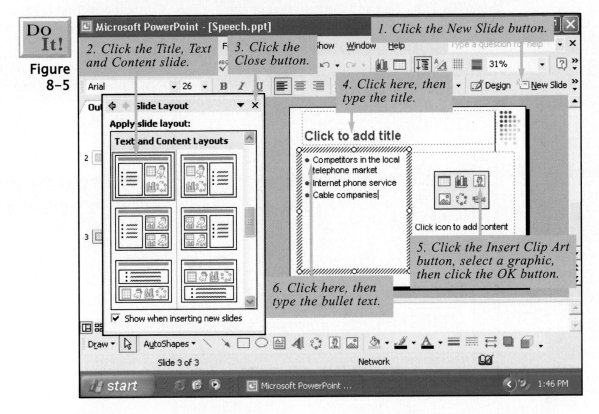

■ To add clip art, click the Insert Clip Art button. The Select Picture dialog box opens. Click any graphic to select it, then click the OK button. The graphic is inserted in the slide, replacing the placeholder.

■ The Select Picture dialog box includes a search tool to look for clip art. Type search text in the *Search text* text box, then click Search. Click a graphic, then click OK. You can find more information on using the Select Picture dialog box in the Microsoft PowerPoint Help.

■ If you've inserted a graphic, then decide that you want to change, click the graphic, then press the Delete key. Click the Insert Clip Art button again to select a new graphic.

■ You can insert clip art into any slide layout. Click Insert on the PowerPoint menu bar, click Picture, then click Clip Art. Select a graphic, then click OK. Use the sizing handles to position and size the graphic.

▪FAQ How do I add a chart?

You can use the Slide Layout task pane to select a slide layout that includes a bar chart, a line chart, or a pie chart. Using the **Title and Content layout**, you can click the Insert Chart button. The chart comes complete with sample data in a datasheet, which you'll change to reflect the data that you want to display on your chart. The **Title, Text and Content layout** and the **Title, Content and Text layout** allow you to add a smaller chart next to a text placeholder, which you can then use to describe the chart data it represents.

Do It!

Figure 8-6

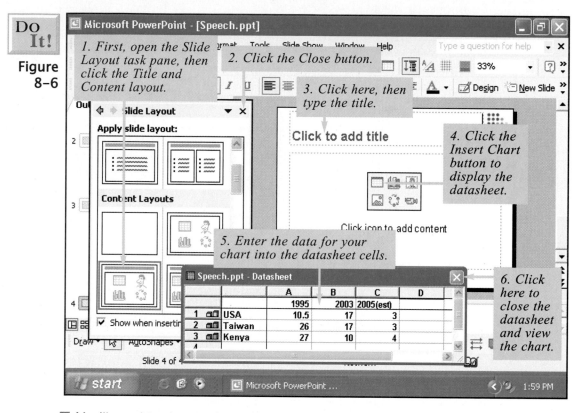

▪ You'll need to change the sample data to suit your needs. Click each cell containing a sample column heading in the first column of the top row, then type your own column heading into the cell. Click each cell containing sample data and type your own data into the cell.

▪ If you need to delete sample data in the datasheet's columns or rows, select the cells, then press the Delete key.

▪ If you need additional columns or rows, use the scroll bars to move to the right or down in the datasheet. Enter the new data to replace sample data, or type it into an empty cell.

▪ If you need to move data in the datasheet, select the cells, then right-click to display the shortcut menu. Click Cut, then right-click the cell where you want to move the data. Click Paste on the shortcut menu.

▪ To insert a row, right-click the cell where you want the row inserted. Click Insert on the shortcut menu, click Entire row, then click the OK button. The steps to insert a column are similar to inserting a row. The steps to delete a row or column are similar to the steps to insert them, except you use the Delete option on the shortcut menu.

■FAQ How do I add a table?

You can use the Slide Layout task pane to select the Title and Content layout that includes a placeholder for a table. You can then enter your own data into the rows and columns of the table.

Do It!

Figure 8-7

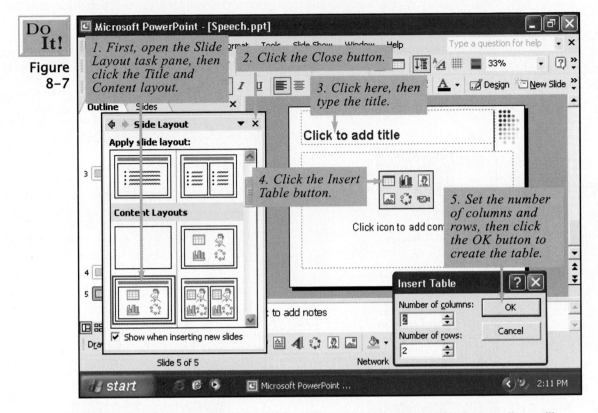

■ When the table is inserted into the slide, the Tables and Borders toolbar will appear. Using the buttons on this toolbar, you can format the table borders, add color shading to the cells, and adjust the alignment of text in the cells. You can find information on the Tables and Borders toolbar in Microsoft PowerPoint Help or in the program documentation.

■ To add text to a cell, click inside the cell, then type the text. You edit and format text inside the table just as you do outside the table. You will learn more about formatting text in the next chapter.

■ To adjust the height or width of the cells, position the pointer over the dividing lines so that the pointer changes to a ↔ or ↥ shape. Drag the dividing line to the correct position.

■ To insert rows, right-click the cell where you want to insert, then click Insert Rows. The steps to insert a column are similar to the steps for inserting a row, except you will click Insert Columns. The steps to delete a row or column are similar to the steps to insert them, except you use the Delete option on the shortcut menu.

■ ■ ■

■FAQ How do I view a slide show?

When you build a presentation, your screen contains menu bars, toolbars, and other objects that will not be visible when you make your presentation before an audience. In this chapter, you have seen how to create and modify a presentation in the Normal View. When you are ready to see how your slides will look to your audience, use the scroll bar to display the first slide, then click the **Slide Show button**.

Do It!

Figure 8-8

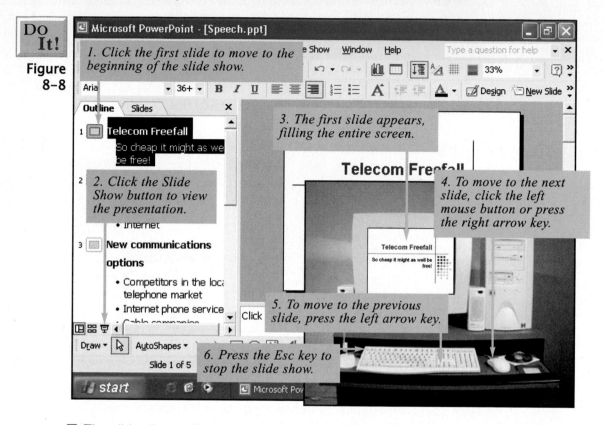

1. Click the first slide to move to the beginning of the slide show.

2. Click the Slide Show button to view the presentation.

3. The first slide appears, filling the entire screen.

4. To move to the next slide, click the left mouse button or press the right arrow key.

5. To move to the previous slide, press the left arrow key.

6. Press the Esc key to stop the slide show.

■ The slide show will start with the current slide, so it's important to move to the first slide in the slide show before starting your presentation.

■ You can navigate through the slides during your presentation in several ways. For instance, you can press the left mouse button or the right arrow key to display the next slide, or the next bullet. Press the left arrow key or the P key to move to the previous slide or the previous bullet.

■ Right-click a slide to display a shortcut menu that allows you to select a specific slide to display. Click Previous on the shortcut menu to go back one slide.

■ Press the Esc key to cancel the slide show and return to the PowerPoint application.

■ Before presenting to an audience, be sure to familiarize yourself with the content of each slide. Then, practice the timing of your presentation.

■ There are many formatting options and other enhancements you can make to finalize a presentation. The next chapter discusses many of them, along with ways to use the Outline tab, the Slides tab, and Slide Sorter View.

■ ■ ■

QuickCheck A

1. After adding a slide, you click the title text [_____] to replace it with your own title.

2. Before viewing a presentation, you should move to the [_____] slide in the presentation.

3. Microsoft PowerPoint is an example of [_____] software.

4. To add a new bullet to a bulleted list, press the [_____] key at the end of the previous bullet.

5. When you add a(n) [_____] to a presentation, you specify the number of rows and columns that will be displayed on the slide.

Check It!

QuickCheck B

Indicate the letter of the desktop element that best matches the following:

1. The New Slide button [_____]

2. The Title Slide layout [_____]

3. The Title and Text layout [_____]

4. The Title, Text and Content layout [_____]

5. The Insert Chart button [_____]

Check It!

Get It?

A	Skill Set A: Creating a new presentation
C	Skill Set C: Adding graphics and charts
B	Skill Set B: Adding titles and bulleted lists
D	Skill Set D: Adding tables and viewing your presentation

Chapter 9

Finalizing a Presentation

What's Inside?

In Chapter 9, you'll learn how to use the different views that are included with Microsoft PowerPoint. In addition, you'll learn formatting techniques, as well as how to add animation and other visual effects to your slides. To finalize your presentations, you'll learn how to print notes for yourself and handouts for your audience, how to save your presentation for sharing on the Internet, and how to use an overhead projector if a computer and projection device are not available.

■ FAQs:

How do I use the Normal View? 91

How do I use the Slide Sorter View? 92

How do I add transitions? 93

How do I format text on a slide? 94

How do I add animation effects to a bulleted list? 95

How do I check the spelling in a presentation? 96

How do I add and print speaker notes? 97

How do I print handouts? 98

How do I save a presentation as Web pages? 99

Can I show my presentation with an overhead projector? 100

■ Assessment 101

■FAQ How do I use the Normal View?

Microsoft PowerPoint provides different views that you can use to build, modify, and view your presentation. Most of the time, you will work in Normal View. To change views, click the buttons in the lower-left corner of the PowerPoint window.

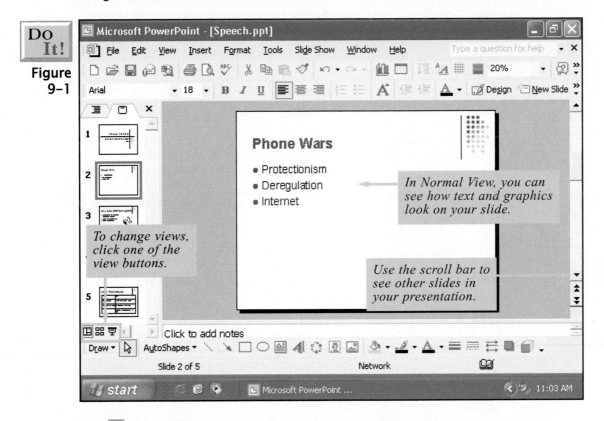

Do It!

Figure 9-1

■ In ▥ Normal View, you can work in any of the three panes—the slide, the notes, or the Outline or Slides tab panes. Normal View is convenient for building the basic structure of your presentation and for adding speaker notes.

■ To work effectively on all the slides' contents, use the ☰ Outline tab. After you have created most of the slides in the presentation, the Outline tab is useful for revising and rearranging the contents of your presentation. Use the ⊞ Increase Indent button to indent a bullet, or use the ⊟ Decrease indent button to return a bullet to its previous level.

■ When you are satisfied with the order of the content in your presentation, use the ▱ Slide tab to add graphics and visual effects to one slide at a time. You can navigate to, and work on other slides by clicking the slide icons in the Slide tab or by using the scroll bar on the right side of the PowerPoint window.

■FAQ How do I use the Slide Sorter View?

Slide Sorter View allows you to view miniaturized versions of all the slides in a presentation. In this view, it is easy to rearrange slides as needed. You can add special effects to your presentation by using the Slide Sorter toolbar.

Do It!

Figure 9-2

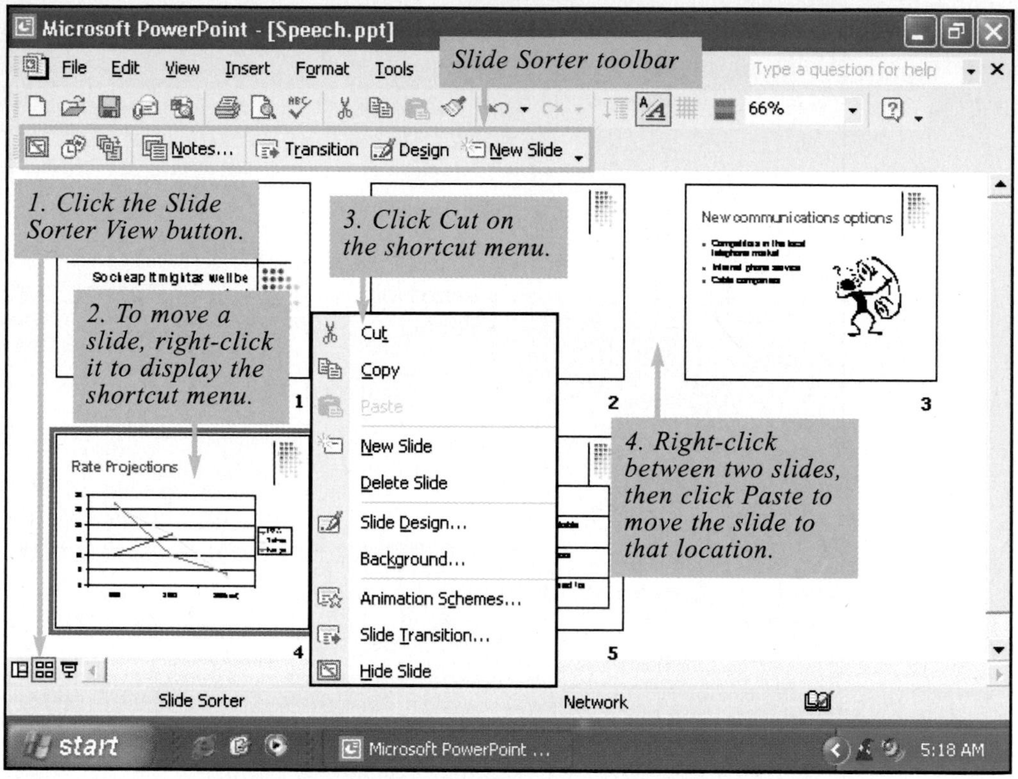

■ You can use the **drag-and-drop** method to move a slide. Select the slide, then drag it to a new location. PowerPoint will display a vertical line between slides to show you the proposed position before you release the mouse button.

■ To delete a slide, click the slide to select it, click Edit, then click Delete Slide. You can also select the slide, then press the Delete key on your keyboard.

■ To duplicate a slide, right-click it, then click Copy from the shortcut menu. Right-click between the slides where you want to insert the copy, then click Paste on the shortcut menu. A copy of the slide will be inserted at the selected location.

■ You can hide a slide so that it won't appear when you view the presentation. Right-click the slide in Slide Show View, then click Hide Slide on the shortcut menu. Repeat this process to make the slide visible again. This feature can be handy when you need to give a shortened version of your presentation. Rather than showing slides without commenting on them, you can just hide the slides that you won't have time to discuss.

■ You will learn how to add transitions using the Slide Sorter toolbar on page 93.

■FAQ How do I add transitions?

A **transition** is an effect that determines how a slide replaces the current slide. Transitions include fades, wipes, and other animated effects. If you do not specify a transition, a new slide replaces the entire current slide all at once. Carefully selected transitions can make a presentation more interesting and help the audience to pay attention, but overuse of transitions can be very irritating and can draw attention away from the content of your presentation.

Do It!

Figure 9-3

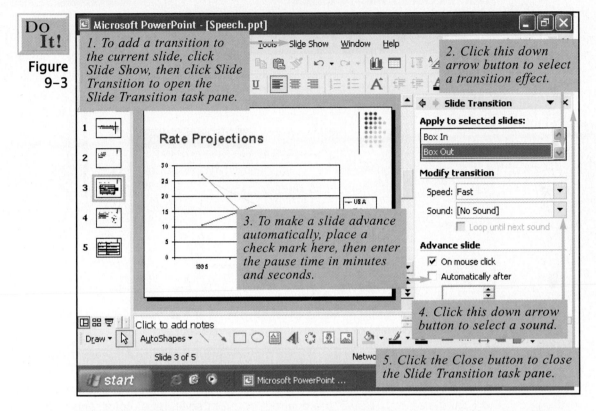

1. To add a transition to the current slide, click Slide Show, then click Slide Transition to open the Slide Transition task pane.

2. Click this down arrow button to select a transition effect.

3. To make a slide advance automatically, place a check mark here, then enter the pause time in minutes and seconds.

4. Click this down arrow button to select a sound.

5. Click the Close button to close the Slide Transition task pane.

■ When you add a transition to a slide, the new slide can move down over the current slide, replace the current slide diagonally, or even replace the current slide from the center to the outside edges. You can also select sound effects to go along with each transition.

■ After you apply a transition, you can view it by moving to the previous slide, then clicking the Slide Show button. Click the left mouse button to display the slide with the transition.

■ In Slide Sorter View, a transition icon will be displayed under the slide. When you click the transition icon, the transition will activate. You can change the transition by selecting the slide, clicking the Slide Transition button on the Slide Sorter toolbar, then selecting a different transition from the Slide Transition task pane.

■ Normally, a presentation will advance from one slide to the next when you click the mouse or press a key. If you want the slide to advance automatically after a specified period of time, click the *Automatically after* check box in the Slide Transition task pane. Use the spin box to set the time after which the next slide will be displayed. The time is displayed as mm:ss, where the first two digits represent the number of minutes and the last two digits represent the number of seconds. To force the slide to advance after 1 minute and 30 seconds, for example, enter 01:30 in the *Automatically after* spin box.

■ ■ ■

■FAQ How do I format text on a slide?

The PowerPoint design templates include fonts and font sizes specially selected to complement the background design. In most cases, these preselected fonts will work fine, but sometimes, you'll find it necessary to modify font attributes.

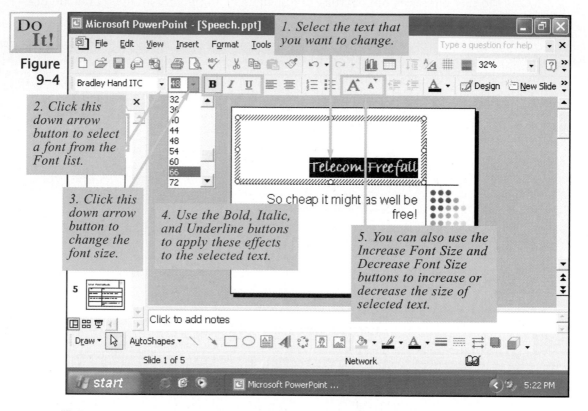

Do It!

Figure 9-4

■ For more font options, select the text, click Format, then click Font to display the Font dialog box. Select the desired font, font style, size, color, and effect, then click the OK button to apply the font changes.

■ When you select font sizes, you should consider the number of people in the audience. If the presentation will be given in a large room, you should use a large font that will be visible even from the back of the room. In order to do so, you might have to use fewer words on each slide.

■ You also need to consider the lighting in the room in which your presentation will be given. In a light room, your slides will be easier to read if you use a dark font color on a light background color. In a dark room, you should use a dark background color with light font colors. You should experiment with font colors to find the combination that works best in the room in which you will give the presentation.

■ You can change the font attributes for all the slides in your presentation at the same time by using the Slide Master. The **Slide Master** is a template that you can modify to create a consistent look for your presentation. Click the View menu, click Master, then click Slide Master. Select all the text in one of the text placeholders, then change the font attributes. Click the Slide Sorter View button to verify that the new font attributes are applied to the text on all the slides in your presentation.

■FAQ How do I add animation effects to a bulleted list?

The Slide Show menu provides options for adding animation effects and sounds to items on a slide. Animation effects are typically used to draw attention to bullets as they appear on the slide during a presentation. For example, each bulleted item can "fly" in from the side when you click the left mouse button. Animation effects can also be accompanied by sound effects to draw attention to each new bullet.

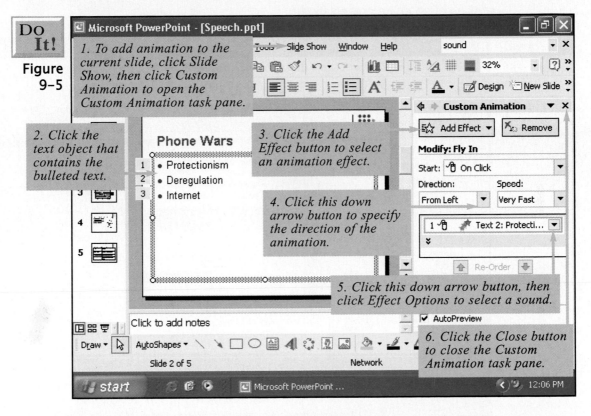

Do It!

Figure 9-5

■ You can apply animation effects to any type of object, including text, graphics, charts, and tables. After you apply an animation effect, you can test it by moving to the previous slide, then clicking the Slide Show button. Click the left mouse button to display the slide with the animation effects. Continue to click the left mouse button to proceed to the next animation effect or to the next slide.

■ After selecting Effect Options, you can use the *After animation* option to indicate whether the object should change to a different color or disappear after animation. For example, a dim bulleted item can appear on the slide but in a lighter shade than the original font color. When the next bulleted item appears, its brighter font color will focus the audience's attention on the new bullet.

■ Use sounds sparingly—a sound effect can be humorous and effective the first time it's used, but the effect can become less amusing after ten or twenty slides. If you use sounds for a presentation, make sure that your presentation equipment includes a sound system with adequate volume for your audience.

■FAQ How do I check the spelling in a presentation?

PowerPoint's spelling checker is very similar to the one that you use in Word. It provides an in-line spelling checker that uses a wavy red line to indicate possible spelling errors. It also provides a way to check the spelling of the entire presentation. You can right-click a word that is marked with a wavy red line to see a list of correctly spelled alternatives. You can also use the Spelling button on the toolbar to check the spelling of an entire presentation.

Do It!

Figure 9-6

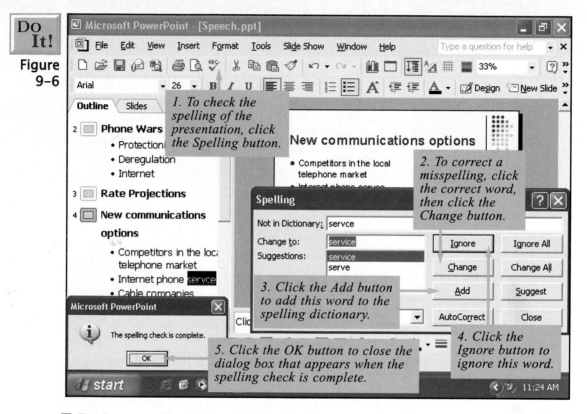

■ Don't worry—the wavy red lines do not appear when you view the presentation.

■ You should always check the spelling of your slides. Misspellings can make your audience doubt the accuracy of the content of your presentation.

■ PowerPoint does not include a grammar checker, so you will have to proofread your presentation for grammar errors yourself. Bulleted items are usually sentence fragments, but sometimes, complete sentences are more appropriate. You should try to be consistent on each slide, using either complete sentences or only phrases.

■ You can correct common typing errors automatically as you work by using the AutoCorrect feature. Click the Tools menu, then click AutoCorrect Options. In the AutoCorrect dialog box, select the options that are useful to you. Options include the automatic capitalization of the first word of a sentence and the names of days, the changing of two capital letters at the beginning of a word to a single capital letter, and the correction of capitalization errors caused by accidental use of the Caps Lock key. You can find more information about using AutoCorrect in Microsoft PowerPoint Help and in the program documentation.

■ ■ ■

■FAQ How do I add and print speaker notes?

You can prepare and print speaker notes to help you remember what you want to say about each slide. Because the speaker notes also contain printed versions of each slide, you won't have to keep looking back at the projected slides. This feature allows you to maintain better eye contact and rapport with the audience.

Do It!

Figure 9-7

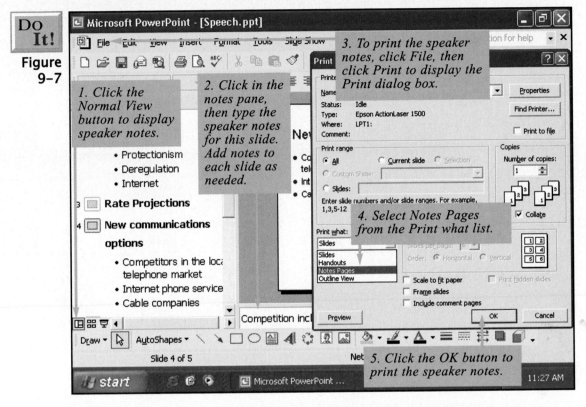

■ Speaker notes shouldn't include the exact text that appears on the slide. Use speaker notes for any additional comments that you want to make.

■ To print the speaker notes, click File, then click Print. Select Notes Pages from the *Print what* section of the Print dialog box. Click the OK button to print the speaker notes.

■ When you print the speaker notes, each slide and its notes will be printed on a page. You can use the printed slide and notes during your presentation so that you don't have to keep looking back at the projected slide.

■ Speaker notes can be included as part of a presentation that is viewed in a Web browser. This feature can be useful for sharing your presentation and comments with others who could not attend the actual presentation. You will learn how to save the slides in your presentation as Web pages on page 99.

∎FAQ How do I print handouts?

Handouts help your audience remember the content of your presentation. Microsoft PowerPoint offers several print layouts that you can use, depending on the content and the number of slides in the presentation.

Do It!

Figure 9-8

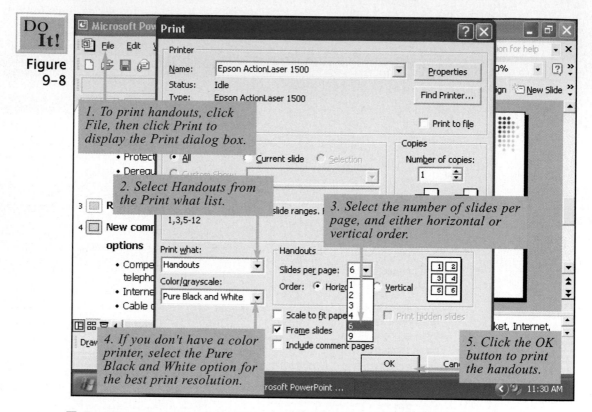

1. To print handouts, click File, then click Print to display the Print dialog box.

2. Select Handouts from the Print what list.

3. Select the number of slides per page, and either horizontal or vertical order.

4. If you don't have a color printer, select the Pure Black and White option for the best print resolution.

5. Click the OK button to print the handouts.

∎ If your presentation is brief, you can print two or three slides per page for handouts. The two-slide layout prints each slide on one-half of the page. It is appropriate to use this layout when the graphics and bullets on the slides include most of the details of your presentation content. The three-slide layout prints blank lines to the right of each slide. It is appropriate to use this layout when you expect your audience to write notes about your detailed comments.

∎ You can save paper by printing four to nine slides per page. You can select either horizontal or vertical order for all of these print layouts. Horizontal order prints multiple slides (in order) across the page; vertical order prints the slides (in order) down the page. The preview in the *Handouts* section illustrates the selected order.

∎ The biggest advantage of using a PowerPoint presentation is the variety of colors and graphics you can include to enhance your comments. Note, however, that your handouts can be printed in black and white, instead of in color, without sacrificing print quality. Select the *Pure Black and White* option to print your handouts with the best resolution for your black and white printer.

∎ The Frame slides option gives your handouts a professional look by drawing a thin black line around each slide.

∎ You can print a text-only version of your presentation by selecting Outline View from the *Print what* list. This handout is useful for very long presentations that include a number of bulleted items. Graphics will not print in the Outline View version.

∎ ∎ ∎

■FAQ How do I save a presentation as Web pages?

If you convert your presentation into Web pages, viewers who didn't take notes during your presentation, as well as potential viewers who didn't attend your presentation at all, can later refer to the Web pages.

It's easy to save your presentation as Web pages. The converted presentation can be viewed over the Internet using a standard Web browser. Each slide appears as a separate Web page with navigation tools to move from slide to slide.

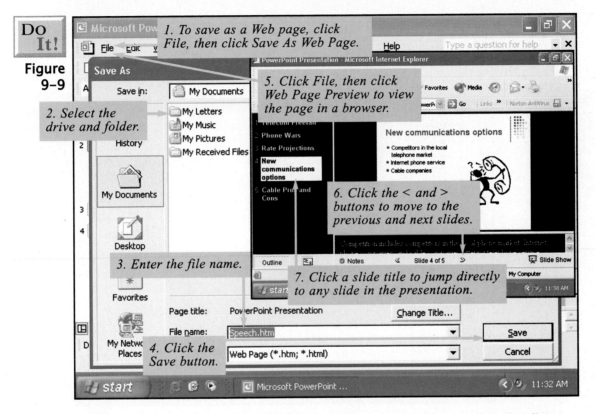

Do It!

Figure 9–9

1. To save as a Web page, click File, then click Save As Web Page.

2. Select the drive and folder.

3. Enter the file name.

4. Click the Save button.

5. Click File, then click Web Page Preview to view the page in a browser.

6. Click the < and > buttons to move to the previous and next slides.

7. Click a slide title to jump directly to any slide in the presentation.

■ Before you convert your presentation to Web pages, include a slide that lists the URL where the presentation will be located. Interested audience members can then make a note of the URL and later review the presentation on the Web.

■ Be sure to select *Web page (*.htm, *.html)* as the *Save as type* option. PowerPoint will create a folder that contains all the files that are necessary for your presentation to be viewed in a Web browser.

■ PowerPoint is useful for converting a presentation to Web pages, but some slide features cannot be duplicated. For instance, a viewer who is looking at the Web presentation might not see transitions and animation effects. If a presentation contains formatting that cannot be duplicated in Web pages, you'll be notified of the problem areas and will have the option of canceling or continuing with the save.

■ You should preview your presentation in a Web browser to see how it will actually look on the Web. If you're not satisfied with how the Web version looks, you can get more information in Microsoft PowerPoint Help.

■FAQ Can I show my presentation with an overhead projector?

Typically, you'll connect your computer to a projection device, then display the presentation directly from PowerPoint. However, sometimes you won't have access to a computer and projection device, which means you'll need to display your presentation the old fashioned way—with transparency film and an overhead projector. You'll lose the transitions, animations, and sound effects, but at least you'll be able to display the content of your PowerPoint slides while you make your comments.

Do It!

Figure 9-10

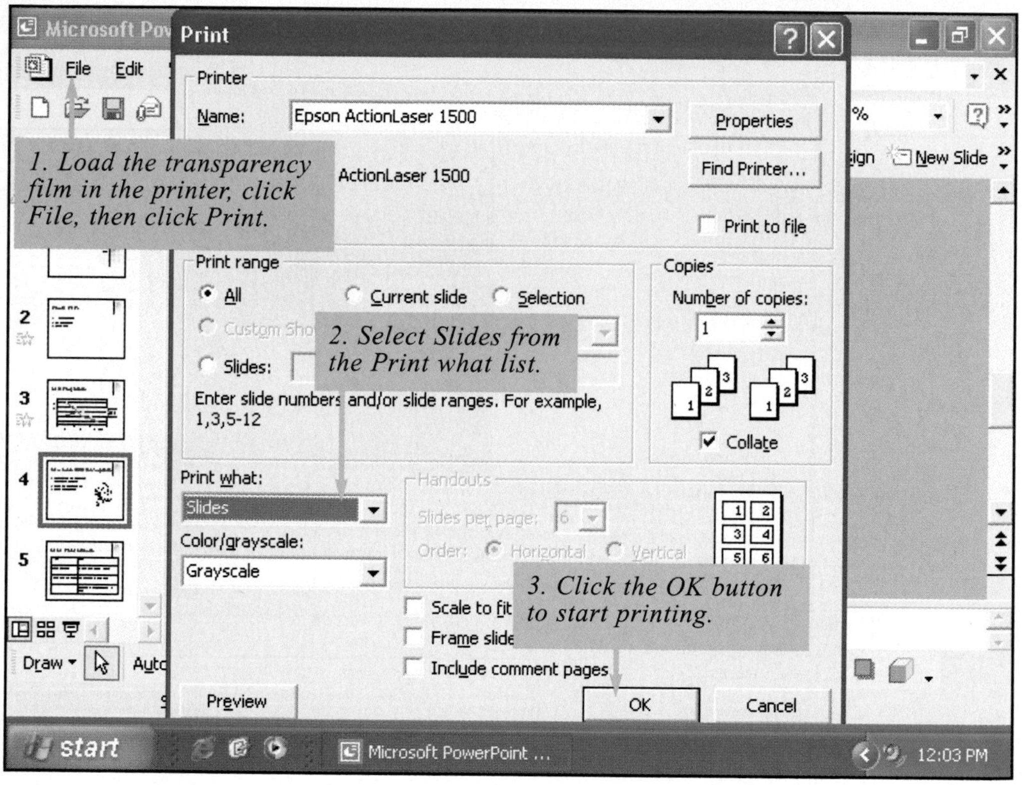

1. Load the transparency film in the printer, click File, then click Print.

2. Select Slides from the Print what list.

3. Click the OK button to start printing.

■ You can purchase transparency film from an office supply store. The type of film that you purchase depends on whether you are printing on a laser printer or an ink jet printer, so read the packaging carefully to make sure that you buy the right kind of transparency film.

■ If your printer will allow it, you can put transparency film into the paper feeder and print directly onto the transparencies. However, you might have to print on regular paper and use a xerographic copier to create the transparencies. Read your printer manual for details.

■ A color printer that accepts transparency film can be used to create color transparencies. If you don't have access to a color printer, you should select the *Pure Black and White* option in the Print dialog box to create slides with the best resolution for your black and white printer.

QuickCheck A

1. [_____] notes consist of text used as a reminder of what to say when the slide is displayed during a presentation.

2. A(n) [_____] effect controls the way bullets appear in a bulleted list.

3. A(n) [_____] controls the way a slide replaces the previous slide during a presentation.

4. True or false? In order to show your PowerPoint presentation to a group of people, you must have a computer connected to a projection device. [_____]

5. If you're going to put your presentation on the Web, you should always include a slide with the [_____] where the presentation will be located.

Check It!

QuickCheck B

Indicate the letter of the desktop element that best matches the following:

1. The Slide Sorter View button [____]

2. The Spelling button [____]

3. The Increase Font Size button [____]

4. The Slide Show button [____]

5. The Normal View button [____]

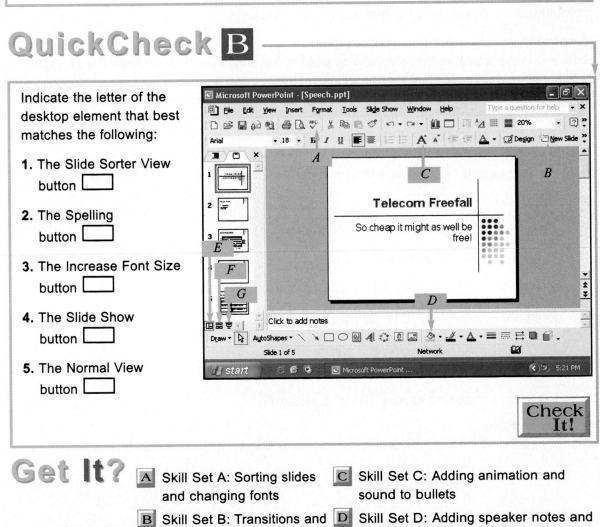

Check It!

Get It?

A Skill Set A: Sorting slides and changing fonts

C Skill Set C: Adding animation and sound to bullets

B Skill Set B: Transitions and spell checking

D Skill Set D: Adding speaker notes and saving slides as Web pages

Chapter 10

Creating a Database

What's Inside?

Microsoft Access is the component of the Microsoft Office suite best suited for working with large collections of data called a **database**. As **database software**, Microsoft Access provides a powerful set of tools for entering and updating information, deleting information, sorting data, searching for specific data, and creating reports.

The databases that you create with Access are technically referred to as "relational databases." A **relational database** contains data that is organized into easy-to-visualize tables, which are composed of fields and records. A **record** contains information about a single "entity" in the database—a person, place, event, or thing. A **field** contains a single unit of information, such as a name, birth date, or ZIP code.

A relational database can contain more than one table and you can define relationships between these tables so that they can be used in conjunction with each other. For example, a video store database might include a table of movies and a table of customers. Suppose a customer checks out one of the Star Wars movies. If the movie is never returned, the relationship between the movie and customer tables allows the clerk to contact the appropriate customer about returning the movie. The customer number, which was entered in the Star Wars record when the movie was checked out, acts as a link to the customer table that displays the customer's address, phone number, and credit card billing information.

■ FAQs:

How is data organized in a database?   103

What's in the Access window?   104

How do I create a new database or open an existing database?   105

How do I create a table using a wizard?   106

How do I enter and edit data in a table?   109

How do I create a table in Design view?   110

How do I create a query using a wizard?   111

■ Assessment   113

■FAQ How is data organized in a database?

Because it's useful for organizing many types of data, database software, like Microsoft Access, can be complex. A few simple concepts, however, will provide you with the background necessary to start working with this important data management tool. An Access database consists of tables. Each table is similar to a stack of index cards. Each card in the stack has the same sort of data written on it, which relates to a single entity. A database record is equivalent to one index card, as shown in the figure below.

Play It!

An Access table is a group of related records, like this stack of index cards containing information about movies.

A record contains fields of data about a single entity—in this case the entity is the movie Shakespeare in Love.

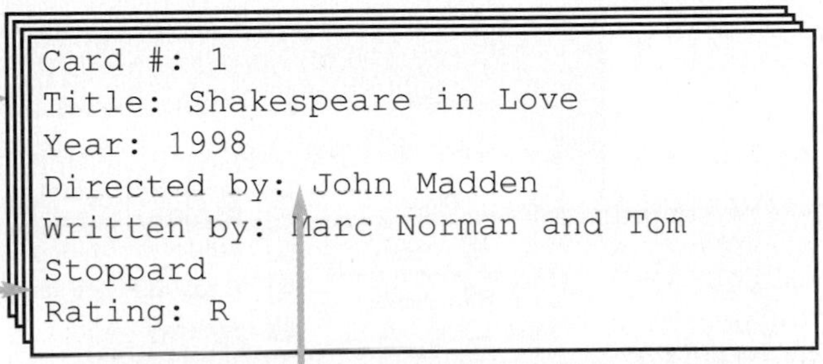

```
Card #: 1
Title: Shakespeare in Love
Year: 1998
Directed by: John Madden
Written by: Marc Norman and Tom
Stoppard
Rating: R
```

A field contains a single fact that describes the record. This field, for example, contains the name of the movie's director.

The data in a database can be displayed in different ways. Most of the time, you'll work with the data arranged in a table such as the one shown below. Data arranged in this way is organized using the same records and fields as in the index cards, shown above—it just looks different because of its arrangement. In the figure below, each row contains one record, equivalent to one index card. Each cell in a row contains the data for one field. The table is made up of all fields in all rows—equivalent to the entire stack of index cards.

Figure 10-1

An Access table consists of a grid of rows and columns.

Each horizontal row contains one record, each of which is equivalent to one index card.

Each cell in a row contains one field of data.

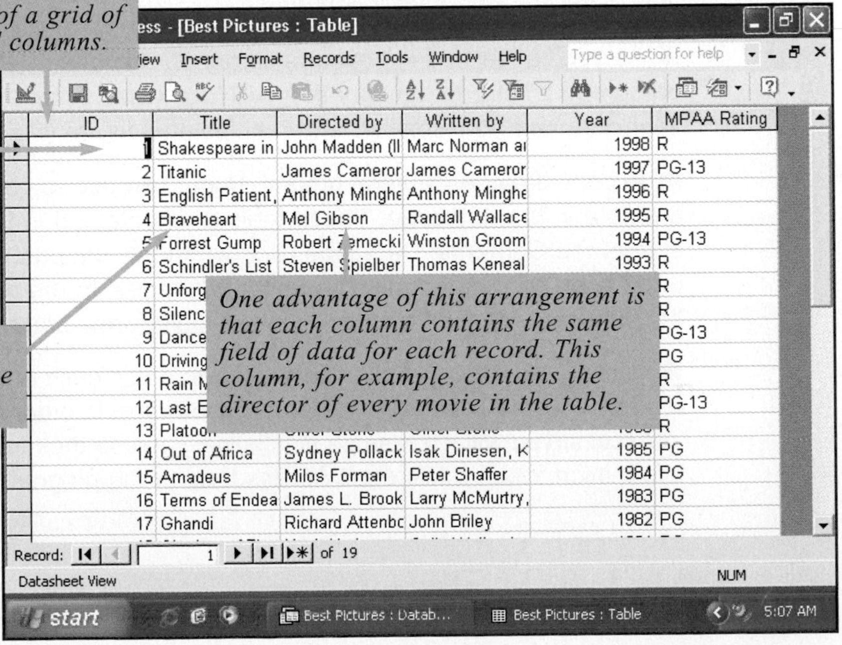

One advantage of this arrangement is that each column contains the same field of data for each record. This column, for example, contains the director of every movie in the table.

ID	Title	Directed by	Written by	Year	MPAA Rating
1	Shakespeare in	John Madden (II	Marc Norman a	1998	R
2	Titanic	James Cameror	James Cameror	1997	PG-13
3	English Patient,	Anthony Minghe	Anthony Minghe	1996	R
4	Braveheart	Mel Gibson	Randall Wallace	1995	R
5	Forrest Gump	Robert Zemecki	Winston Groom	1994	PG-13
6	Schindler's List	Steven Spielber	Thomas Keneal	1993	R
7	Unforg				R
8	Silenc				R
9	Dance				PG-13
10	Driving				PG
11	Rain M				R
12	Last E				PG-13
13	Platoo	Oliver Stone	Oliver Stone	1986	R
14	Out of Africa	Sydney Pollack	Isak Dinesen, K	1985	PG
15	Amadeus	Milos Forman	Peter Shaffer	1984	PG
16	Terms of Endea	James L. Brook	Larry McMurtry,	1983	PG
17	Ghandi	Richard Attenbc	John Briley	1982	PG

Record: 1 of 19

Datasheet View — NUM

start — Best Pictures : Datab... — Best Pictures : Table — 5:07 AM

■FAQ What's in the Access window?

To start Access, click Start, point to Programs or All Programs, then click Microsoft Access. Unlike other Microsoft Office applications, Access doesn't automatically display an empty document window when you start the program. When you start Access, the New File task pane appears. You can use this task pane to create a new database or open an existing database.

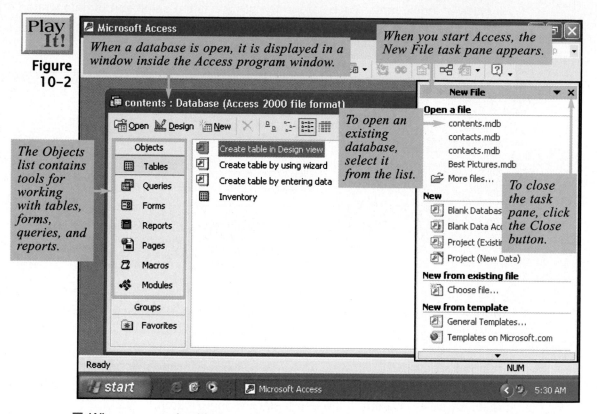

Play It!

Figure 10-2

When a database is open, it is displayed in a window inside the Access program window.

When you start Access, the New File task pane appears.

The Objects list contains tools for working with tables, forms, queries, and reports.

To open an existing database, select it from the list.

To close the task pane, click the Close button.

■ When you work with Access, you won't need to create a new database each time you use the program. Usually, you'll open an existing database in order to add to, or edit, the data it contains.

■ As you've learned in previous chapters, documents and spreadsheets appear on-screen similar to the way they will look when printed. Databases are different—their data can be displayed and manipulated in many different ways.

■ Access provides several tools that you can use to create, modify, and display the data in the database. These tools are contained in the Objects list on the left side of the Contents: Database window. In this chapter, you'll learn how to use these tools to create tables and simple queries. In the next chapter, you'll learn how to use additional tools to create simple forms and reports.

■ Access also offers many different ways to use each of the tools. You should remember that Access is very complex software. In order to simplify your introduction to Access, you will learn some simple ways to use the most common tools. For more information, refer to Microsoft Access Help or the program documentation.

■FAQ How do I create a new database or open an existing database?

Creating a database is different from creating a document, worksheet, or presentation. With Word, for example, you create the document, then save it later. With Access, first you save an empty database, then you create the elements that will make up the database. These elements include tables, reports, forms, and queries.

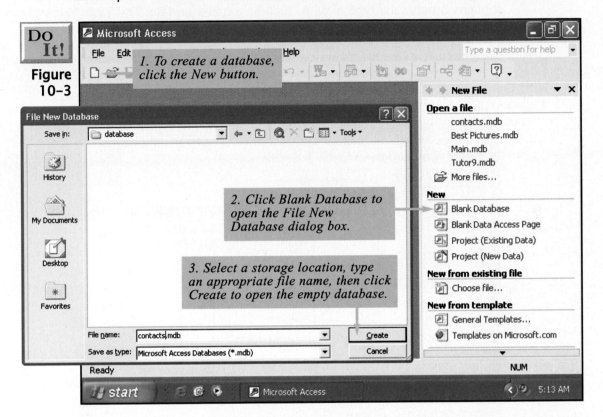

Do It!

Figure 10-3

1. To create a database, click the New button.

2. Click Blank Database to open the File New Database dialog box.

3. Select a storage location, type an appropriate file name, then click Create to open the empty database.

■ You only need to save a database once, when you first create it. As you add or change data in the database, the changes are automatically saved in the database file. When you're finished using the database, you just close it—there's no need to save it because all changes were saved as you made them.

■ If you have already created a database, select the name of the database from the New File task pane, as shown on page 104.

■ To open a database that is not listed on the New File task pane, you can use the More files link on the New File task pane or the ☞ Open button on the Database toolbar. Select the appropriate storage device and file name, then click OK.

■ ■ ■

■FAQ How do I create a table using a wizard?

A newly created database is empty. Before you can enter data, you must specify the structure of the tables, records, and fields in your database. The **Table Wizard** makes it easy to create tables for common business and personal databases. A table contains records. Each record consists of one or more fields, each of which contains a particular type of data, such as a name or date. The Table Wizard will assist you in creating fields correctly.

Do It!

Figure 10-4

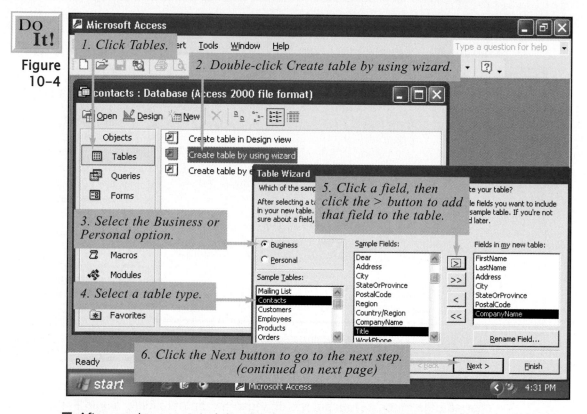

1. Click Tables.

2. Double-click Create table by using wizard.

3. Select the Business or Personal option.

4. Select a table type.

5. Click a field, then click the > button to add that field to the table.

6. Click the Next button to go to the next step. (continued on next page)

■ After you have created the database, make sure that Tables is selected in the Objects list, then double-click *Create table by using wizard*.

Table Wizard - Step 1

■ Access includes sample tables for common business and personal database needs. Click the Business or Personal option button to display the personal or business sample tables. Select the most appropriate table type from the Sample Tables list.

■ The sample tables include many fields that you probably won't need for your database. It's possible to add new fields to a table later, so it's best to keep your tables simple and choose the minimum number of fields that will adequately describe the records in your database.

■ To add an individual field, click the field in the Sample Fields list, then click the ▸ button. To add all sample fields to your table, click the ▸▸ button. To remove a field, click the ◂ button. To remove all selected fields, click the ◂◂ button.

■ **How do I create a table using a wizard? (continued)**

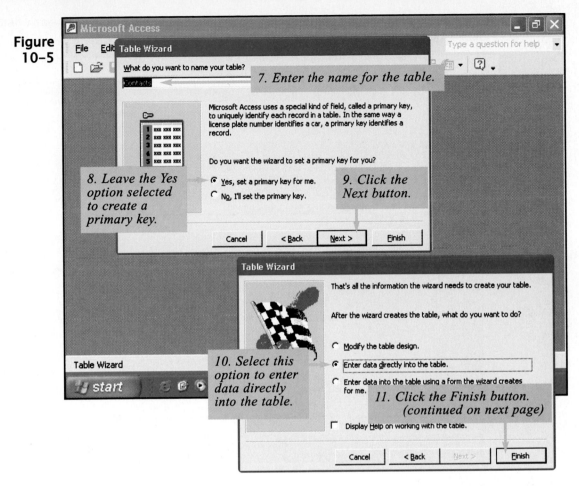

Figure
10–5

Table Wizard - Step 2

■ The name that you enter in this step is the name for the table, which is not necessarily the same as the name for the database. For example, a database called "Contacts.mdb" might have tables called "Contacts," "Meetings," and so on. All tables in the database are stored in the same database file.

■ A **primary key** is a field that uniquely identifies each record. It's very important that no two records are ever assigned the same value for this unique field. For this reason, it's usually best to have Access create the primary key. Access will then be responsible for assigning a unique value to each record. As an alternative, you can select your own primary key. For example, you could use each contact's social security number as the primary key.

■ Each *table* in the database is also assigned its own primary key. In a relational database, these fields are used to link the tables together as described in the introduction to this chapter on page 102.

Table Wizard - Step 3

■ Generally, you'll want to enter data directly into the table, so make sure that the *Enter data directly into the table* option is selected.

■ How do I create a table using a wizard? (continued)

The completed table is displayed and ready for data entry. The title of each field is displayed at the top of each column. The first blank record appears as the first row of fields in the table. You'll learn how to enter and edit data on page 109.

Figure 10-6

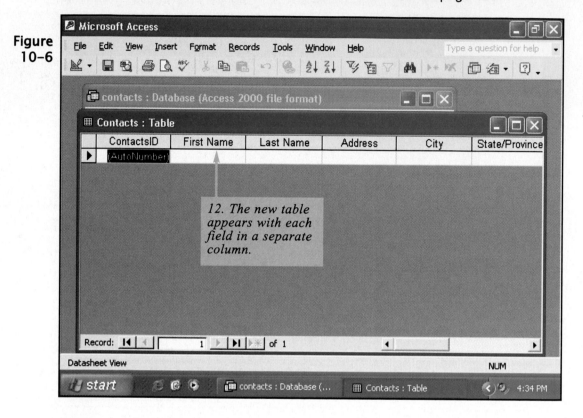

12. The new table appears with each field in a separate column.

■ The database is saved when you click the Finish button. You don't have to save it again when you exit Access—just close the Access program window when you're through.

■ If you are saving on a floppy disk, leave the disk in the floppy disk drive until the Access window closes. If you remove the disk too soon, your database file may become corrupted and some of your data may be lost.

■ To open the database the next time you start Access, click the file name from the New File task pane or click the Open button on the toolbar to display the Open dialog box.

■FAQ How do I enter and edit data in a table?

Once you've created the fields and data types for a table, you can enter data. The data for each entity in your table, such as a person or an inventory item, becomes one record, or row, in the table.

If you have just created a table using the Table Wizard, the table will be open. If the table is not open, click Tables in the Objects list in the database window, then double-click the name of the table.

Do It!

Figure 10-7

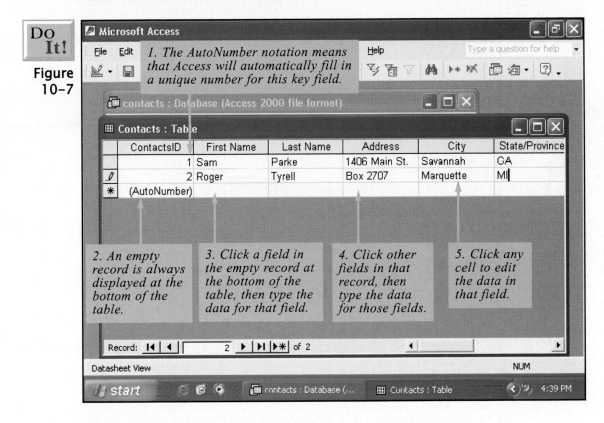

1. *The AutoNumber notation means that Access will automatically fill in a unique number for this key field.*

2. *An empty record is always displayed at the bottom of the table.*

3. *Click a field in the empty record at the bottom of the table, then type the data for that field.*

4. *Click other fields in that record, then type the data for those fields.*

5. *Click any cell to edit the data in that field.*

■ An empty record is always displayed at the bottom of a table. Each time you enter data into that empty record, a new empty record appears.

■ Be careful to enter data in a consistent manner. For example, don't use inconsistent entries, such as MI and Michigan, in the same database. If you're entering state names, always use either the state abbreviation or the entire state name. Later, when the database contains many records, it will be easier to locate the records that contain specific data if the data has been entered consistently. In this example, if you ask the database to list all of the contacts in the state of "MI," any records for contacts in "Michigan" might not be included in the list.

■ To edit data, click the cell containing the data. Use the left and right arrow keys to move the insertion point within the field. Use the Backspace and Delete keys to delete text to the left or to the right of the insertion point.

■ To delete an entire record, right-click the grey box to the left of the row that contains that record. Click Delete Record on the shortcut menu, then click the Yes button to delete the record.

■ ■ ■

■FAQ How do I create a table in Design view?

If the sample tables offered by the Table Wizard don't meet your needs, you'll need to create your own table using Design view. This option requires just a bit more planning because you must specify a data type for each field. The **data type** determines what kind of data can be entered into the field.

Do It!

Figure 10-8

1. Click Tables.

2. Double-click Create table in Design view.

3. Type the name of each field in the Field Name column.

4. For each field, use the down arrow button to select a data type.

5. Click the Save button.

6. Type the name of the table, then click the OK button to save the table.

7. Click the Yes button to create a primary key.

There is no primary key defined.

Although a primary key isn't required, it's highly recommended. A table must have a primary key for you to define a relationship between this table and other tables in the database. Do you want to create a primary key now?

■ Use the **Text** data type for fields that will contain text data of up to 255 characters in length.

■ Use the **Memo** data type for fields that will contain variable length data more than 255 characters in length.

■ Use the **Number** data type for fields that will contain numeric data. Don't use the Number data type for data that looks like a number, but that will never be calculated. For example, a field for telephone numbers should be defined as Text.

■ Use the **Date/Time** data type for dates and times. This special data type makes it much easier, for example, to determine if one date occurs before or after another date.

■ When you allow Access to define the primary key, the ID field is created, using the **AutoNumber** data type. A unique number is automatically entered in this field as you enter each new record.

■ The **Yes/No** data type can be useful for fields designed to hold simple Yes/No or True/False data. For example, you might use a Yes/No data type for the field "Have you received any awards?"

■ After you have finished defining all of the fields, save and then close the Table window to begin entering data into your new table.

■FAQ How do I create a query using a wizard?

After you have organized your data into one or more tables, you can manipulate the data in many ways. For example, you can search a company database for all contacts in a specific state or search an inventory database for all products that cost more than $10. You can create a **query** to search your database for records that contain particular data. A query contains criteria that specify what you would like to find. You can also use a query to display some, but not all, of the fields in a table. Using the **Query Wizard** is a quick way to learn how to create and use a simple query.

Do It!

Figure 10-9

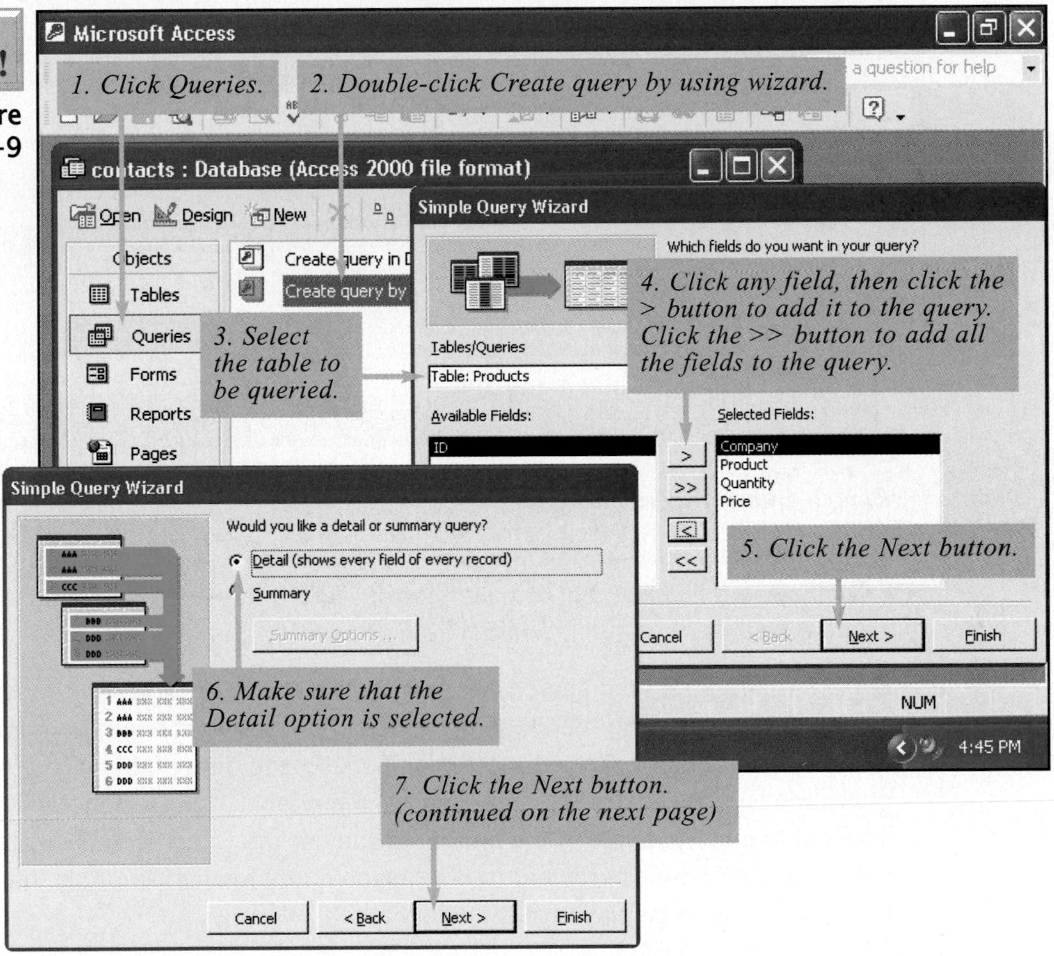

1. Click Queries.

2. Double-click Create query by using wizard.

3. Select the table to be queried.

4. Click any field, then click the > button to add it to the query. Click the >> button to add all the fields to the query.

5. Click the Next button.

6. Make sure that the Detail option is selected.

7. Click the Next button. (continued on the next page)

■ After a query is saved, you can run it repeatedly to display all the records—including new and updated data—that match the criteria you've specified.

Simple Query Wizard - Step 1

■ Click a field, then click the > button to add an individual field to the query. Click the >> button to add all fields to the query. Click the < button to remove a field from the query. Click the << button to remove all fields from the query.

Simple Query Wizard - Step 2

■ Selecting the Detail option for all records shows all of the specified fields for the records, whereas selecting the Summary option only displays how many records match your criteria.

■ ■ ■

How do I create a query using a wizard? (continued)

Figure 10-10

8. Type the title for the query.

9. Click the Finish button to view the results of the query.

10. The query results are displayed in a window.

Simple Query Wizard

What title do you want for your query?

| Products Query |

That's all the information the wizard needs to query.

Do you want to open the query or modify?

☑ Open the query to view information.
☐ Modify the query design.

☐ Display Help on working with the query

| Cancel | < Back | Next > | Finish |

Products Query : Select Query

Company	Product	Quantity	Price
General Plastic	6 oz mug	47	$3.98
AwardTech	drink holder	13	$2.45
General Plastic	12 oz mug	52	$4.95
General Plastic	8 oz cup	38	$2.25
AwardTech	car compass	24	$1.99
GizmoDirect	sun visor	41	$4.58
GizmoDirect	dash protector	17	$12.95
AwardTech	insulated mug	61	$4.48
General Plastic	car broom	13	$8.75
GizmoDirect	drink holder	48	$3.48
		0	$0.00

Record: |◄ ◄ 1 ► ►| ►* of 10

11. Click the Close button to close the query.

Table Wizard   NUM

start   Microsoft Access   4:45 PM

Simple Query Wizard - Step 3

■ After you click the Finish button, the results of the query appear in a new window. In this example, the query specified only selected fields, so all records are displayed, but the ID field is not displayed.

■ To further refine your search, you can define **query criteria**. For example, instead of a query that returns all of the records, you might want to see only those records for products that cost more than $10. To add query criteria, close the query window, then right-click the name of the query. Click Design View on the shortcut menu. Type >10 in the criteria row under the Price field. Click the **!** Run button on the Database toolbar to display the query results. Records that match the criteria will be displayed in the query results window.

■ When you close the query window after viewing the results of a query for which you specified query criteria, you'll see a message asking "Do you want to save changes to the design of query 'Query Name'?" Click Yes if you would like to use the same query criteria every time you use this query.

■ For more information on ways to customize a query, refer to Microsoft Access Help or the program documentation.

QuickCheck A

1. True or false? A structured database contains information that is organized into tables that contain columns and rows. [＿＿＿＿＿]

2. A(n) [＿＿＿＿＿＿＿＿＿] contains a single piece of information such as a name or ZIP code.

3. A(n) [＿＿＿＿＿＿＿＿＿] contains fields of information about a single entity in the database, such as a person, event, or thing.

4. True or false? Each time you enter new data into a database table, you must save the table. [＿＿＿＿＿]

5. A(n) [＿＿＿＿＿] contains criteria that specify the data you want to find in the database.

Check It!

QuickCheck B

Indicate the letter of the desktop element that best matches the following:

1. A text field [＿＿＿]

2. A number field [＿＿＿]

3. A primary key field [＿＿＿]

4. A currency field [＿＿＿]

5. A blank field in a new record [＿＿＿]

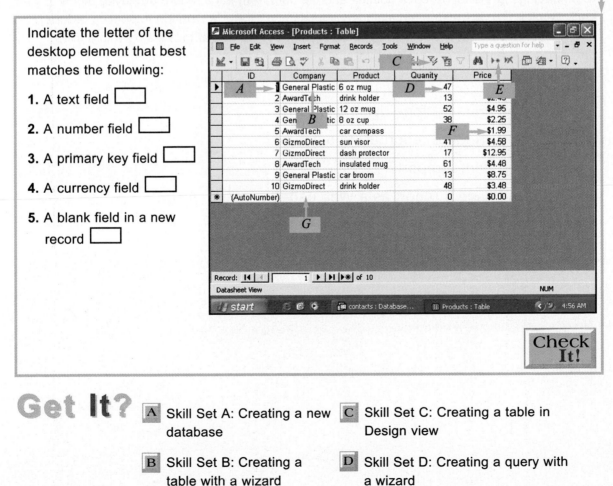

Check It!

Get It?

A Skill Set A: Creating a new database

B Skill Set B: Creating a table with a wizard

C Skill Set C: Creating a table in Design view

D Skill Set D: Creating a query with a wizard

Chapter 11

Finalizing a Database

What's Inside?

In this chapter, you'll learn how to create forms, generate reports, print reports, and convert reports for display on the Internet.

A **form** allows you to customize the way Access displays records by selecting particular fields, specifying the field order, and adding descriptive field labels. Forms are designed to simplify the data entry process by making the screen-based record look like a printed form.

A **report** is typically a printed document containing data selected from a database. Like a query, a report can be based on criteria that determine which data will be included in the report. Reports can be formatted in various ways. Many reports are formatted in columns, with headings at the top of each column and the data from each record displayed below each header. Reports also often include subtotals and totals. In addition to printing reports, Microsoft Access makes it easy to export reports to HTML format for viewing with a Web browser.

■ FAQs:

How do I create a form using a wizard?   115

How do I create a report using a wizard?   118

How do I print a report?   121

How do I save a report as a Web page?   122

■ Assessment   123

■FAQ How do I create a form using a wizard?

You can organize your data into rows and columns using a table, which is the best way to view the data contained in a large number of records. Another way to display your data is with a form. A form allows you to view your data one record at a time, with the fields of each record arranged on your computer screen as they might be arranged on a printed form. The **Form Wizard** helps you to design an on-screen form in which you can enter and manipulate data in each record of a database.

Do It!

Figure 11-1

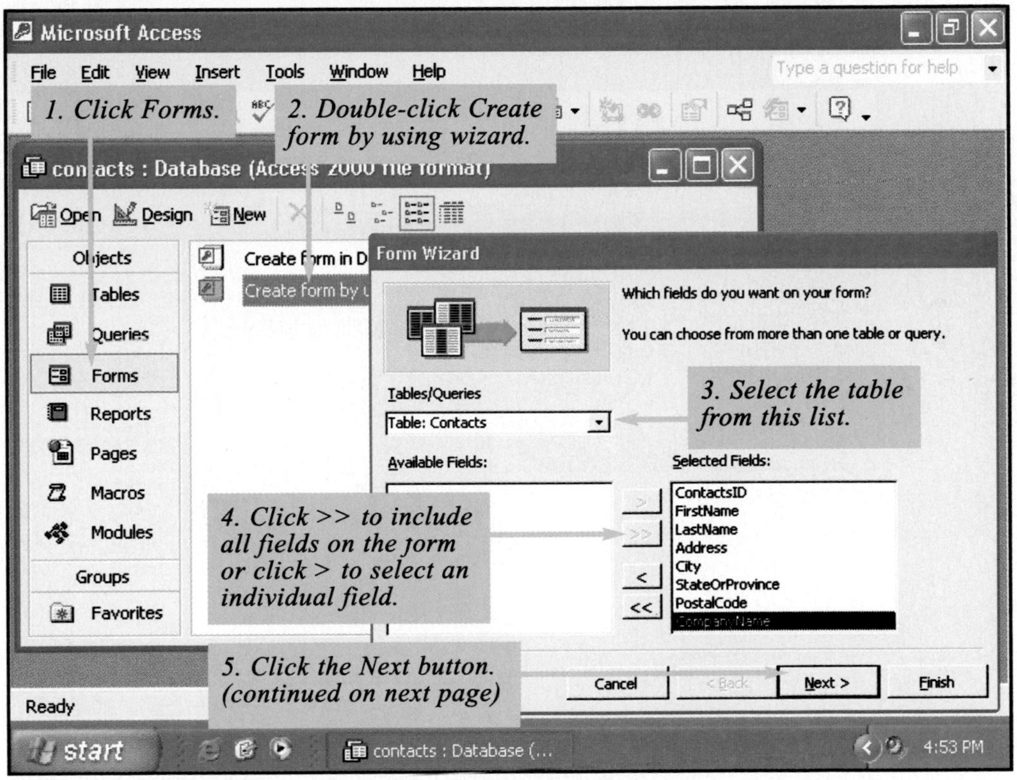

1. Click Forms.

2. Double-click Create form by using wizard.

3. Select the table from this list.

4. Click >> to include all fields on the form or click > to select an individual field.

5. Click the Next button. (continued on next page)

Form Wizard - Step 1

■ Most of the time, you'll want to include all fields on the form. To do so, click the >> button to automatically include all fields.

■ As an alternative, you can select individual fields. For example, if you are entering specific data, such as today's purchases, you might use a form that shows only ContactsID, FirstName, and LastName, along with a field for the amount of purchase. You don't need to see the contact's address information while you are entering this data. To select a specific field, click one of the fields, then click the > button. Repeat these steps for each field that you want to include on the form.

■ You can remove an individual field from the Selected Fields list by clicking the < button.

■ How do I create a form using a wizard? (continued)

Figure
11-2

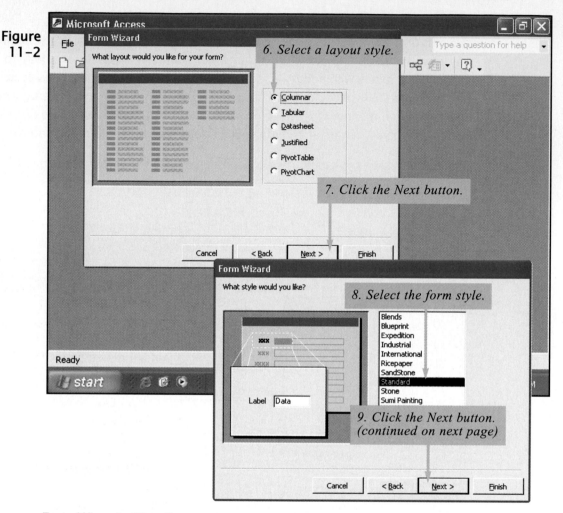

Form Wizard - Step 2

■ You might want to experiment with layouts to see how they work for different types of data. The Columnar layout places the label next to the field, and lists the fields in columns. The Tabular layout places the field label at the top of a column, which makes it appear like a table. The Datasheet layout resembles a spreadsheet, with cells for entering data. The Justified layout displays the fields across the screen in rows, with the label above each field. The PivotTable and PivotChart layouts allow you to create a form with an interactive table or chart that helps you to analyze your data.

Form Wizard - Step 3

■ The form style determines the font, font color, and background for the form. Choose a style that seems appropriate for your data. The preview area to the left of the list of styles is useful for selecting the form style.

■ How do I create a form using a wizard? (continued)

Figure 11-3

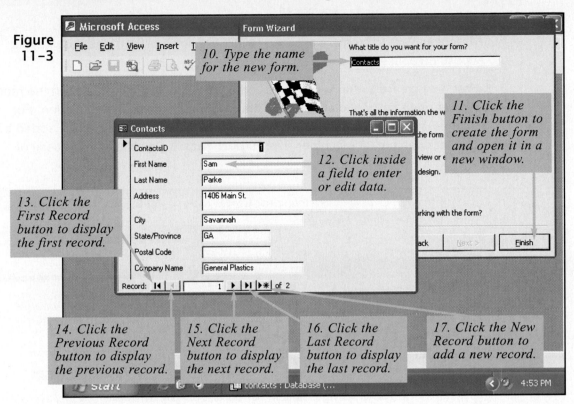

10. Type the name for the new form.

11. Click the Finish button to create the form and open it in a new window.

12. Click inside a field to enter or edit data.

13. Click the First Record button to display the first record.

14. Click the Previous Record button to display the previous record.

15. Click the Next Record button to display the next record.

16. Click the Last Record button to display the last record.

17. Click the New Record button to add a new record.

Form Wizard - Step 4

■ When the Form Wizard closes, the first record of the table is displayed in the new form. You can now use the form to view, edit, or add records to the table. Use the navigation controls (see Steps 13 through 17 in the figure above) to move from one record to the next and to add new records to the database.

■ The form will be automatically saved in the database file, so you don't need to save the form separately. The changes that you make to data while using the form will automatically update the corresponding table in your database.

■ You can modify the form, if needed. To do so, close the form, then right-click the name of the form. Click Design View on the shortcut menu. Click any label to edit it. To move a label and the associated data field, move the pointer over the label until the pointer changes to a ♛ shape, then drag the label and data field as needed. To delete a label and data field from the form, right-click the label, then click Cut on the shortcut menu.

■ As you become more familiar with Access, you might eventually want to explore creating forms using Design view. When you create a form using Design view, start with a blank form, then add the labels and controls needed for that form. Design view provides maximum flexibility for designing the form, but requires more time on your part. Before you begin to experiment with Design view, refer to Microsoft Access Help or the program documentation for more information.

■FAQ How do I create a report using a wizard?

When you want to create a polished printout of some or all of the data in your Access database, you can create a **report**.

When you create a report, you specify the fields that will be included in the report. Reports often include totals and subtotals as well as detailed information. For example, you might create a report that shows all the inventory items, sorted by manufacturer and item number. The **Report Wizard** simplifies the process of creating a report.

Do It!

Figure 11-4

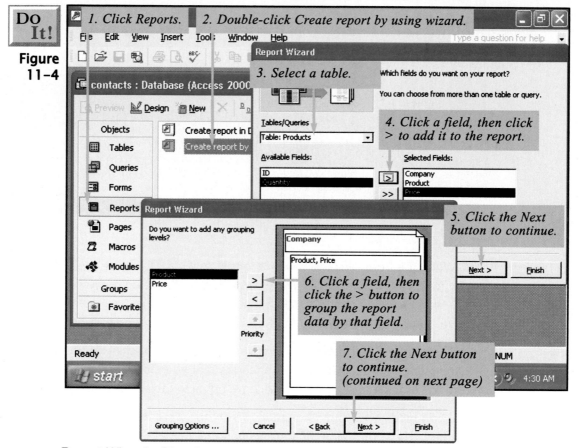

Report Wizard - Step 1

■ To add individual fields to the report, click a field, then click the > button. Click the >> button to add all available fields to the report.

Report Wizard - Step 2

■ When you add a grouping level, records will be sorted according to the entries in the group field. You can add several grouping levels to the report. For example, you might group a list of products by the manufacturer, then group them by item number.

■ How do I create a report using a wizard? (continued)

Figure 11-5

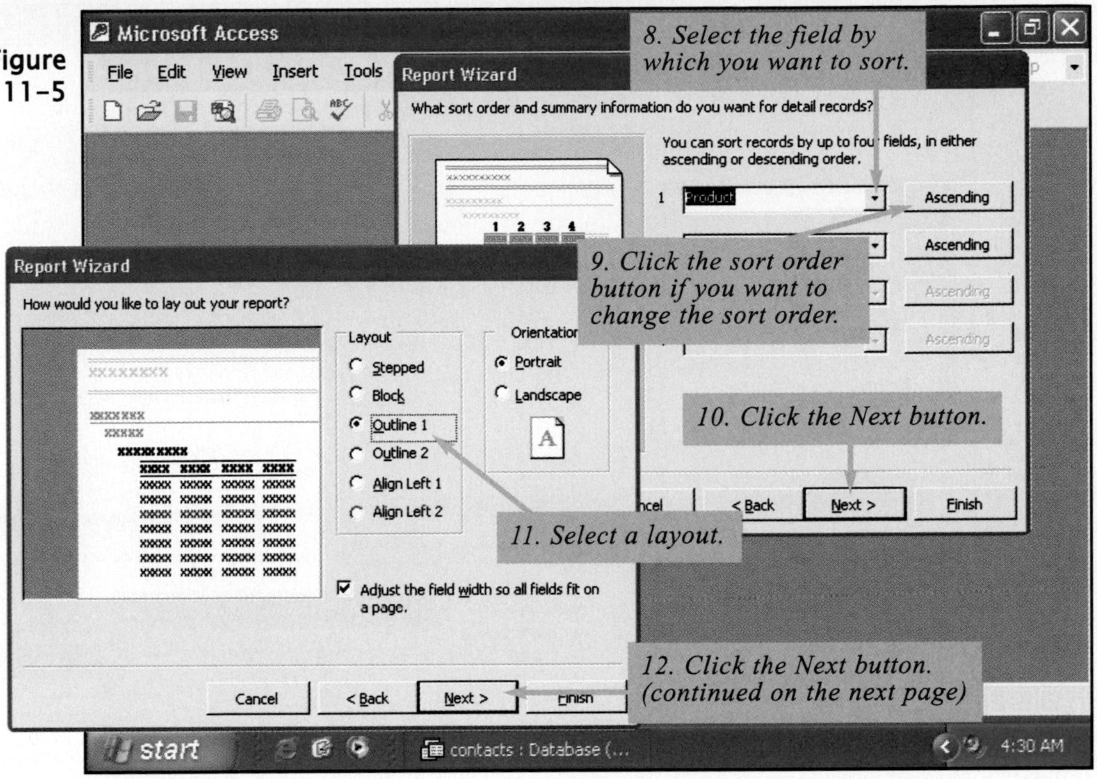

Report Wizard - Step 3

■ To sort records within a group, click the down arrow button and select the field by which you want to sort. Click the sort order button if you want to change the sort order from ascending order to descending order.

■ Use the `Ascending` button for an ascending sort and the `Descending` button for a descending sort.

Report Wizard - Step 4

■ If you want to use a different layout, click the appropriate option button in the Layout section. The Stepped layout is a tabular layout that uses field names for column headings, and it displays grouped reports very effectively. The Block layout is similar to the Stepped layout, with gridlines added for easier reading. There are two Outline layouts that vary the location of the field names within the columns and that vary the indention of grouped reports. The two Align Left layouts also vary the location of the field names; however, neither indents the rows of the report.

■ How do I create a report using a wizard? (continued)

Figure 11-6

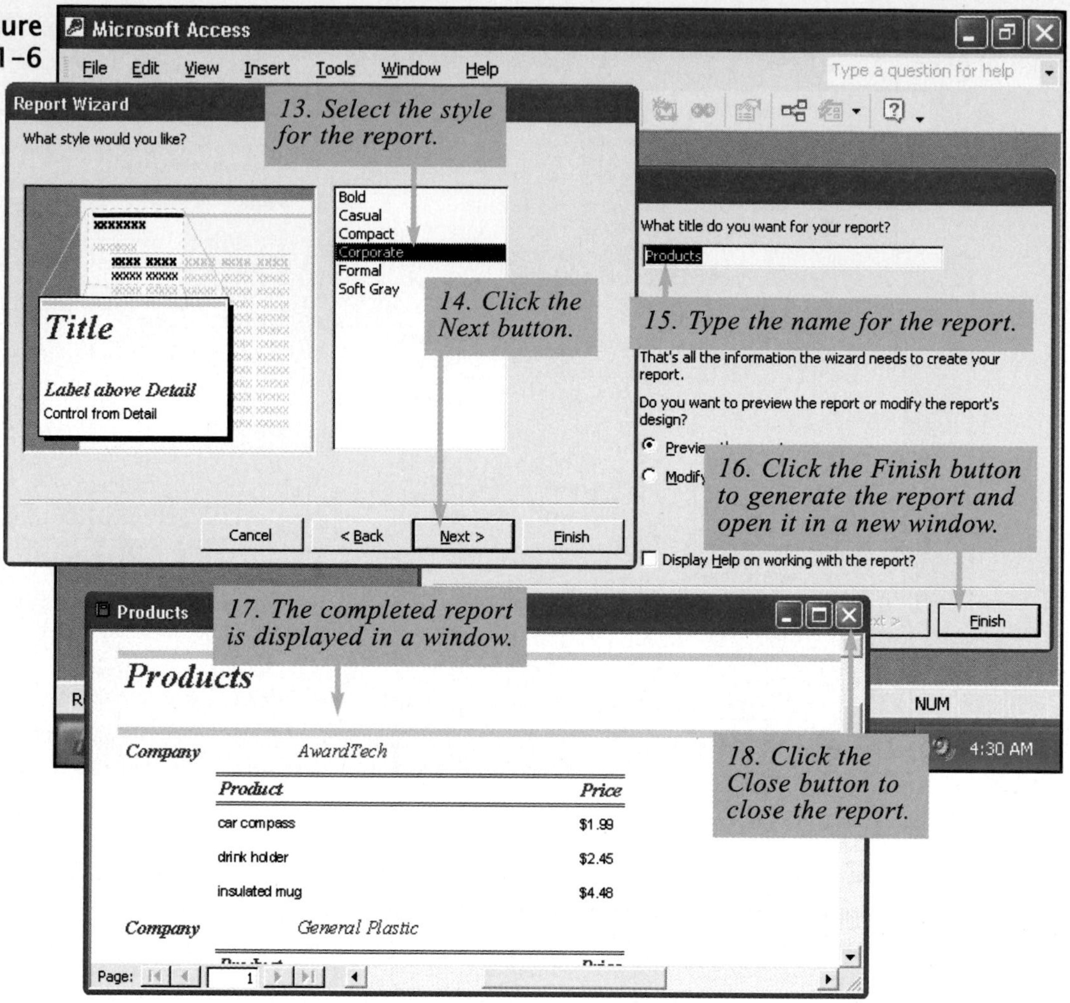

13. Select the style for the report.

14. Click the Next button.

15. Type the name for the report.

16. Click the Finish button to generate the report and open it in a new window.

17. The completed report is displayed in a window.

18. Click the Close button to close the report.

Report Wizard - Step 5

■ Select the style that seems most suitable for your report. The preview area to the left of the list of styles is useful for selecting the report style.

Report Wizard - Step 6

■ Type the name of the report, which is used to identify the report so that you can open it in the future. The report itself is automatically saved in the database file along with the tables, queries, and forms that you have already created.

■ When you click the Finish button, the report is displayed in a window. Use the vertical scroll bar to view pages of the report that aren't visible. You may also need to use the horizontal scroll bar to view columns of the report that will print on the right half of the page.

■ You can modify the completed report if needed. Close the report, then right-click the report name. Click Design View from the shortcut menu. Use the sizing handles to resize objects on the report. To move an object, move the pointer over the object until it changes to a ♥ shape, then drag the object to the new location.

■FAQ How do I print a report?

Each time that you display or print a report, the contents of the report are automatically updated to reflect the current data stored in the database. For example, suppose that you print a report today. Over the next week, you add and change data in the database. If you display or print the report next week, the report will include all of the updated data.

Do It!

Figure 11-7

To print one copy of all pages of the report, click the name of the report, then click the ⎙ button on the Database toolbar.

■ The data in a printed report is a "snapshot" that shows the status of your database at a particular point in time. When you edit or add data to the database, your report will include the new data. It's a good idea to include the date the report was printed on all pages of the report so that you know how current the data in the report is.

■ To add the date or times as a header to your report, right-click the report, then click Design View on the shortcut menu. Click Insert, then click Date and Time on the Access menu bar. Select the date or time formats, then click the OK Button. Select the fields that were inserted into the report by holding down the Shift key as you click each field. Move the pointer over the edge of the fields until the pointer changes to a 🖐 shape, then drag the fields to the desired location in the report.

■FAQ How do I save a report as a Web page?

Once you've created a report, you can either print it or you can post it on the Web. As with other Web pages, your report must be in HTML format to be accessible to Web browsers.

Do It!

Figure 11-8

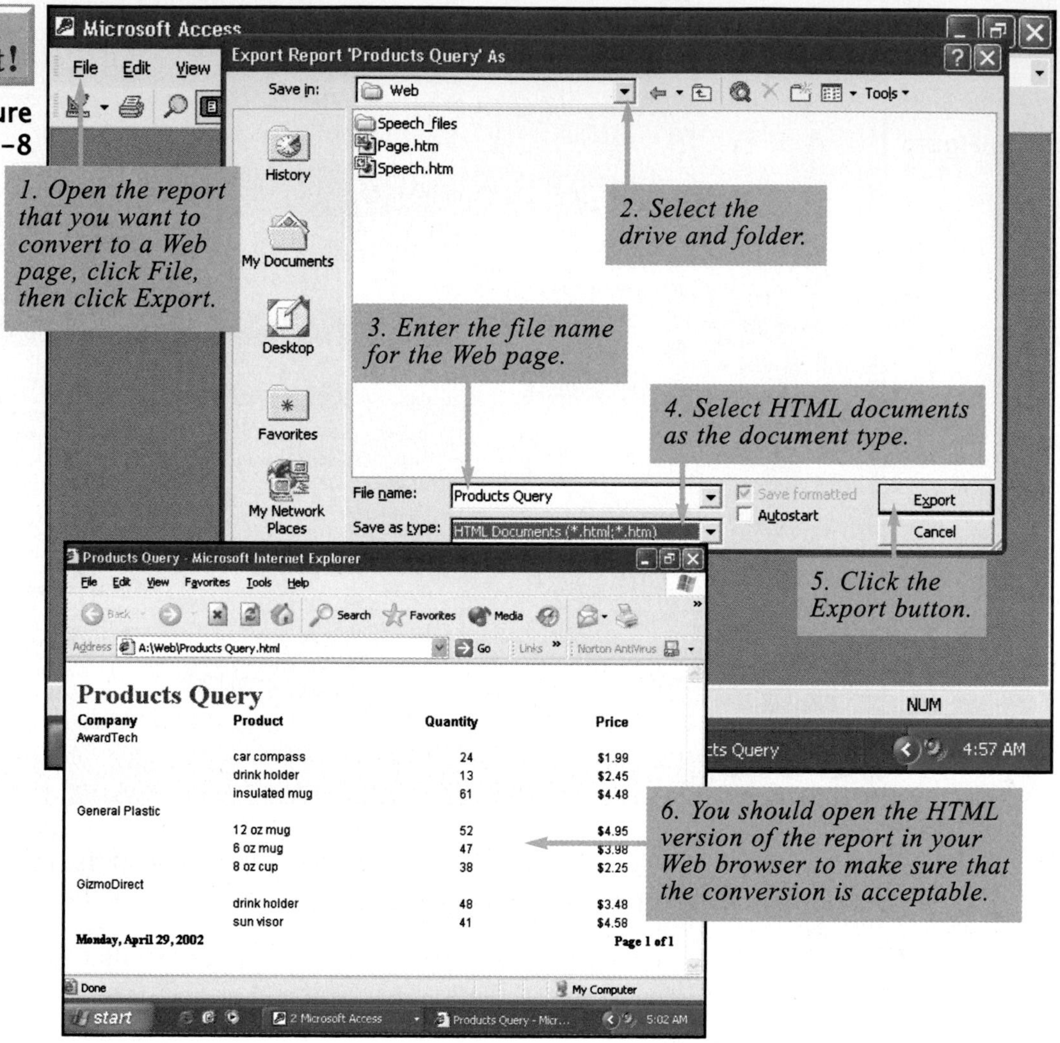

1. Open the report that you want to convert to a Web page, click File, then click Export.

2. Select the drive and folder.

3. Enter the file name for the Web page.

4. Select HTML documents as the document type.

5. Click the Export button.

6. You should open the HTML version of the report in your Web browser to make sure that the conversion is acceptable.

■ Be sure to select *HTML Documents (*.html,*.htm)* in the Save as Type pull-down list.

■ Use a Web browser to preview the report as a Web page. Microsoft Access usually does a fairly good job when converting the report to a Web page, but you'll want to check it yourself to make sure that everything appears correctly.

■ As the data in your database changes, the Web page version of the report will become increasingly out of date. You should, periodically, open the report and export it again as a Web page. This action ensures that all new data is included in the Web-based version of the report.

■ Contact your Internet Service Provider (ISP) if you need instructions for posting your Web pages to the Internet.

QuickCheck A

1. A(n) [_____] displays the fields of a record in the way that they might be printed on a paper form, such as on an application or questionnaire.

2. A(n) [_____] is typically a formatted printout of some or all of the data contained in a database.

3. True or false? You can use a form to view, edit, and add data to a table. [_____]

4. True or false? Reports are automatically saved in the database file. [_____]

5. True or false? The data in a printed report or in a report exported as a Web page will become increasingly out of date. [_____]

Check It!

QuickCheck B

Indicate the letter of the desktop element that best matches the following:

1. A text field [____]

2. The New Record button [____]

3. The First Record button [____]

4. The Last Record button [____]

5. The Next Record button [____]

Check It!

Get It?

A Skill Set A: Creating a form

B Skill Set B: Creating a report

C Skill Set C: Printing a report

D Skill Set D: Saving a report as a Web page

Projects

■ Introduction to Projects — 125

    Submitting an Assignment as a Printout or on Disk — 126

    Submitting an Assignment as an E-mail Attachment — 127

    Microsoft Office XP Configuration — 129

■ Projects for Microsoft Windows

    Project 1-1: Working with Programs and Windows — 130

    Project 1-2: Working with Files — 132

■ Projects for Microsoft Word

    Project 2-1: Creating a Word Document — 134

    Project 2-2: Using a Document Wizard — 136

    Project 3-1: Formatting a Document — 138

    Project 3-2: Using Tabs and Paragraph Alignment — 140

    Project 4-1: Finalizing a Document — 142

    Project 4-2: Creating a Table — 144

■ Projects for Microsoft Excel

    Project 5-1: Creating a Worksheet — 146

    Project 5-2: Using Functions — 148

    Project 6-1: Formatting a Worksheet — 150

    Project 6-2: Using Absolute and Relative References — 152

    Project 7-1: Finalizing a Worksheet — 154

    Project 7-2: Creating Charts — 156

■ Projects for Microsoft PowerPoint

    Project 8-1: Creating a Presentation — 158

    Project 8-2: Creating Slides with Charts and Tables — 160

    Project 9-1: Using Animations, Transitions, and Sounds — 162

    Project 9-2: Finalizing a Presentation — 164

■ Projects for Microsoft Access

    Project 10-1: Creating a Database Table — 166

    Project 10-2: Creating Queries — 168

    Project 11-1: Creating Forms — 170

    Project 11-2: Creating Reports — 172

■Introduction to Projects

The projects in this section are designed to help you review and develop the skills that you learned in each chapter of this book. They serve as a valuable intermediate step between *The Practical Office XP* learning environment and working on your own. Even if you don't have to complete the projects for a class, you'll find that trying some of the projects will greatly enhance your ability to use Microsoft Office XP.

Although it was not required for interacting with the screen tours in Chapters 1–11, Microsoft Office XP must be installed on the computer that you will use to complete the projects in this section. To discover if this software has been installed on your computer, click the Start button, click Programs or All Programs, then look for Microsoft Word, Microsoft Excel, Microsoft Access, and Microsoft PowerPoint on the Programs or All Programs menu. When you open any of these programs, the splash screen should display the "Microsoft Office XP" logo.

If you don't remember how to complete a task for a project, refer to *The Practical Office XP* book. It is designed to serve as a handy reference guide to the skills that you've learned—keep it handy as you work on the projects and when working on your own.

For many of the projects, you'll start by creating a Project Disk. A Project Disk is a blank, formatted disk onto which project files have been copied using the Project Disk menu option. To copy the file for a project, click the Project Disk menu option on the Welcome screen of *The Practical Office XP* CD-ROM. Click the menu option for the project and follow the instructions to copy the project file to a blank floppy disk. You can also click the Copy It! button on the first page of a project to copy the file for that project to your floppy disk.

At the completion of each project, you'll have created a file that demonstrates your ability to apply your Office XP skills. To submit a completed project to your instructor, use one of the methods indicated by the instructions at the end of the project. Most projects can be printed, saved on a floppy disk, or sent as an e-mail attachment. Your instructor might have a preference for one of these methods. You'll find additional information about printing, saving, and e-mailing projects on the next three pages.

■Submitting an Assignment as a Printout or on Disk

You can print or save your project files using the File menu, as shown in the figure below.

Figure Pr–01

To print a completed project, click the Print button or click File, then click Print.

Close
Save
Save As...

Click File, then click Save As to save a project file. Be sure to save the file on the floppy disk in drive A using the file name specified in the instructions for each project.

Save as Web Page...
Search...
Versions...
Web Page Preview
Page Setup...
Print Preview
Print...   Ctrl+P
Send To   ▶
Properties
1 C:\Work\POXP\...\opening bmps.doc

■ To print a project file:

1. Make sure that a printer is attached to your computer and that it is turned on.

2. Click the Print button or click File, then click Print.

3. If the printout doesn't already include your name, student ID, section number, and date, be sure to write this information on the printout.

■ To save your file on a floppy disk:

1. Click the Save As option on the File menu.

2. When the Save As dialog box appears, use the ▼ button on the *Save in* box to select 3½ Floppy (A:).

3. In the *File name* box, enter the name specified by the project instructions.

4. Click the Save button to complete the process.

5. Before you submit your disk to your instructor, make sure that you've labeled it with the project name, your name, your student ID, your section number, and date.

■Submitting an Assignment as an E-mail Attachment

You can typically use either Method 1 or Method 2, as explained below, to submit a Word, Excel, or PowerPoint project as an e-mail attachment. Access projects, however, require Method 1. America Online (AOL) users must use Method 1 for all projects. For information on setting up your e-mail, refer to the next page.

■ Method 1—Use your usual e-mail software to send a project

With Method 1, you'll send your project file using your usual e-mail software, such as Microsoft Outlook, Outlook Express, Eudora, Hotmail, or AOL mail. To use Method 1, first make sure that you have saved the project file. Next, start your e-mail software. Then, follow your software's procedures for sending an e-mail attachment. The procedure usually consists of the following steps:

1. Start a new message by using a toolbar button, such as Compose Message (Outlook Express) or Write Mail (AOL mail).

2. Address the new message to your instructor.

3. Click the Attachment button or select the Attachment option from a menu.

4. When prompted, specify the disk that contains the attachment—usually 3½ Floppy (A:)—and then select the project file from the list.

5. Click the Send button to send the e-mail message and attachment.

■ Method 2—Use Microsoft Office XP's Send To feature

If Microsoft Office XP is set up in conjunction with your e-mail software, you can send your project file directly from Word, Excel, or PowerPoint by using the following steps:

1. After saving your project, keep your application (Paint, Word, Excel, or PowerPoint) window open.

2. Click File on the menu bar.

3. Select the *Send To* option from the File menu. *Hint:* If you do not see the *Send To* option, point to the ⌄ arrows at the bottom of the menu. In less than a second, additional File menu options should appear, including the *Send To* option.

4. From the Send To submenu, select the option *Mail Recipient (as Attachment)*.

5. Enter your instructor's e-mail address into the To: box.

6. For the subject line, enter your student ID number, the project number, and your class section.

7. Click the Send button.

■ ■ ■

■E-mail attachments (continued)

■ To configure your e-mail:

You can send e-mail attachments only if your computer has an Internet connection and a functioning e-mail account. To use e-mail from a school or business computer, you should consult with your instructor or technical support person for instructions.

To use e-mail on your home computer, you will need an Internet connection and an e-mail account from an Internet Service Provider (ISP), such as America Online (AOL), AT&T WorldNet, or any local ISP that you might find by looking in the Yellow Pages. Many ISPs will provide software that automatically creates your e-mail account. If your ISP does not supply such software, you will need to obtain the following information from your ISP and ask for help to set up your account:

The phone number that provides access to the Internet

Your e-mail address (such as hfinn5678@worldnet.att.net)

Your e-mail password (such as huck2finn)

The incoming mail server type (usually POP3)

Your incoming mail server (often the part of your e-mail address that comes after the @ symbol, i.e., aol.com)

Your outgoing SMTP mail server (such as mailhost.worldnet.att.net)

The primary and secondary domain name server (DNS) numbers (such as 204.127.129.1)

■Microsoft Office XP Configuration

Microsoft Office XP provides many ways for you to configure and modify the way its applications look and operate. While this adaptability can be a positive feature, it can potentially cause confusion if your version of Microsoft Office XP is not configured to look or work the same way as the version used for the examples in *The Practical Office XP*. Here's how to configure your software to match the settings that were used for *The Practical Office XP* figures and animations.

■ To configure Microsoft Word, Excel, and PowerPoint:

1. Click View, then click Toolbars. Make sure that a check mark appears next to the Standard and Formatting toolbars. Check marks should *not* appear next to any of the other toolbars.

2. Click View, click Toolbars, then click Customize to display the Customize dialog box. Click the Options tab. Make sure that a check mark *does* appear in the *Show Standard and Formatting toolbars on two rows* check box. The *Large icons* check box should not contain a check mark. Click the Close button to apply these settings.

■ To configure Microsoft Access:

1. Click View, click Toolbars, then click Customize to display the Customize dialog box. Click the Options tab. Make sure that a check mark does *not* appear next to the *Large icons* check box. Click the Close button to apply these settings.

Figure Pr–02

■Project 1-1: Working with Programs and Windows

In this project, you'll apply what you've learned about Microsoft Windows to start several programs and arrange the program windows.

Requirements: This project requires Microsoft Windows.

Project files: No project files are needed to complete this project.

1. Start the WordPad program, which is located in the Accessories group of the Programs or All Programs menu on the Start menu.

2. Make sure that the WordPad window is maximized.

3. Start the Paint program, which is located in the Accessories group of the Programs or All Programs menu on the Start menu.

4. Make sure that the Paint window is maximized.

5. Switch to the WordPad window.

6. Switch back to the Paint window.

7. Restore the Paint window.

8. Adjust the size and position of the Paint window so that your screen looks similar to the one on the next page.

Figure Pr–03

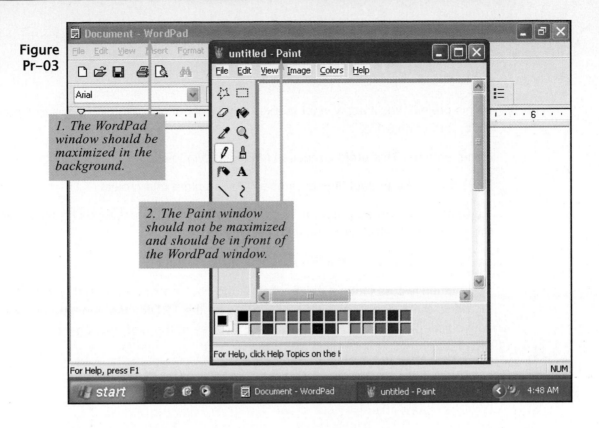

1. The WordPad window should be maximized in the background.

2. The Paint window should not be maximized and should be in front of the WordPad window.

9. Press the PrtSc or Print Screen key on your keyboard.

10. Maximize the Paint window. Click Edit on the Paint menu bar, then click Paste. If you are given the option of enlarging the bitmap, click the Yes button.

11. Save the graphic as Project 1-1 XXXXX 9999, where XXXXX is your student ID number and 9999 is your section number. *Hint:* If a message indicates that your disk is full, remove the floppy disk from your computer and replace it with a blank, formatted disk, then try the save operation again.

12. Use one of the following options to submit your project on disk, as a printout, or as an e-mail attachment, according to your instructor's directions:

■ To submit the project on a floppy disk, use a blank, formatted floppy disk. Click File on the Paint menu bar, then click Save As to display the Save As dialog box. Use the ▼ button on the *Save in* box to select 3½ Floppy (A:). In the *File name* box, enter the project name that you used in Step 11. Write your name, student ID number, section number, date, and Project 1-1 on the disk label.

■ To print the project, click File on the Paint menu bar, then click Print. Click the OK button. Write your name, student ID number, section number, date, and Project 1-1 on the printout.

■ To e-mail the file, use Method 1 or Method 2, as described on page 127. Type your instructor's e-mail address in the To: box. Click the Subject: box, then type Project 1-1, your student ID number, and your class section number. Click the Send button or perform any additional steps required by your e-mail software to send an e-mail message.

■ ■ ■

■Project 1-2: Working with Files

In this project, you'll apply what you've learned about Microsoft Windows to create, save, and open a file.

Requirements: This project requires Microsoft Windows.

Project files: No project files are needed to complete this project.

1. Start the WordPad program, which is located in the Accessories group of the Programs or All Programs menu on the Start menu.

2. Make sure that the WordPad window is maximized.

3. Click anywhere in the blank section of the document window and type the following short memo. Type your own name on the FROM: line and type today's date on the DATE: line. *Hint:* Press the Enter key at the end of each line.

MEMO
TO: Professor Greer
FROM: [Your name]
DATE: [Today's date]
SUBJECT: This week's lesson
I will not be able to attend my music lesson this week.

4. Save the document on your Project Disk in drive A as Project 1-2.

5. Stop the WordPad application by closing its window.

6. Start WordPad again. Open the file Project 1-2 from your Project Disk.

7. Type the word IMPORTANT so that the first line of the document reads IMPORTANT MEMO. Your document should now look like the one shown on the next page.

Figure Pr-04

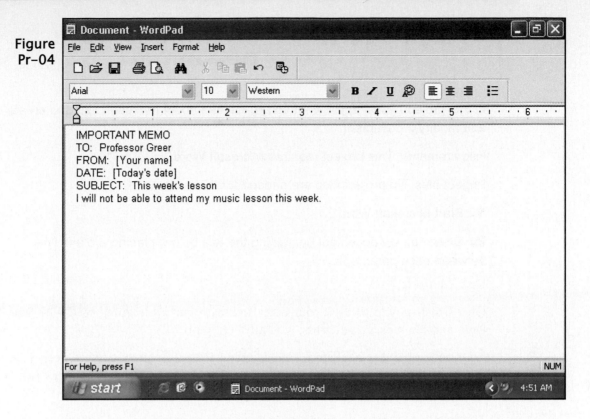

8. Save the new version of your document under a different name on your Project Disk. Use Project 1-2 XXXXX 9999 as the new name, where XXXXX is your student number and 9999 is your section number.

9. Use one of the following options to submit your project on disk, as a printout, or as an e-mail attachment, according to your instructor's directions:

■ To submit the memo on the Project Disk where it is currently stored, stop the WordPad program by closing its window. Remove your Project Disk from the disk drive. Write your name, student ID number, class section number, date, and Project 1-2 on the disk label.

■ To print the project, click File on the WordPad menu bar, then click Print. Click the OK button. Write your name, student ID number, section number, date, and Project 1-2 on the printout.

■ To e-mail the memo file, use Method 1 or Method 2, as described on page 127. Type your instructor's e-mail address in the To: box. Click the Subject: box and type Project 1-2, your student ID number, and your class section number. Click the Send button or perform any additional steps required by your e-mail software to send an e-mail message.

■Project 2-1: Creating a Word Document

In this project, you'll apply what you've learned about Microsoft Word to create and modify a document.

Requirements: This project requires Microsoft Word.

Project files: No project files are needed for this project.

1. Start Microsoft Word.

2. Create a new document containing the text below, placing a blank line between each paragraph.

Dear Marjorie,

Hi! I was happy to receive your letter and learn that all is going well with you, Bob, and the kids. I really miss you all!

Your new job at the bookstore sounds great! How do you manage to keep your mind on work where there are so many fascinating books and magazines just begging to be read?

You mentioned that your first big assignment is to create a display appropriate for the month of February, but without featuring Valentine's Day or Presidents' Day. Did you know that I keep a database of offbeat events, like International Tuba Day and National Accordion Awareness Month? Let me know if you're interested and I'll create a query and send you a list of interesting events.

Sorry for the shortness of this note, but I have to run off to class. I promise to write more soon.

Good luck with the new job!

3. Compare the text that you typed with the text shown above and correct any typing mistakes that you might have made.

4. Delete the phrase create a query and from the last sentence of the third paragraph.

5. Copy the phrase for the month of February from the paragraph that starts with the words You mentioned. Paste the copied phrase before the period at the end of the sentence that ends with send you a list of interesting events.

6. Select the sentence I really miss you all! in the first paragraph. Cut the sentence from the document, then paste it into the document after the sentence Good luck with the new job! at the end of the document.

7. Delete the fourth paragraph of the document, which starts with the words Sorry for the shortness.

8. Use the Undo button to restore the deleted paragraph.

9. Compare your letter with the document in the figure on the next page. Don't worry if the sentences in your document break in different places at the right margin.

Figure Pr-05

> Dear Marjorie,
>
> Hi! I was happy to receive your letter and learn that all is going well with you, Bob, and the kids.
>
> Your new job at the bookstore sounds great! How do you manage to keep your mind on work where there are so many fascinating books and magazines just begging to be read?
>
> You mentioned that your first big assignment is to create a display appropriate for the month of February, but without featuring Valentine's Day or Presidents' Day. Did you know that I keep a database of offbeat events, like International Tuba Day and National Accordion Awareness Month? Let me know if you're interested and I'll send you a list of interesting events for the month of February.
>
> Sorry for the shortness of this note, but I have to run off to class. I promise to write more soon.
>
> Good luck with the new job! I really miss you all!

10. Add your name as the last line of the letter.

11. Save your document on a floppy disk as Project 2-1 XXXXX 9999, where XXXXX is your student ID number and 9999 is your class section number.

12. Use one of the following options to submit your project on disk, as a printout, or as an e-mail attachment, according to your instructor's directions:

■ To submit the file on the Project Disk where it is currently stored, stop the Word program by closing its window. Remove your Project Disk from the drive. Write your name, student ID number, class section number, date, and Project 2-1 on the disk label.

■ To print the project, click File on the Word menu bar, then click Print. Click the OK button. Write your name, student ID number, section number, date, and Project 2-1 on the printout.

■ To e-mail the file, use Method 1 or Method 2, as described on page 127. Type your instructor's e-mail address into the To: box. Click the Subject: box and type Project 2-1, your student ID number, and your class section number. Click the Send button or perform any additional steps required by your e-mail software to send an e-mail message.

■Project 2-2: Using a Document Wizard

In this project, you'll use a document wizard to create and modify a fax cover sheet.

Requirements: This project requires Microsoft Word.

Project files: No project files are needed for this project.

1. Start Microsoft Word.

2. Open the Fax Wizard from the Letters & Faxes tab of the Template dialog box.

3. As you step through the Wizard dialog boxes, make selections as indicated below:

Create just a fax cover sheet with a note.
Print the document on paper so that you can send it on a separate fax machine.
Address the fax to your instructor. You can make up a fax number if you don't
know your instructor's real one.
Select the Contemporary style.
Enter your name, address, phone number, and fax number (make one up, if
necessary).

4. Click the Finish button to complete the wizard entries.

5. Replace the bracketed items in the header with the following:
Phone: Your instructor's phone number
Pages: 1
Re: Missing class

6. Click the bracketed text in the CC: line, then press the Delete key on your keyboard to delete the text Click here and type name.

7. Double-click the Urgent box to insert a check mark.

8. In the Notes: section, type the following:

I will not be able to attend class next week because I will be participating in
an internship program in Washington, D. C. I will be keeping up with my
coursework according to the syllabus.

9. Compare your fax cover sheet with the one on the next page. Your version should be customized with your name, address, and phone number, as well as with your instructor's name, fax number, and phone number.

Figure Pr–06

[Student Address]
Phone: [Student phone here]
Fax:

facsimile transmittal

To: [Instructor name here]   **From:** [Student's name here]

Fax: (706)542-3001   **Date:** May 13, 2003

Phone: (706)542-3000   **Pages:** 1

Re: Missing class   **CC:**

☑ Urgent   ☐ For Review   ☐ Please Comment   ☐ Please Reply   ☐ Please Recycle

Notes: I will not be able to attend class next week because I will be participating in an internship program in Washington, D. C. I will be keeping up with my coursework according to the syllabus.

10. Save your fax cover sheet on a Project Disk using the file name Project 2-2 XXXXX 9999, where XXXXX is your student ID number and 9999 is your class section number. Use one of the following options to submit your project:

■ To submit the fax cover sheet on the Project Disk where it is currently stored, stop the Word program by closing its window. Remove your Project Disk from the drive. Write your name, student ID number, class section number, date, and Project 2-2 on the disk label.

■ To print the project, click File on the Word menu bar, then click Print. Click the OK button. Write your name, student ID number, section number, date, and Project 2-2 on the printout.

■ To e-mail the file, use Method 1 or Method 2, as described on page 127. Type your instructor's e-mail address into the To: box. Click the Subject: box and type Project 2-2, your student ID number, and your class section number. Click the Send button or perform any additional steps required by your e-mail software to send an e-mail message.

■Project 3-1: Formatting a Document

In this project, you'll apply what you've learned about Microsoft Word to format an existing document.

Requirements: This project requires Microsoft Word.

Project file: Proj3-1.doc.

1. Copy the file Proj3-1 to your Project Disk using either the Project Disk menu or the Copy It! button on this page in the Book-on-CD.

2. Start Microsoft Word.

3. Open the file Proj3-1 from your Project Disk.

4. Apply the bold text attribute to the line MEMORANDUM - Novel-Tea & Coffee, Inc.

5. Apply italics to the phrase air-tight in the sentence that begins Please don't forget.

6. Apply bold and underlining to the phrase number one in the last sentence.

7. Select the MEMORANDUM line, then change its font to Arial, size 18.

8. Center the MEMORANDUM line.

9. Select the list of items starting with Bean quality, then format the list as a bulleted list.

10. Indent the first line of the main paragraphs by .4". The three paragraphs that you'll indent begin Just a reminder, Please don't forget, and Thanks for helping.

11. Change the line spacing to 1.5 lines for the paragraphs that begin Just a reminder, Please don't forget, and Thanks for helping.

12. Justify the paragraphs that begin Just a reminder, Please don't forget, and Thanks for helping so that both the left and right margins are straight.

13. Remove the underlining from the phrase number one in the last sentence.

14. Compare your document with the document in the figure on the next page.

■ ■ ■

Figure Pr–07

MEMORANDUM - Novel-Tea & Coffee, Inc.

To: Tea n' Coffee Shop Managers
From: Food and Beverage Director, Novel-Tea & Coffee
RE: Reminder – Fundamentals of Coffee-making

Just a reminder to all Tea n' Coffee Shop managers that it takes more than our fine beans to make a quality cup of coffee. Sometimes our employees are so busy frothing cream or sprinkling cinnamon that they can forget the five key factors to creating the best possible cup of coffee. Listed below are the five fundamentals of superb coffee creation:

- Bean quality
- Water purity
- Elapsed time from roasting beans to perking
- Cleanliness of equipment
- Elapsed time from grinding beans to perking

Please don't forget to store all beans in clean, glass, *air-tight* containers to retain the freshness and aroma of the coffee beans. Beans from your weekly shipment that you don't anticipate using within the week must be kept in the refrigerator or freezer. This retains flavor by preventing chemical reactions in the beans.

Thanks for helping to make Tea n' Coffee Shops **number one** in the tri-state area.

---

15. Save your document on a Project Disk using the file name Project 3-1 XXXXX 9999, where XXXXX is your student ID number and 9999 is your class section number.

16. Use one of the following options to submit your project on disk, as a printout, or as an e-mail attachment, according to your instructor's directions:

■ To submit the file on the Project Disk where it is currently stored, stop the Word program by closing its window. Remove your Project Disk from the disk drive. Write your name, student ID number, class section number, date, and Project 3-1 on the disk label.

■ To print the project, click File on the Word menu bar, then click Print. Click the OK button. Write your name, student ID number, section number, date, and Project 3-1 on the printout.

■ To e-mail the file, use Method 1 or Method 2, as described on page 127. Type your instructor's e-mail address into the To: box. Click the Subject: box and type Project 3-1, your student ID number, and your class section number. Click the Send button or perform any additional steps required by your e-mail software to send an e-mail message.

■Project 3-2: Using Tabs and Paragraph Alignment

In this project, you'll focus on font formats and tabs.

Requirements: This project requires Microsoft Word.

Project file: Proj3-2.doc.

1. Copy the file Proj3-2 to your Project Disk using either the Project Disk menu or the Copy It! button on this page in the Book-on-CD.

2. Start Microsoft Word.

3. Open the file Proj3-2 from your Project Disk.

4. Select the document title How Much Lead Is in Your Cup?, then use the Font dialog box to change the title font to size 26, dark blue, bold italic with a shadow effect.

5. Select the list of items starting with Perked coffee 90-150 mg and ending with Tea 30-70 mg. Use the Tabs dialog box to set a left tab at the 1" position. Set another left tab at the 3" position, with a dotted leader. Close the Tab dialog box.

6. Position the insertion point to the left of Perked coffee, then press the Tab key to move it to the first tab position. Place the insertion point to the left of 90-150 mg, then press the Tab key to move it to the second tab position and display the dotted leader. Use a similar process with the remaining two list items.

7. Position the insertion point at the end of the line that ends with 30-70 mg, then press Enter to create a new line. Add this fourth list item, with appropriate tabs: Colas 30-45 mg.

8. At the top of the document, replace Juan T. Sposito with your name.

9. Compare your completed document with the document in the figure on the next page.

■ ■ ■

Figure Pr–08

Novel-Tea News
Reporter: [Student name here]

How Much Lead Is in Your Cup?

Caffeine is a product found in many popular beverages. Yet most people are trying to curb their daily caffeine intake. After all, the effects of excessive caffeine have recently received a lot of press coverage.

As employees of Novel-Tea & Coffee, you will often get caffeine-related questions from customers. The following list of common drinks paired with their caffeine content may help you answer many of those questions.

Perked coffee	90-150 mg
Instant coffee	60-80 mg
Tea	30-70 mg
Colas	30-45 mg

Most customers also associate caffeine with chocolate. A typical chocolate bar contains 30 mg of caffeine. Yes, a cup of perked coffee does have three to five times the caffeine of a chocolate bar, but doesn't a chocolate bar have a few more calories than a cup of perked coffee?

So hopefully this information will help you answer commonly asked questions about caffeine and help us better serve our customers.

10. Save your document on a Project Disk using the file name Project 3-2 XXXXX 9999, where XXXXX is your student ID number and 9999 is your class section number.

11. Use one of the following options to submit your project on disk, as a printout, or as an e-mail attachment, according to your instructor's directions:

■ To submit the file on the Project Disk where it is currently stored, stop the Word program by closing its window. Remove your Project Disk from the disk drive. Write your name, student ID number, class section number, date, and Project 3-2 on the disk label.

■ To print the project, click File on the Word menu bar, then click Print. Click the OK button. Write your name, student ID number, section number, date, and Project 3-2 on the printout.

■ To e-mail the file, use Method 1 or Method 2, as described on page 127. Type your instructor's e-mail address into the To: box. Click the Subject: box and type Project 3-2, your student ID number, and your class section number. Click the Send button or perform any additional steps required by your e-mail software to send an e-mail message.

■Project 4-1: Finalizing a Document

In this project, you'll apply what you've learned about Microsoft Word to check a document for errors, correct mistakes, set margins, use styles, add headers, and add footers.

Requirements: This project requires Microsoft Word.

Project file: Proj4-1.doc.

1. Copy the file Proj4-1 to your Project Disk using either the Project Disk menu or the Copy It! button on this page in the Book-on-CD.

2. Start Microsoft Word.

3. Open the file Proj4-1 from your Project Disk.

4. Set the left margin of the document to 1.25" and the right margin to 1.5".

5. Use the right-click method to check the spelling of any words with a wavy red underline. Do not change the spelling of any names or proper nouns.

6. Use the right-click method to correct the grammar of any words or phrases with wavy green underlines.

7. Use the thesaurus to select a more appropriate word or phrase to replace get in touch with in the third sentence of the paragraph that begins The deal involves.

8. Add a left-justified, two-line header to the document that includes your name and your student ID number on line one; add your class section number and Project 4-1 on line two.

9. Add a centered footer that shows the word "Page" followed by the page number.

10. Apply the Heading 1 style to the first line in the document.

11. Compare your document in Print Preview to the document shown in the figure on the next page.

**Figure
Pr–09**

Fred A. Student 345-78-2222
Section #4444 Project 4-1

Press Release for Immediate Publication

Novel-Tea & Coffee has selected Brooks & Barney to handle all of its public relations needs. The decision was reportedly based on the firm's excellent track record of dealing with mid-sized retail stores. Its extensive client list, as well as the satisfaction expressed by those clients, made Brooks & Barney the obvious choice, according to sources at the coffee vendor.

As specified in preliminary meetings, the retail coffee business requires a full-service approach to public relations. All press inquiries will be referred to Brooks & Barney, who will also soon update and revamp all Novel-Tea & Coffee printed materials.

The deal involves a two-year contract, and financial arrangements are yet to be finalized. Nevertheless, rumors indicate that several urgent marketing concerns dictate that the firms establish regular weekly meeting times. Efforts to contact either firm to confirm these rumors were unsuccessful.

Rod McGuire, CEO for Novel-Tea & Coffee, commented, "Brooks & Barney is an excellent firm, and we are looking forward to input from its excellent staff. Let's hope this is the beginning of a long and profitable relationship for everyone involved."

Novel-Tea & Coffee and Brooks & Barney are both privately held companies.

Page 1

12. Save your document on a Project Disk using the file name Project 4-1 XXXXX 9999, where XXXXX is your student ID number and 9999 is your class section number.

■ To submit the file on the Project Disk where it is currently stored, stop the Word program by closing its window. Remove your Project Disk from the disk drive. Write your name, student ID number, class section number, date, and Project 4-1 on the disk label.

■ To print the project, click File on the Word menu bar, then click Print. Click the OK button. Write your name, student ID number, section number, date, and Project 4-1 on the printout.

■ To e-mail the file, use Method 1 or Method 2, as described on page 127. Type your instructor's e-mail address into the To: box. Click the Subject: box and type Project 4-1, your student ID number, and your class section number. Click the Send button or perform any additional steps required by your e-mail software to send an e-mail message.

■   ■   ■

▪Project 4-2: Creating a Table

In this project, you'll apply what you've learned about Microsoft Word to create a table in a document.

Requirements: This project requires Microsoft Word.

Project file: Proj4-2.doc.

1. Copy the file Proj4-2 to your Project Disk using either the Project Disk menu or the Copy It! button on this page in the Book-on-CD.

2. Start Microsoft Word.

3. Open the file Proj4-2 from your Project Disk.

4. Insert a table before the paragraph that starts Because of the special nature. The table should consist of three columns and four rows and have a fixed column width.

5. Enter the following data into the cells of the table:

COFFEE	CALORIES	FAT (grams)
Black Coffee	0	0
8 oz. Cappuccino	63	3
8 oz. Cafe Latte	117	3.8

6. Insert one more row into the table and enter the following data:

8 oz. Cafe Mocha	190	6

7. Use the Table AutoFormat feature to format the table using the Table Professional format.

8. If needed, insert a blank line so that the table is separated from the paragraphs above and below it.

9. At the top of the document, replace the reporter's name with your own name.

10. Compare your document to the document shown in the figure on the next page.

Figure Pr–10

Novel-Tea News
Reporter: [Your name here]

How Much Fat Is in Your Cup?

Lots of people today are trying to limit their daily calorie and fat intake. As employees of Novel-Tea & Coffee, you may be asked about the calories and the fat content of some of our standard and specialty drinks. The following list of standard drinks with their caloric and fat contents may help you answer those questions.

COFFEE	CALORIES	FAT (grams)
Black Coffee	0	0
8 oz. Cappuccino	63	3
8 oz. Café Latte	117	3.8
8 oz. Café Mocha	190	6

Because of the special nature of our monthly spotlight drinks, they are likely to be higher in both calories and fat content than any of the above drinks. We'll try to get you the data on a spotlight drink when we announce the drink.

If a customer is troubled by the calories or fat content of a particular drink, suggest a drink that's similar, but with fewer calories or less fat. For example, suggest a cappuccino instead of a café latte. Or point out that a typical one-ounce chocolate bar contains 160 calories, with 85 of those calories coming from more than 9 grams of fat. You might also point out that the specialty drinks all have considerably less caffeine than an equal amount of regular coffee.

Hopefully this information will help you answer commonly asked questions and help us better serve our customers.

11. Save your document on a Project Disk using the file name Project 4-2 XXXXX 9999, where XXXXX is your student ID number and 9999 is your class section number.

12. Use one of the following options to submit your project on disk, as a printout, or as an e-mail attachment, according to your instructor's directions:

■ To submit the file on the Project Disk where it is currently stored, stop the Word program by closing its window. Remove your Project Disk from the disk drive. Write your name, student ID number, class section number, date, and Project 4-2 on the disk label.

■ To print the project, click File on the Word menu bar, then click Print. Click the OK button. Write your name, student ID number, section number, date, and Project 4-2 on the printout.

■ To e-mail the file, use Method 1 or Method 2, as described on page 127. Type your instructor's e-mail address into the To: box. Click the Subject: box and type Project 4-2, your student ID number, and your class section number. Click the Send button or perform any additional steps required by your e-mail software to send an e-mail message.

■Project 5-1: Creating a Worksheet

In this project, you'll apply what you've learned to create a worksheet using Microsoft Excel.

Requirements: This project requires Microsoft Excel.

Project file: No file is required for this project.

1. Start Microsoft Excel.

2. Enter the labels and values shown below:

Figure Pr–11

	A	B	C	D	E	F
1	Phone Charges Per Roommate for February					
2	Basic Monthly Service Rate			20.44		
3	Long Distance Charges for Each Roommate:					
4			Jamesson	Coleman	Depindeau	Struthers
5			5.65	0.25	1.35	3.75
6			0.45	0.65	2.15	0.88
7			1.68	0.56	3.78	1.23
8				4.15	5.77	0.95
9				1.25		0.88
10				3.67		1.95
11						3.88
12	Total Long Distance					
13	Share of Basic Rate					
14	Total					

3. In cell C12, use the AutoSum button to calculate the sum of the cells in column C. Use a similar procedure to calculate the long distance call totals for Coleman, Depindeau, and Struthers in cells D12, E12, and F12.

4. In cell C13, create a formula to calculate Jamesson's share of the $20.44 basic monthly service rate by dividing the contents of cell D2 by 4. Create a similar formula for each roommate in cells D13, E13, and F13.

5. In cell C14, create a formula to calculate Jamesson's share of the total phone bill by adding the contents of cell C12 to the contents of cell C13. Create a similar formula for each roommate in cells D14, E14, and F14.

6. Compare your worksheet to the one shown in the figure on the next page.

Figure Pr–12

```
Microsoft Excel - 5-1.xls
File   Edit   View   Insert   Format   Tools   Data   Window   Help          Type a question for help

Arial         ▾ 10 ▾   B  I  U   ≡ ≡ ≡ 国  $ % ,  ‰ ‰ 律  国 ▾ ♦ ▾ A ▾

      A15        ▾        fx
```

	A	B	C	D	E	F	G	H	I
1	Phone Charges Per Roommate for February								
2	Basic Monthly Service Rate		20.44						
3	Long Distance Charges for Each Roommate:								
4			Jamesson	Coleman	Depindeau	Struthers			
5			5.65	0.25	1.35	3.75			
6			0.45	0.65	2.15	0.88			
7			1.68	0.56	3.78	1.23			
8				4.15	5.77	0.95			
9				1.25		0.88			
10				3.67		1.95			
11						3.88			
12	Total Long Distance		7.78	10.53	13.05	13.52			
13	Share of Basic Rate		5.11	5.11	5.11	5.11			
14	Total		12.89	15.64	18.16	18.63			
15									
16									

```
I◀ ◀ ▶ ▶I \ Sheet1 ⟨ Sheet2 ⟨ Sheet3 /            |◀                          ▶|
Ready                                                              NUM
```

7. Save your worksheet on a Project Disk using the file name Project 5-1 XXXXX 9999, where XXXXX is your student ID number and 9999 is your class section number.

8. Use one of the following options to submit your project on disk, as a printout, or as an e-mail attachment, according to your instructor's directions:

■ To submit the file on the Project Disk where it is currently stored, stop the Excel program by closing its window. Remove your Project Disk from the disk drive. Write your name, student ID number, class section number, date, and Project 5-1 on the disk label.

■ To print the project, click File on the Excel menu bar, then click Print. Click the OK button. Write your name, student ID number, section number, date, and Project 5-1 on the printout.

■ To e-mail the file, use Method 1 or Method 2, as described on page 127. Type your instructor's e-mail address into the To: box. Click the Send button or perform any additional steps required by your e-mail software to send an e-mail message.

■Project 5-2: Using Functions

In this project, you'll apply what you've learned about functions to complete a Microsoft Excel worksheet.

Requirements: This project requires Microsoft Excel.

Project file: Proj5-2.xls.

1. Copy the file Proj5-2 to your Project Disk using either the Project Disk menu or the Copy It! button on this page in the Book-on-CD.

2. Start Microsoft Excel.

3. Open the file Proj5-2 from your Project Disk.

4. Use the AutoSum button to display the total number of flights in cells B11 and C11.

5. In cell B12, use the MIN function to display the lowest number of Mango Air flights from the list that begins in cell B4 and ends in cell B10. Enter a similar function in cell C12 for Econo Air flights.

6. In cell B13, use the MAX function to display the highest number of Mango Air flights from the list that begins in cell B4 and ends in cell B10. Enter a similar function in cell C13 for Econo Air flights.

7. In cell B14, use a function to display the average number of Mango Air flights from the list that begins in cell B4 and ends in cell B10. Enter a similar function in cell C14 for Econo Air flights.

8. Enter your name in cell E1.

9. Compare your worksheet to the one shown in the figure on the next page, but don't save it yet. You have one change to make in Step 10.

**Figure
Pr–13**

10. Change the number in cell C9 to 85.

11. Save your worksheet on a Project Disk using the file name Project 5-2
XXXXX 9999, where XXXXX is your student ID number and 9999 is your class
section number.

12. Use one of the following options to submit your project on disk, as a printout,
or as an e-mail attachment, according to your instructor's directions:

■ To submit the file on the Project Disk where it is currently stored, stop the
Excel program by closing its window. Remove your Project Disk from the disk
drive. Write your name, student ID number, class section number, date, and
Project 5-2 on the disk label.

■ To print the project, click File on the Excel menu bar, then click Print. Click
the OK button. Write your name, student ID number, section number, date, and
Project 5-2 on the printout.

■ To e-mail the file, use Method 1 or Method 2, as described on page 127. Type
your instructor's e-mail address into the To: box. Click the Send button or perform
any additional steps required by your e-mail software to send an e-mail message.

■Project 6-1: Formatting a Worksheet

In this project, you'll apply what you've learned about Microsoft Excel to complete and format a worksheet.

Requirements: This project requires Microsoft Excel.

Project file: Proj6-1.xls.

1. Copy the file Proj6-1 to your Project Disk using either the Project Disk menu or the Copy It! button on this page in the Book-on-CD.

2. Start Microsoft Excel.

3. Open the file Proj6-1 from your Project Disk.

4. Copy the formula from cell C6 to cells D6 and E6.

5. Copy the formula from cell C15 to D15 and E15.

6. Copy the formula from cell F4 to cells F5 through F6, and F9 through F15.

7. Insert a new, empty row before row 15.

8. Change the color of the text in cell A1 to dark blue.

9. Change the font in cell A1 to Times New Roman, size 14, bold.

10. Merge the contents of cells A1 through F1 so that the title is centered across those columns.

11. Format cells B3 through F3 as bold text.

12. Format the numbers in cells C4 through E16 as currency.

13. Format the numbers in cells F4 through F16 as percentages.

14. Right-align the labels in cells C3 through F3.

15. Add both inside and outline borders to two cell ranges: B4 through F5 and B9 through F13.

16. Adjust the width of all columns so that all labels and values fit within the cells.

17. Compare your worksheet to the one shown on the next page.

Figure Pr-14

```
Microsoft Excel - 6-1.XLS
File  Edit  View  Insert  Format  Tools  Data  Window  Help        Type a question for help
Arial          10    B  I  U                    $ %
      G2              fx
        A        B          C          D          E          F        G        H
1                    Income and Expense Summary
2
3   Income                   Previous    Current    Increase % Increase
4            Misc.Income  $  1,450.00  $  2,208.00  $    758.00      52%
5            Sales        $53,200.00  $72,850.00  $19,650.00      37%
6            Total        $54,650.00  $75,058.00  $20,408.00      37%
7
8   Expenses
9            Salaries     $22,180.00  $23,850.00  $  1,670.00       8%
10           Inventory    $18,462.00  $24,502.00  $  6,040.00      33%
11           Rent         $  4,500.00  $  5,250.00  $    750.00      17%
12           Advertising  $  2,240.00  $  3,810.00  $  1,570.00      70%
13           Misc.        $  1,860.00  $  2,602.00  $    742.00      40%
14           Total        $49,242.00  $60,014.00  $10,772.00      22%
15
16  Profit                $  5,408.00  $15,044.00  $  9,636.00     178%
17
    Sheet1 / Sheet2 / Sheet3 / Sheet4 / Sheet5 / She
Ready                                                                NUM
start              Microsoft Excel                              5:24 AM
```

18. Save your worksheet on a Project Disk using the file name Project 6-1 XXXXX 9999, where XXXXX is your student ID number and 9999 is your class section number.

19. Use one of the following options to submit your project on disk, as a printout, or as an e-mail attachment, according to your instructor's directions:

■ To submit the file on the Project Disk where it is currently stored, stop the Excel program by closing its window. Remove your Project Disk from the disk drive. Write your name, student ID number, class section number, date, and Project 6-1 on the disk label.

■ To print the project, click File on the Excel menu bar, then click Print. Click the OK button. Write your name, student ID number, section number, date, and Project 6-1 on the printout.

■ To e-mail the file, use Method 1 or Method 2, as described on page 127. Type your instructor's e-mail address into the To: box. Click the Send button or perform any additional steps required by your e-mail software to send an e-mail message.

■Project 6-2: Using Absolute and Relative References

In this project, you'll apply what you've learned about absolute and relative references to complete a sales commission worksheet.

Requirements: This project requires Microsoft Excel.

Project file: Proj6-2.xls.

1. Copy the file Proj6-2 to your Project Disk using either the Project Disk menu or the Copy It! button on this page in the Book-on-CD.

2. Start Microsoft Excel.

3. Open the file Proj6-2 from your Project Disk.

4. Notice that cell B2 contains a sales commission rate. Each salesperson receives a commission equal to his or her total sales multiplied by the commission rate. The commission rate changes periodically. The worksheet is set up so that if the sales manager changes the rate in cell B2, all the sales commissions will be recalculated.

5. Create a formula in cell B10 to calculate the sales commission for column B by multiplying the Total Sales in cell B9 by the Commission Rate in cell B2. *Hint:* You must use an absolute reference for the Commission Rate in the formula.

6. Copy the formula from cell B10 to cells C10 through E10.

7. Check the results of the copied formulas to make sure that they show the correct results. If cells C10 through E10 contain zeros, you did not use the correct absolute reference for the formula that you entered in Step 5. If necessary, modify the formula in B10, then recopy it to cells C10 through E10.

8. Compare your worksheet to the worksheet shown in the figure on the next page, but don't save it until you complete Steps 9 and 10.

■　　■　　■

Figure Pr-15

9. Change the contents of cell B2 to 0.03.

10. Enter your name in cell B4.

11. Save your worksheet on a Project Disk using the file name Project 6-2 XXXXX 9999, where XXXXX is your student ID number and 9999 is your class section number.

12. Use one of the following options to submit your project on disk, as a printout, or as an e-mail attachment, according to your instructor's directions:

■ To submit the file on the Project Disk where it is currently stored, stop the Excel program by closing its window. Remove your Project Disk from the disk drive. Write your name, student ID number, class section number, date, and Project 6-2 on the disk label.

■ To print the project, click File on the Excel menu bar, then click Print. Click the OK button. Write your name, student ID number, section number, date, and Project 6-2 on the printout.

■ To e-mail the file, use Method 1 or Method 2, as described on page 127. Type your instructor's e-mail address into the To: box. Click the Send button or perform any additional steps required by your e-mail software to send an e-mail message.

■Project 7-1: Finalizing a Worksheet

In this project, you'll apply what you've learned about Microsoft Excel to finalize a worksheet.

Requirements: This project requires Microsoft Excel.

Project file: Proj7-1.xls.

1. Copy the file Proj7-1 to your Project Disk using either the Project Disk menu or the Copy It! button on this page in the Book-on-CD.

2. Start Microsoft Excel.

3. Open the file Proj7-1 from your Project Disk.

4. Sort the data in cells A3 through F16 in ascending order by Description.

5. Check the spelling of the worksheet and correct misspellings as needed.

6. Add a right-justified custom header to the worksheet that includes your name, your student ID, your section, today's date, and Project 7-1.

7. Add a centered footer to the worksheet that includes the word "Page" followed by the page number.

8. Use the Page Setup options to print the page on a single piece of paper.

9. Preview your worksheet. It should now look similar to the worksheet shown in the figure on the next page.

Figure
Pr–16

Nancy A. Student
345-666
Section A
January 20, 2003
Project 7-1

Gothic Gargoyle Collection				
Description	**Product Size**	**Weight**	**Price**	**Shipping**
Ancient Burden Gargoyle	872 4"Wx2"H	16	$32.95	$5.95
Dwarf Dragon Gargoyle	561 3"Wx5"H	4	$12.95	$5.95
Dwarf Dragon Gargoyle	731 3"Wx7"H	5	$19.95	$5.95
Dwarf Florentine Gargoyle	810 2"Wx4"H	9	$14.95	$5.95
Dwarf Gnawing Gargoyle	994 3"Wx7"H	8	$10.95	$5.95
Dwarf Gothic Gruff	741 3"Wx7"H	7	$19.95	$5.95
Gargoyle Candelabra	782 3"Wx4"H	11	$22.95	$5.95
Gothic Gargoyle Snow Globe	792 3"Wx4"H	18	$12.95	$5.95
Guardian of the Flame Gargoyle	736 3"Wx4"H	14	$29.95	$5.95
Guardians of the Gate Gargoyle	824 4"Wx2"H	15	$34.95	$5.95
Keeper of the Castle Gargoyle	777 3"Wx4"H	7	$27.95	$5.95
Keeper of the Castle Gargoyle	721 4"Wx2"H	19	$32.95	$5.95
Le Petite Florentine Gargoyle	731 3"Wx4"H	7	$15.95	$5.95
The Emmett Gargoyle	735 3"Wx4"H	11	$12.95	$5.95

Page 1

10. Save your worksheet on a Project Disk using the file name Project 7-1 XXXXX 9999, where XXXXX is your student ID number and 9999 is your class section number.

11. Use one of the following options to submit your project on disk, as a printout, or as an e-mail attachment, according to your instructor's directions:

■ To submit the file on the Project Disk where it is currently stored, stop the Excel program by closing its window. Remove your Project Disk from the disk drive. Write your name, student ID number, class section number, date, and Project 7-1 on the disk label.

■ To print the project, click File on the Excel menu bar, then click Print. Click the OK button.

■ To e-mail the file, use Method 1 or Method 2, as described on page 127. Type your instructor's e-mail address into the To: box. Click the Send button or perform any additional steps required by your e-mail software to send an e-mail message.

■ ■ ■

■Project 7-2: Creating Charts

In this project, you'll apply what you've learned about Microsoft Excel to create a column chart and a pie chart for an e-commerce worksheet.

Requirements: This project requires Microsoft Excel.

Project file: Proj7-2.xls.

1. Copy the file Proj7-2 to your Project Disk using either the Project Disk menu or the Copy It! button on this page in the Book-on-CD.

2. Start Microsoft Excel.

3. Open the file Proj7-2 from your Project Disk.

4. Select the data in cells B3 through C6. Use the Chart Wizard to create a 3-D pie chart. For the title of the chart, enter Which Activities Lead?. Use the Data Labels tab to show percents on the pie slices. Place the chart on the current worksheet. When the chart is complete, position the chart so that the top-left corner of the chart is in cell A10.

5. Select the data in cells H4 through H8. Use the Chart Wizard to create a Clustered Column chart. On Step 2 of 4, click the Series tab, click the 🔣 button to select Category (X) axis labels, then select cells G4 through G8. Click the 🖼 button to return to the Chart Wizard, then go to the next step. For the title of the chart, enter U.S. Projections. Label the Y-axis $ Billions. In Step 3 of the Wizard, remove the check mark from the *Show legend* check box. Place the chart as an object in the current worksheet. When the chart is complete, position it so that it is located to the right of the previous pie chart.

6. Click a blank cell in the worksheet, then click the Print Preview button. Use Page Setup options to change the page orientation to Landscape and fit the worksheet on one page. The worksheet preview should look like the one shown in the figure on the next page.

Figure Pr-17

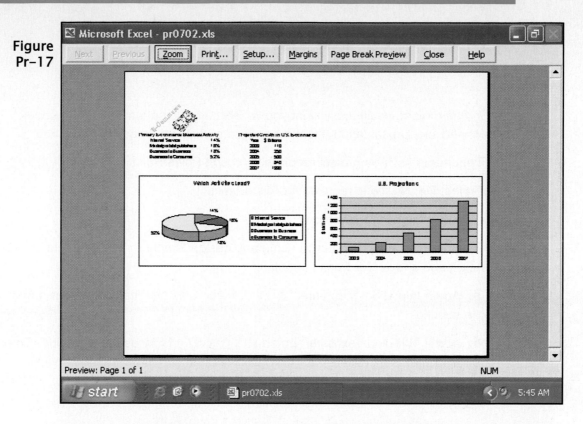

7. Save your worksheet on a Project Disk using the file name Project 7-2 XXXXX 9999, where XXXXX is your student ID number and 9999 is your class section number.

8. Use one of the following options to submit your project on disk, as a printout, or as an e-mail attachment, according to your instructor's directions:

■ To submit the file on the Project Disk where it is currently stored, stop the Excel program by closing its window. Remove your Project Disk from the disk drive. Write your name, student ID number, class section number, date, and Project 7-2 on the disk label.

■ To print the project, click File on the Excel menu bar, then click Print. Click the OK button. Write your name, student ID number, section number, date, and Project 7-2 on the printout.

■ To e-mail the file, use Method 1 or Method 2, as described on page 127. Type your instructor's e-mail address into the To: box. Click the Send button or perform any additional steps required by your e-mail software to send an e-mail message.

■Project 8-1: Creating a Presentation

In this project, you'll apply what you've learned to create a "tongue-in-cheek" PowerPoint presentation about e-commerce business trends.

Requirements: This project requires Microsoft PowerPoint.

Project file: No file is required for this project.

1. Start Microsoft PowerPoint.

2. Create a new presentation using any design template. The example on the next page shows the Ocean template.

3. Add a title slide, then enter Money Machine as the title. Enter your name as the subtitle.

4. Add a Title and Text slide. Enter The Web Economy as the slide title. Enter the following items as bullets:

> Growth is more important than profit.
> Scalability is crucial–we must be able to grow faster than the competition.
> It's OK to lose money–as long as we keep growing.

5. Add a Title, Text, and Content slide. Enter We don't need profits because: as the slide title. Add the following items as bullets:

> Even if we lose money on every item, we can make it up on volume.
> What we can't make up in volume, we'll make up by selling banner ads.

Add whatever clip art you decide is appropriate.

6. Add a Title and Text slide. Enter Here's the Plan! as the slide title. Add the following items as bullets:

> Quickly expand to credit card sales!
> Expand into major international markets!

7. Compare your slides to those shown in the figure on the next page.

**Figure
Pr-18**

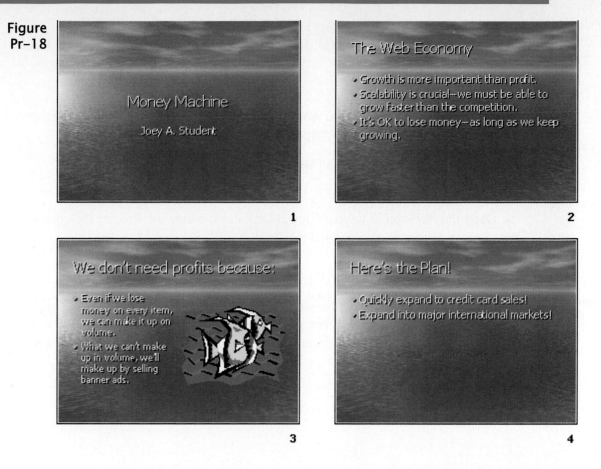

8. Save your presentation on a Project Disk using the file name Project 8-1 XXXXX 9999, where XXXXX is your student ID number and 9999 is your class section number.

9. Use one of the following options to submit your project on disk, as a printout, or as an e-mail attachment, according to your instructor's directions:

■ To submit the file on the Project Disk where it is currently stored, stop the PowerPoint program by closing its window. Remove your Project Disk from the disk drive. Write your name, student ID number, class section number, date, and Project 8-1 on the disk label.

■ To print the project, click File on the PowerPoint menu bar, then click Print. In the Print dialog box, look for the *Print what* section and use its pull-down list to select Handouts. Make sure that the *Handouts* section specifies 6 slides per page in Horizontal order. Also, make sure that the *Scale to fit paper* check box contains a check mark. Click the OK button. Write your name, student ID number, section number, date, and Project 8-1 on the printout.

■ To e-mail the file, use Method 1 or Method 2, as described on page 127. Type your instructor's e-mail address into the To: box. Click the Send button or perform any additional steps required by your e-mail software to send an e-mail message.

■Project 8-2: Creating Slides with Charts and Tables

In this project, you'll apply what you've learned about charts and tables to create PowerPoint slides for a fitness center.

Requirements: This project requires Microsoft PowerPoint.

Project file: Proj8-2.ppt.

1. Copy the file Proj8-2 to your Project Disk using either the Project Disk menu or the Copy It! button on this page in the Book-on-CD.

2. Start Microsoft PowerPoint.

3. Open the file Proj8-2 from your Project Disk.

4. Add a Title and Content. Enter Target Heart Rates as the slide title. Add a table consisting of three columns and four rows, then enter the following data into the table:

Age	Minimum Rate	Maximum Rate
20	120	170
30	114	162
40	108	163

5. Add a Title and Content after the Target Heart Rates slide. Enter Caloric Expenditures by Body Weight as the slide title. Create a column chart that shows the following data:

	125 Lbs.	175 Lbs.
Jogging	7.3	10.4
Swimming	6.9	9.8

6. Compare your slides to those shown in the figure on the next page.

Figure Pr–19

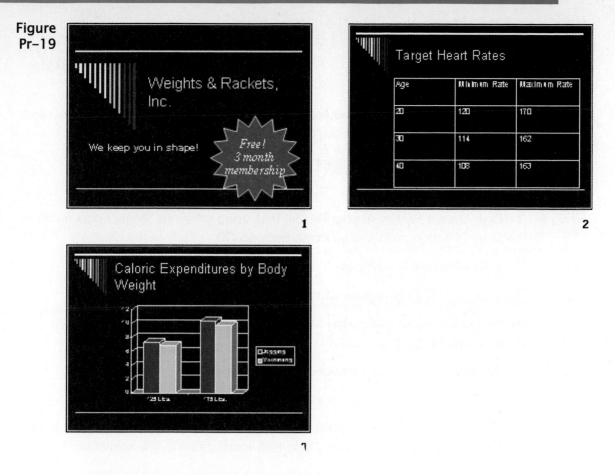

7. Save your presentation on a Project Disk using the file name Project 8-2 XXXXX 9999, where XXXXX is your student ID number and 9999 is your class section number.

8. Use one of the following options to submit your project on disk, as a printout, or as an e-mail attachment, according to your instructor's directions:

■ To submit the file on the Project Disk where it is currently stored, stop the PowerPoint program by closing its window. Remove your Project Disk from the disk drive. Write your name, student ID number, class section number, date, and Project 8-2 on the disk label.

■ To print the project, click File on the PowerPoint menu bar, then click Print. In the Print dialog box, look for the *Print what* section and use its pull-down list to select Handouts. Make sure that the *Handouts* section specifies 6 slides per page in Horizontal order. Also, make sure that the *Scale to fit paper* check box contains a check mark. Click the OK button. Write your name, student ID number, section number, date, and Project 8-2 on the printout.

■ To e-mail the file, use Method 1 or Method 2, as described on page 127. Type your instructor's e-mail address into the To: box. Click the Send button or perform any additional steps required by your e-mail software to send an e-mail message.

■Project 9-1: Using Animations, Transitions, and Sounds

In this project, you'll apply what you've learned to add animations, transitions, and sounds to a PowerPoint presentation.

Requirements: This project requires Microsoft PowerPoint.

Project file: Proj9-1.ppt.

1. Copy the file Proj9-1 to your Project Disk using either the Project Disk menu or the Copy It! button on this page in the Book-on-CD.

2. Start Microsoft PowerPoint.

3. Open the file Proj9-1 from your Project Disk.

4. On the first slide, change the subtitle text The time is right! to Times New Roman, size 44, bold, and italic.

5. Add the Uncover Down transition to the second slide.

6. Add the Fade Through Black transition to the third slide.

7. Add the Fly In animation (coming from the left) to the bulleted list on the third slide in the presentation. Add the Drum Roll sound effect to the animation.

8. View the presentation to see how the transition and animation effects work.

9. Switch to Slide Sorter View. You should see transition and animation icons under slides 2 and 3, as shown on the next page. *Note:* Don't worry about spelling errors. You will have an opportunity to fix them in the next project.

**Figure
Pr-20**

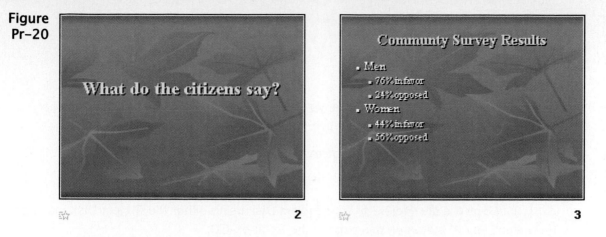

2   3

10. Save your presentation on a Project Disk using the file name Project 9-1 XXXXX 9999, where XXXXX is your student ID number and 9999 is your class section number.

11. Use one of the following options to submit your project on disk, as a printout, or as an e-mail attachment, according to your instructor's directions:

■ To submit the file on the Project Disk where it is currently stored, stop the PowerPoint program by closing its window. Remove your Project Disk from the disk drive. Write your name, student ID number, class section number, date, and Project 9-1 on the disk label.

■ To print the project, click File on the PowerPoint menu bar, then click Print. On the Print dialog box, look for the *Print what* section and use its pull-down list to select Handouts. Make sure that the *Handouts* section specifies 6 slides per page in Horizontal order. Also, make sure that the *Scale to fit paper* check box contains a check mark. Click the OK button. Write your name, student ID number, section number, date, and Project 9-1 on the printout.

■ To e-mail the file, use Method 1 or Method 2, as described on page 127. Type your instructor's e-mail address into the To: box. Click the Send button or perform any additional steps required by your e-mail software to send an e-mail message.

■Project 9-2: Finalizing a Presentation

In this project, you'll apply what you've learned as you finalize a version of the Microsoft PowerPoint presentation that you worked with in Project 9-1.

Requirements: This project requires Microsoft PowerPoint.

Project file: Project 9-2.ppt.

1. Copy the file Proj9-2 to your Project Disk using either the Project Disk menu or the Copy It! button on this page in the Book-on-CD.

2. Start Microsoft PowerPoint.

3. Open the file Proj9-2 from your Project Disk.

4. Use Slide Sorter View to move the Questions & Answers? slide to the end of the presentation.

5. Move the Best Site slide so that it comes immediately after the Potential Sites slide.

6. Add the following speaker note to the first slide in the presentation: Introduce team members Jill Smith, David Byrne, and Tom Woods.

7. Add the following speaker note to the last slide in the presentation: Let's get a general idea of your reaction to the proposed golf course... raise your hand if you would like the project to proceed.

8. Delete the We need to proceed as quickly as possible! slide.

9. Check the spelling of all slides and make any necessary corrections.

10. In Slide Sorter View, compare your presentation to the one shown in the figure on the next page.

**Figure
Pr–21**

11. Save your presentation on a Project Disk using the file name Project 9-2 XXXXX 9999, where XXXXX is your student ID number and 9999 is your class section number.

12. Use one of the following options to submit your project on disk, as a printout, or as an e-mail attachment, according to your instructor's directions:

■ To submit the file on the Project Disk where it is currently stored, stop the PowerPoint program by closing its window. Remove your Project Disk from the disk drive. Write your name, student ID number, class section number, date, and Project 9-2 on the disk label.

■ To print the project, click File on the PowerPoint menu bar, then click Print. On the Print dialog box, look for the *Print what* section and use its pull-down list to select Handouts. Make sure that the *Handouts* section specifies 6 slides per page in Horizontal order. Also, make sure that the *Scale to fit paper* check box contains a check mark. Click the OK button. Write your name, student ID number, section number, date, and Project 9-2 on the printout.

■ To e-mail the file, use Method 1 or Method 2, as described on page 127. Type your instructor's e-mail address into the To: box. Click the Send button or perform any additional steps required by your e-mail software to send an e-mail message.

■Project 10-1: Creating a Database Table

In this project, you'll apply what you've learned about Microsoft Access to create a database, create a table, and enter data into the table.

Requirements: This project requires Microsoft Access.

Project file: No project file is required for this project.

1. Start Microsoft Access.

2. Create a new database on a floppy disk in drive A. Name the database Project 10-1.mdb.

3. Use the Table Wizard to create a table using the Contacts sample table in the Business group. Include the following fields in the table: ContactsID, FirstName, LastName, Address, City, StateOrProvince, PostalCode, Country/Region, CompanyName, Title, WorkPhone, FaxNumber, and EmailName. Name the table Contacts. Have Access create a primary key for you. Select the option to enter data directly into the table.

4. Add the following records to the database. Leave fields, such as CompanyName, blank if you don't have the data.

1 Luke Brown 4702 Lakewood Lane, Stone's Throw, GA 83928 USA (812)928-3828 luke_brown@csm.com

2 Alison Cho 337 Center Street, Stockton, KY 83748 USA (702)737-2781 acho@centnet.net

3 Joe McGuire 1147 Old Mill Road, Hanover, OH 57373 USA (303)383-7478 jmc@cnet.net

5. Check the data that you entered and correct any typing mistakes.

Figure
Pr-22

6. Use one of the following options to submit your project on disk, as a printout, or as an e-mail attachment, according to your instructor's directions:

■ To submit the file on disk, close Access and remove the floppy disk. Write your name, student ID, section number, date, and Project 10-1 on the disk label.

■ To print the file, make sure that the Contacts table is open. Click the Print button on the Access toolbar. Write your name, student ID, section number, date, and Project 10-1 on the first page of the printout.

■ To e-mail the file, exit Access and start your usual e-mail program. [Note that you should *not* use the File menu's *Send To* option for this project.] Type your instructor's e-mail address into the To: box. Type Project 10-1, your student ID number, and your class section number into the Subject: box. Attach the file Project 10-1.mdb from your Project Disk to the e-mail. Click the Send button and perform any additional steps required to send an e-mail message.

■Project 10-2: Creating Queries

In this project, you'll apply what you've learned about Microsoft Access to create queries for finding specific information in a database.

Requirements: This project requires Microsoft Access.

Project file: Proj10-2.mdb.

1. Copy the file Proj10-2 to your Project Disk using either the Project Disk menu or the Copy It! button on this page in the Book-on-CD.

2. Start Microsoft Access.

3. Open the file Proj10-2 from your Project Disk.

4. Use the Query Wizard to create a query that includes all fields from the Products table. Name the query Products Under $10. Add query criteria to limit the query results to products that cost less than $10. Run the query and compare your results to those shown in the figure below:

Figure Pr–23

	ID	Product Numbe	Description	Price
▶	1	72838	8 oz Coffee Mug	$3.45
	2	82892	12 oz Coffee Mug	$4.15
	3	18372	Cup Holder	$2.85
	5	83827	Auto Trash Bag	$7.95
	7	23702	Lock De-icer	$2.89
	8	37027	Windshield Scrape	$3.25
＊	(AutoNumber)	0		$0.00

Products Under $10 : Select Query

Record: 1 of 6

5. Use the Query Wizard to create a query that includes all fields from the Contacts table. Name the query Ohio Contacts. Add query criteria to limit the query results to records of people located in the state of Ohio (OH). Run the query and compare your results to those shown in the figure below.

Figure Pr–24

	ContactsID	First Name	Last Name	Address	City	State/Province	Postal Code
▶	3	Joe	McGuire	1147 Old Mill Road	Hanover	OH	57373-
	5	Yukiko	Nakamura	1010 Dill St.	Cleveland	OH	58348-
	6	Candace	Glenn	1717 Oak Lane	Cleveland	OH	58348-
*	(AutoNumber)						

Ohio Contacts : Select Query

Record: 1 of 3

6. Use one of the following options to submit your project on disk, as a printout, or as an e-mail attachment, according to your instructor's directions:

■ To submit the file on disk, close Access and remove the floppy disk. Write your name, student ID, section number, date, and Project 10-2 on the disk label.

■ To print the project, make sure that the Products Under $10 query is open, then click the Print button on the Access toolbar. Close the Products Under $10 query, then open the Ohio Contacts query. Click the Print button on the Access toolbar. Staple the pages together, then write your name, student ID number, class section number, date, and Project 10-2 on the first page.

■ To e-mail the file, exit Access and start your usual e-mail program. [Note that you should *not* use the File menu's *Send To* option for this project.] Type your instructor's e-mail address into the To: box. Type Project 10-2, your student ID number, and your class section number into the Subject: box. Attach the file Project 10-2.mdb from your Project Disk to the e-mail. Click the Send button and perform any additional steps required to send an e-mail message.

■Project 11-1: Creating Forms

In this project, you'll apply what you've learned about Microsoft Access to create forms that would allow a data entry person to easily update the Products and Contacts tables.

Requirements: This project requires Microsoft Access.

Copy It! Project file: Proj11-1.mdb.

1. Copy the file Proj11-1.mdb to your Project Disk using either the Project Disk menu or the Copy It! button on this page in the Book-on-CD.

2. Start Microsoft Access.

3. Open the file Proj11-1.mdb from your Project Disk.

4. Use the Form Wizard to create a form containing all the fields from the Products table. Specify the Columnar layout and the International style. Enter Product Inventory as the form title.

5. Compare your form to the one shown below:

Figure Pr–25

Product Inventory
ID	1
Product Number	72838
Description	8 oz Coffee Mug
Price	$3.45
Record: 1 of 10

6. Use the Product Inventory form to add a new record for product # 54431, which is Fix-a-Flat priced at $1.89.

7. Close the Product Inventory form.

8. Use the Form Wizard to create a form containing the following fields from the Contacts table: FirstName, LastName, and EmailName. Use the Justified layout and the Blends style. Enter E-Mail List as the form title.

9. Compare your form to the one shown on the next page.

Figure Pr-26

10. Add your own name and e-mail address to the list. If you don't have an e-mail address, just make one up.

11. Close the E-Mail List form.

12. Use one of the following options to submit your project on disk, as a printout, or as an e-mail attachment, according to your instructor's directions:

■ To submit the file on disk, close Access and remove the floppy disk. Write your name, student ID, section number, date, and Project 11-1 on the disk label.

■ To print the data as it appears in the form, make sure that the Product Inventory form is open. Click the Print button on the Access toolbar. Close the Product Inventory form and open the E-Mail List form. Click the Print button on the Access toolbar. Staple the pages together, then write your name, student ID number, class section number, date, and Project 11-1 on the first page.

■ To e-mail the file, exit Access and start your usual e-mail program. [Note that you should *not* use the File menu's *Send To* option for this project.] Type your instructor's e-mail address into the To: box. Type Project 11-1, your student ID number, and your class section number into the Subject: box. Attach the file Project 11-1.mdb from your Project Disk to the e-mail. Click the Send button and perform any additional steps required to send an e-mail message.

■ ■ ■

■Project 11-2: Creating Reports

In this project, you'll apply what you've learned about Microsoft Access to generate printed reports.

Requirements: This project requires Microsoft Access.

Project file: Proj11-2.mdb.

1. Copy the file Proj11-2.mdb to your Project Disk using either the Project Disk menu or the Copy It! button on this page in the Book-on-CD.

2. Start Microsoft Access.

3. Open the file Proj11-2.mdb from your Project Disk.

4. Use the Report Wizard to create a report containing only the FirstName, LastName, and EmailName fields from the Contacts table. Do not add any grouping levels. Sort the records by last name in ascending order. Use the Tabular layout and the Casual style for the report. Enter Contact E-Mail Addresses for the report title.

5. Compare your report to the one shown in the figure below, then close the report.

Figure Pr–27

Contact E-Mail Addresses

Last Name	First Name	Email Name
Brown	Kim	brown_kim@mindspring.com
Brown	Luke	luke_brown@csm.com
Cho	Alison	acho@centnet.net
Glenn	Candace	cglenn120@aol.com
Lowe	Sharon	slowe@aol.com
Maki	John	john_maki_aol.com
McGuire	Joe	jmc@cnet.net
Nakamura	Yukiko	ynaka@cnet.net
Smith	Heidi	heidis@aol.com

6. Use the Report Wizard to create a report containing all fields *except the ID field* in the Query: Products Under $10 table. Group by department. Sort the records by Description in ascending order. Use the Stepped layout and Formal style for the report. Enter Products Under $10 by Department for the report title.

7. Compare your report to the one shown in the figure below, then close the report.

Figure Pr-28

Products Under $10 by Department

Department	Description	Product Number	Price
Automotive			
	Auto Trash Bag	83827	$7.95
	Cup Holder	18372	$2.85
	Fix-a-Flat	54431	$1.89
	Lock De-icer	23702	$2.89
	Windshield Scraper	37027	$3.25
Floral			
	Herb Garden	77543	$3.49
Housewares			
	12 oz Coffee Mug	82892	$4.15
	8 oz Coffee Mug	72838	$3.45
	Plastic Hangers/12	78662	$3.99
	Rock Key Safe	986443	$5.99
	Votive Candles	887611	$0.99

8. Use one of the following options to submit your project on disk, as a printout, or as an e-mail attachment, according to your instructor's directions:

■ To submit the file on disk, close Access and remove the floppy disk. Write your name, student ID, section number, date, and Project 11-2 on the disk label.

■ To print the project, open the Contact E-Mail Addresses report, then use the Print button on the Access toolbar. Open the Products Under $10 by Department report, then click the Print button on the toolbar. Write your name, student ID, section number, date, and Project 11-2 on the printouts.

■ To e-mail the file, exit Access and start your usual e-mail program. [Note that you should *not* use the File menu's *Send To* option for this project.] Type your instructor's e-mail address into the To: box. Type Project 11-2, your student ID number, and your class section number into the Subject: box. Attach the file Project 11-2.mdb from your Project Disk to the e-mail. Click the Send button and perform any additional steps required to send an e-mail message.

■Index

> button, 106, 111, 115, 118
>> button, 106, 111, 115, 118
< button, 106, 111, 115
<< button, 106, 111

A

absolute references, 65
Access, 102
  tools, 104
  windows, 104
actions, redoing and undoing, 21
active cell, 49–50
active window, 7
addition (+) operator, 52
Align Center button, 63
Align Left button, 32, 63
Align Left layouts, 119
Align Right button, 32, 63
aligning cell contents, 63
All Programs command, 5, 17, 49, 81
All Programs menu, 5, 17, 49, 81
animation effects, 84, 93, 95
application programs
  menu bar, 8
  toolbars, 9
  windows, 6
arguments, 55
arithmetic operators, 52, 53
AutoCorrect Options command, 96
AutoCorrect dialog box, 96
automatically
  advancing slides, 93
  entering values, 51
AutoNumber data type, 110
AutoSum button, 56
Average function, 54, 55

B

background colors for worksheets, 59
Backspace key, 18, 50, 109
bar charts, 72, 86
Bar tab icon, 35
bar tab stop, 35
blank
  documents, 17
  line, 18
Blank layout, 83
Block layout, 119
Bold button, 94
bold text, 30, 60
boot process, 3
booting up computers, 3

borders for cells and worksheets, 59
bugs, 14
bulleted lists, 33, 84, 95
bullets, 33
Bullets and Numbering command, 33
Bullets and Numbering dialog box, 33
Bullets button, 33, 84
buttons, 9

C

calculating total of column or row, 56
cell references, 52-53, 55
cells, 43, 49, 103
  absolute references, 65
  aligning contents, 63
  automatically filling, 51
  borders, 59
  centering contents, 63
  comma in values, 61
  copying, 64
  currency format, 61
  formula too long, 62
  formulas, 52
  label too long, 62
  labels, 50
  marquee, 52
  moving, 64
  number formats, 61
  one digit less or more after decimal, 61
  as percentage, 61
  relative references, 65
  resizing, 62
  value too long, 62
  values, 51
  word wrap, 43
Cells command, 50, 59, 60, 61, 63
Center button, 32
Center tab icon, 35
center tab stop, 35
centering
  cell contents, 63
  labels, 63
  text, 32, 35
  titles, 32
channels, 4
Chart Wizard, 72–73
Chart Wizard button, 72
charts, 72–73, 86
check boxes, 10
clearing tabs, 35
clip art, 85
Clip Art command, 85

■ ■ ■

Clipboard, 20
Close button, 6, 74
Close command, 6
color transparencies, 100
colors and fonts, 60, 94
Columnar layout, 116
columns, 103
    inserting and deleting, 66
    merging range of cells in, 63
    resizing, 43, 62
Columns command, 66
Comma Style button, 61
commands, 17
    ellipsis (...) after, 8
    redoing, 21
    selecting, 8
    shortcuts to, 9
    undoing, 21
complex formulas, 53
computers, 3, 14
consistency, 96
Contents: Database window, 104
controls, 10–11
copy and paste, 20
Copy button, 20
Copy command, 92
copying
    cells, 64
    ranges, 64
    text, 20
Currency Style button, 61
Custom Animation command, 95
custom document templates, 22
Customize command, 9
Customize dialog box, 9
Cut button, 20
Cut command, 86, 92

D
data
    organization in databases, 103
    storing, 12
Data menu, 70
data type, 110
Database icon, 105
database software, 102
databases, 102
    cells, 103
    columns, 103
    creation of, 105
    data organization in, 103
    displaying data, 103-104
    fields, 103
    opening, 104-105, 108
    queries, 111–112
    records, 103

rows, 103
saving, 105, 108
structure of tables, fields, and records, 106
tables, 103
datasheet, 86
Datasheet layout, 116
Date/Time data type, 110
Date and Time command, 121
Decimal tab icon, 35
decimal tab stop, 35
Decrease Decimal button, 61
Decrease Font Size button, 94
Decrease Indent button, 33, 91
default margins, 42
defining styles, 45
Delete command, 66, 86, 87, 92
Delete dialog box, 66
Delete key, 11, 18, 50, 85, 92, 109
Delete record command, 109
deleting
    columns and rows, 66
    datasheet sample data, 86
    fields from queries, 111
    form fields, 115
    form labels, 117
    graphics, 85
    records, 109
    rows and columns, 43
    slides, 92
    styles, 45
    text, 18
    text box contents, 11
deselecting text, 19
Design button, 82
design templates, 81, 83
Design view
    forms, 117
    table creation, 110
Design View command, 117, 120, 121
Design view command, 112
desktop, 3–5
device letter, 12
diagnostic messages, 3
dialog boxes, 8, 10
disk drive, floppy disk left in, 3
division (/) operator, 52
document templates, 22
document window, 17–18
document wizards, 24–25
documents, 12, 16, 41
    blank, 17
    blank line, 18
    checking spelling and grammar, 39
    creation of, 18, 24–25
    current location, 18
    double-spacing, 34

as e-mail attachment, 26
file type, 23
fonts, 29
footers, 41
headers, 41
HTML format, 46
line spacing, 34
margins, 42
naming, 17, 23
paragraphs, 18
previewing, 26
printing, 26, 44
saving, 23
saving as Web pages, 46
selecting entire, 29
selecting text, 19
styles, 45
views, 17
double-clicking, 19
double-spacing documents, 34
drag-and-drop to move slides, 92
drag-and-fill, 51
dragging windows, 6
Drawing toolbar, 83
duplicating slides, 92

E
Edit menu, 19, 34, 51, 66, 92
editing, 19
Effect Options, 95
electronic spreadsheets, 48
e-mail
    attachments, 26
    one-click access, 4
empty records, 109
Enter key, 18
Entire row command, 86
Excel, 48–49
Export command, 122

F
fades, 93
fields, 102-103, 110
    adding or deleting, 106
    reports, 118
    structure of, 106
    titles, 108
file extension, 13
File menu, 22, 24, 26, 42, 44, 46, 74, 77–78,
    82, 97–100, 121–122
File New Database dialog box, 105
files, 12–13
Fill command, 51
floppy disks
    left in disk drive, 3
    saving database to, 108

folders, 12-13, 23
Font command, 31, 94
Font dialog box, 31, 94
Font list, 94
fonts, 29, 60, 94
footers, 41-42
    See also headers
    worksheets, 74–76
Form Wizard, 115–117
Format Cells dialog box, 50, 59–61, 63
Format menu, 31–32, 34–36, 45, 50, 60–61,
    63, 94
formatting
    cell data, 60–61
    slide text, 94
Formatting toolbar, 9, 29, 32, 59–61, 82, 84
forms, 114–117
Formula bar, 50, 52, 60
formulas, 52-53, 62, 64-65
Function button, 54
functions, 54–56

G
grammar checking, 39
graphical user interface, 2
graphics, 85
grouping files, 12

H
handouts, 81, 98
hanging indent, 36
hard disk drive, 3
hardware, 4
Header and Footer command, 41, 76
Header and Footer toolbar, 41
Headers, 41-42, 74-76
help, 4, 55
hidden menu options, 8
Hide Slide command, 92
hiding
    slides, 92
    taskbar, 7
HTML (hypertext markup language), 46
HTML format, 46

I
icons, 2, 4–5, 7
ID field, 110
identifying icons, 7
Increase Decimal button, 61
Increase Font Size button, 94
Increase Indent button, 33, 84, 91
indenting text, 36
Insert Chart button, 86
Insert Clip Art button, 85
Insert Columns command, 87

Insert command, 43, 86
Insert menu, 66, 85, 121
Insert Rows command, 87
Insert Table dialog box, 43
insertion point, 18
installing programs, 4
Internet Explorer, 4
ISP (Internet Service Provider), 46
Italic button, 30, 94
italic text, 30

J
Justified layout, 116
Justify button, 32
justifying text, 32

K
kerning, 31
keyboard
    displaying menus from, 8
    selecting text, 19

L
labels, 50, 62–63
Landscape orientation, 42, 75
Language command, 40
layouts, 116
leaders, 35
left arrow key, 109
Left tab icon, 35
left tab stop, 35
left-aligning text, 32, 35
letters, 16
line charts, 72, 86
lists, 11, 33
loans, calculating payment, 54

M
magic wand icon, 24
margins, 42, 74
Margins button, 74
marquee, 52
Master Command, 94
Maximize button, 6
maximizing windows, 6
Maximum function, 54
Memo data type, 110
menu bar, 8, 17
menus, 8
Merge and Center button, 63
merging range of cells in columns, 63
Microsoft Excel. *See* Excel
Microsoft Office XP. *See* Office XP
Microsoft PowerPoint. *See* Power Point
Microsoft Windows. *See* Windows
Microsoft Word, 12, 16–17

Microsoft Word command, 17
Microsoft Word Help, 22
minimizing windows, 6
Minimum function, 54
monitors, 3
moving
    cells, 64
    insertion point, 18
    ranges, 64
    tab stops, 35
    text, 20
    toolbars, 9
    windows, 6
multiplication (*) operator, 52
My Documents folder, 12, 23

N
negative (-) value, 51
New button, 105
New command, 22, 24, 82
New Presentation task pane, 82
New Slide button, 83, 84, 85
New Style dialog box, 45
Next button, 111
Next Slide button, 81
"non-system disk" message, 3
Normal View, 17, 81, 91
notes pane, 91
Number data type, 110
number formats, 61
numbered lists, 33
Numbering button, 33
numbers
    aligning on decimal, 35
    as labels, 51

O
Objects list, 109
Office XP, 2, 7–9
Open button, 12, 105
Open dialog box, 12, 108
option button, 10
optional arguments, 55
Options command, 39
Options dialog box, 39
organizing files, 12
Outline layout, 119
Outline tab, 81, 84, 91
Outline View, 17
overhead projector, 100

P
page numbers, 41
Page Setup command, 42
Page Setup dialog box, 42, 74–76
paper size and orientation, 42

Paragraph command, 34, 36
Paragraph dialog box, 34, 36
paragraphs, 18
    alignment, 32
    indenting, 36
    line spacing, 34
    selecting, 19
parentheses (), 53
passwords, 3
Paste button, 20
Paste command, 86, 92
Paste Function dialog box, 54
pasting text, 20
PCs, booting up, 3
Percent Style button, 61
Picture command, 85
pie charts, 72, 86
PivotChart layout, 116
PivotTable layout, 116
placeholders, 22, 25, 83
PMT (Payment) function, 54
pointers, 4
Portrait orientation, 42
positioning toolbars, 9
PowerPoint, 12, 80–81, 91
power-saving feature, 3
.ppt extension, 82
predefined formulas, 54
predefined styles, 45
presentation software, 80
presentations, 80
    AutoContent wizard, 81
    basic structure, 91
    bulleted items, 84
    creation of, 81–82
    design templates, 81
    Normal View, 81
    with overhead projector, 100
    .ppt extension, 82
    saving as Web page, 99
    slides, 82
    spell checking, 96
    templates, 82
    title slide, 83
    transitions, 93
    viewing slide show, 88
previewing documents, 26
Previous command, 88
Previous Slide button, 81
primary key, 107, 110
Print button, 26, 74, 121
Print command, 26, 44, 74, 77, 97–98, 100, 121
Print dialog box, 26, 44, 74, 77, 97-98, 100, 121
Print Layout View, 17, 41
Print Preview, 26, 41, 74
Print Preview button, 26, 74

printed pages, 41
printer options, 42
printing, 44
    documents, 26, 44
    handouts, 98
    orientation, 42
    reports, 121
    speaker notes, 97
    worksheets, 75, 77
program buttons on taskbar, 6
programs
    See also application programs
    adding to Programs menu, 5
    bugs, 14
    Close button, 6
    closing unused, 5
    frozen up, 14
    as icon on desktop, 5
    installing, 4
    Maximize button, 6
    menu bar, 8
    minimizing all icons, 7
    Restore button, 6
    starting and stopping, 4–5
    switching between, 4, 7
    windows, 4, 6
Programs command, 5, 17, 49, 81
Programs menu, 5, 17, 49, 81
pull-down lists, 11

Q
queries, 111–112
Query Wizard, 111
Quick launch icons, 4

R
ranges, 49, 56
    aligning, 63
    as arguments in function, 55
    copying, 64
    moving, 64
    number formats, 61
records, 102, 103
    deleting, 109
    details, 111
    empty, 109
    fields, 106
    grouping level, 118
    structure of, 106
    unique identification, 107
Redo button, 21
redoing actions or commands, 21
relational databases, 102, 107
relative reference, 64
removing styles, 45
Report Wizard, 118–120

reports, 16, 114
  adding fields, 118
  dating, 121
  fields, 118
  layouts, 119
  modifying, 120
  naming, 120
  printing, 121
  saving as Web Page, 122
  scrolling, 120
  sorting group records, 119
  styles, 120
  subtotals, 118
  totals, 118
  wizards, 118–120
required arguments, 55
resizing
  cells, 62
  columns, 43, 62
  placeholders, 83
  taskbar, 7
  text, 31
  windows, 6
Restore button, 6
resume wizard, 24
revealing taskbar, 7
right arrow key, 109
Right tab icon, 35
right tab stop, 35
right-aligning text, 32, 35
rows, 43, 66, 103
Rows command, 66
ruler, setting tabs from, 35

S
sample tables, 106
Save As command, 13
Save As dialog box, 13, 23, 78
Save As Web Page command, 46, 78, 99
Save button, 13, 23
saving
  databases, 105, 108
  documents, 23
  documents as Web pages, 46
  files, 13
  presentations as Web page, 99
  reports as Web page, 122
  worksheet before sorting, 70
  worksheets as Web page, 78
  worksheets before testing, 71
ScanDisk, 14
scientific notation, 62
Screen Tips, 7, 9
Select All command, 19, 29, 34
Select Picture dialog box, 85
selecting text, 19, 29

Setup button, 74–75
Shift key, 18
shortcut menus, 6
Shut Down command, 14
Shut Down Windows dialog box, 14
shutting down process, 14
sizing handles, 83
Slide Design task pane, 82
Slide Layout task pane, 82-83, 85, 86-87
Slide Master, 94
slide pane, 91
Slide Show button, 88, 93
Slide Show menu, 93, 95
Slide Show view, 88
slide shows, 81, 88
Slide Sorter, 92
Slide Sorter toolbar, 92
Slide Sorter View, 92–93
Slide Transition command, 93
Slide Transition task pane, 93
slides, 82
  adding graphics and visual effects, 91
  animation effects, 95
  AutoCorrect feature, 96
  automatically advancing, 93
  Blank layout, 83
  bulleted lists, 84
  charts, 86
  clip art, 85
  consistency, 96
  deleting, 92
  drag-and-drop, 92
  duplicating, 92
  fonts, 94
  formatting text, 94
  grammar errors, 96
  graphics, 85
  hiding, 92
  layouts and graphics, 85
  miniaturized versions, 92
  moving between, 81
  placeholders, 83
  rearranging, 91, 92
  revising, 91
  selecting objects to animate, 95
  sounds, 95
  spell checking, 96
  tables, 87
  thumbnail sketches of, 83
  title, 83
  Title Only layout, 83
  Title Slide layout, 82, 83
  transitions, 93
  typing errors, 96
Slides tab, 81, 91
Sort Ascending button, 70

Sort command, 70
Sort Descending button, 70
Sort dialog box, 70
Sort Order button, 119
sorting
    group records, 119
    worksheet data, 70
sound and slides, 95
space between words, 18
Spacebar, 18
speaker notes, 91, 97
spell checking, 39
    presentations, 96
    worksheets, 69
Spelling and Grammar button, 39
Spelling and Grammar dialog box, 39
Spelling button, 96
Spelling dialog box, 69
spin boxes, 10
spreadsheet software, 48
Standard toolbar, 9
Start button, 4, 5, 14
Start menu, 4, 17, 49, 81
status bar, 17
Stepped layout, 119
storage devices, 12
storing data and files, 12
Style command, 45
styles, 45
Styles and Formatting task pane, 45
subdirectories, 12
submenus, 5, 8
subtraction (-) operator, 52
Sum function, 54, 56
switching
    between headers and footers, 41
    between programs, 7
    worksheets, 49
synonyms, 40
Synonyms command, 40

T
tab stops, 35
    leaders, 35
    moving, 35
Table AutoFormat command, 43
Table AutoFormat dialog box, 43
Table command, 43
Table menu, 43
Table Wizard, 106–108
tables, 103
    adding fields, 106
    adding text, 43, 87
    cells, 43
    columns, 43
    creation of, 106–108

data consistency, 109
deleting fields, 106
deleting records, 109
deleting rows or columns, 43
Design view creation, 110
editing data, 109
empty records, 109
entering data, 107–108, 109
formatting, 43
inserting rows or columns, 43, 87
naming, 107
primary key, 107
records, 106
resizing cells, 87
resizing columns, 43
rows, 43
sample, 106
slides, 87
structure of, 106
Web pages, 78
word wrap, 43
Tables and Borders toolbar, 87
Tables tool, 106
tabs, 35
Tabs command, 35
Tabs dialog box, 35
Tabular layout, 116
Task pane, 17
taskbar, 4, 7
technical support person, 46
Template dialog box, 24
templates, 22, 82, 94
testing
    animation effect, 95
    worksheets, 71
text
    animation effects, 31
    applying attributes, 30
    attributes, 29, 31
    bold, 30
    centering, 32, 35
    combining attributes, 30
    copy and paste, 20
    copying, 20
    cut and paste, 20
    deleting, 18
    deselecting, 19
    double-clicking, 19
    drag method of selecting, 19
    editing, 19
    fields, 110
    formatting on slides, 94
    indenting, 36
    inserting, 18
    italic, 30
    justifying, 32

■ ■ ■

kerning, 31
left-aligning, 32, 35
line selection, 19
moving, 10
multiple copies of, 20
multiple formatting options, 31
paragraph selection, 19
pasting, 20
resizing, 29, 31
right-aligning, 32, 35
selecting, 19
spacing, 31
tabs, 35
triple-clicking, 19
underlined, 30
uppercase letters, 18
vertical bar, 35
vertical position, 31
wavy green line under, 39
wavy red line under, 39
word selection, 19
word wrap, 18
text box button, 83
text boxes, 11
Text data type, 110
thesaurus, 40
Thesaurus command, 40
Thesaurus dialog box, 40
Title and 2-Column Text, 84
Title and 2 Content over Text, 84
Title and Content layout, 86, 87
Title and Text, 84
Title and Text layout, 84
Title and Text over Content, 84
title bar, 7, 17
Title, Content and Text layout, 86
Title Only layout, 83
Title Slide layout, 82, 83
Title, Text and Content layout, 86
titles
  centering, 32
  fields, 108
  slides, 83
toolbar, 9, 17
  applying and removing attributes, 30
  Bold button, 30
  Copy button, 64
  Cut button, 64
  Italic button, 30
  Open button, 108
  Paste button, 64
  Print button, 26, 44, 121
  Print Preview button, 26, 74
  Run button, 112
  Spelling button, 96
  Underline button, 30

tools, 17
Tools menu, 8–9, 39–40, 96
ToolTips, 7
transitions, 93
transparency film, 100
triple-clicking, 19
Turn Off Computer, 14
Turn Off Computer dialog box, 14

U
Underline button, 30, 94
underlined text, 30
Undo button, 21, 70
undoing actions or commands, 21
unused programs, closing, 5
Up One Level button, 12
uppercase letters, 18
user ID, 3

V
values
  automatically entering, 51
  editing, 51
  formulas, 53
  as function argument, 55
  too long for cell, 62
vertical bar, 35
View menu, 41, 76, 94
views, 91

W
Warm Boot (Control+Alt+Del) key combination, 14
Web browser
  previewing presentation, 99
  previewing report, 122
Web Layout View, 17
Web Page Preview command, 46, 99
Web pages
  previewing, 46, 78
  saving documents as, 46
  saving presentation as, 99
  saving report as, 122
  saving worksheet as, 78
  tables, 78
Windows
  controls, 10–11
  graphical user interface, 2
windows, 2, 4
  Access, 104
  activating, 7
  arranging on-screen, 7
  attaching toolbars, 9
  automatically sizing and positioning, 7
  bringing to top, 7
  dragging, 6
  Excel, 49

maximizing, 6
minimizing, 6
moving to new location, 6
open, 7
PowerPoint, 81
resizing, 6
resorting size and location, 7
title bar, 6
Windows desktop, 3–4
wipes, 93
wizards, 24
   forms, 115–117
   generating documents, 25
   reports, 118–120
Word. *See* Microsoft Word
word processing software, 16
word wrap, 18, 43
words, selecting, 19
workbooks, 49
worksheets, 48
   active cell, 49
   ascending order sort, 70
   background colors, 59
   bold text, 60
   borders, 59
   cells, 49
   charts, 72–73
   close-up view, 74
   consistent and easily verified values, 71
   descending order sort, 70
   font attributes, 60
   footers, 75, 76
   formatting data, 60–61
   formulas, 52
   gridlines, 75
   headers, 75, 76
   inserting and deleting columns and rows, 66
   labels, 50
   landscape orientation, 75
   location of header and footer, 74
   manually adjusting margins, 74
   margin settings, 75
   normal view, 74
   printing, 77
   ranges, 49
   real-world values, 71
   resizing columns, 62
   saving as Web page, 78
   saving before testing, 71
   scaling, 75
   sorting data, 70
   spell checking, 69
   switching, 49
   testing, 71
   values, 51

X

Y
Yes/No data type, 110

Z
Zoom button, 74

■   ■   ■